Pocahontas and Nathan Hale

1793 engraving of Pocahontas based on the 1616 oil painting by renowned artist Simon van de Passe.

Photograph of Nathan Hale bronze statue by Bela Lyon Pratt for Yale University. It was created in 1915.

Pocahontas and Nathan Hale

The Biographies of Two Brave Individuals Who Made an Impact on American History

SPECIAL EDITION
Edited by Gary Brin

Condensed from the works by
Elizabeth Eggleston Seelye and Jean Christie Root

LIST OF TITLES USED FOR THIS COLLECTION

Pocahontas was originally published in 1879. It was one of the first-length biographies about the life and times of Pocahontas from historical archives.

Nathan Hale was originally published in 1915. It was based on the research from personal accounts and records kept by Nathan Hale's family.

BOTH TITLES CAN BE FOUND AT THE SITE LISTED BELOW
www.nancyhankslincolnpubliclibrary.org

Spelling errors and visible publishing mistakes found in the original versions listed above were corrected or slightly adjusted whenever necessary for this edition. Original text was left intact to preserve the historical accuracy of the writings.

BOTH BOOKS USED FOR THIS EDITION HAS BEEN REFORMATTED FROM THE ORIGINAL 1879 AND 1915 PUBLISHED VERSIONS.

Images of Pocahontas and Nathan Hale displayed in this book are courtesy of the National Portrait Gallery and New York Public Library. All photographs were digitally restored for this edition. Image of Pocahontas was cropped from the original.
Cover design and book layout © 2023 by Standish Press
Compilation © 2023 by Standish Press

FIRST EDITION

ALL NEW MATERIAL AND CORRECTIONS
Copyright © 2023 by Standish Press

All rights reserved. No part of this book may be reproduced by any means whatsoever without written permission from the publisher.

For more information about reprint rights please visit
www.standishpress.com

ISBN—978-1-945510-11-3

Library of Congress Control Number
2023933199

MANUFACTURED IN THE UNITED STATES OF AMERICA

In Remembrance of

Pocahontas and Nathan Hale

They lived centuries apart and had vastly different lives but achieved immortality in British and American history because of what they did—rather than what they set out to do.

This book is also dedicated in memory of

John Rolfe and Frederick Mackenzie

To John Rolfe for giving Pocahontas a moment of happiness during her short life and to Frederick Mackenzie who recorded in his diary the courage Nathan Hale displayed in his final hours.

Contents

Page 11
Foreword
Page 13
Pocahontas
Page 167
Nathan Hale
Page 255
Afterword
Page 257
Additional Notes
Page 264
About the Series Editor

Foreword

What else can be said about Pocahontas and Nathan Hale? They changed history—guaranteed that they would never be forgotten by historians and schoolchildren alike because of unselfish actions they took which drastically changed the course of their lives. Centuries later they remain central parts of United States history despite having the events that guaranteed them immortality be questioned as to whether what was stated actually took place—or was embellished after the fact.

Pocahontas is best known by American schoolchildren for having saved the life of Captain John Smith of Jamestown fame. From his writings it appears without the help of Pocahontas, he and his fellow settlers would have perished as they struggled to adjust to life in the Virginia wilderness during the early part of the seventeenth century. There have been more than one version of the events that made an unknown Native American girl famous, but withstanding the possibility Smith embellished the events about being saved by Pocahontas in his memoirs, the fact remains that even without saving John Smith's life, Pocahontas was important to American history. Her life was short but over four centuries later she remains very much a part of the fabric of the history of two mighty nations separated by a vast ocean.

Many well-intentioned books have been written about her over the centuries but none were done from actual interviews with people who knew her. What we know about her life comes from history books, personal writings, and reports on interactions she had with John Smith and others in his circle. Of course many have tried to claim they have a definitive account of her life but always fall short of delivering on that promise. There also have been attempts by many to recreate history as they wished it to have been—some going as far as to fictionalize events about her life that never happened in order to rewrite history to their liking. Pocahontas died in March 1617 and was buried in Gravesend, just outside of London. Today many people from around the world travel to the rebuilt church where her remains lie buried in an unknown location to pay respects to the young woman who made such an impact on so many without ever knowing it.

Nathan Hale led an ordinary life until the American Revolution altered the course of British history. Hale was one of the first to join the cause which led him to volunteer to become a spy for George Washington's army. Hale was a schoolteacher by trade and most certainly was not experienced in being a spy. But the brave young man was not deterred and knew what he had chosen to do could possibly result in his death if he was captured, but he forged ahead and began his mission anyway. It's still not clear centuries later how he was betrayed, but nevertheless his fate was sealed after he was found out. He was ordered hung but refused to show any weakness to his captors. His last words before he was hung by British troops has become famous the world over, and rightly so. "*I only regret that I have but one life to lose for my country.*" Exactly what he said has been disputed—but from what eyewitnesses stated—it was something close to the statement above as found in records the British army kept.

Nathan Hale and Pocahontas left indelible legacies of heroism behind—which few has been able to duplicate.

Gary Brin
Series Editor

Pocahontas

Pocahontas

Preface

This book, like those that have gone before it, is intended for popular use, and especially is it meant to attract young people to the early history of our own country. We have not sought, therefore, to confine our story to a personal biography of Pocahontas, for which the materials are not very abundant. The adventures of Smith in the Turkish Wars, as related by himself, and the explorations, trials, and battles of the early settlers at Jamestown, serve to make a romantic passage in history. The story has not often been told so fully before, and we sincerely hope that this book will prove of interest even to those already acquainted with its general features, and that it will stimulate many young readers to go farther in the study of the history of their own country. While we have sought to be interesting we have tried sincerely to be correct, at most, whatever romancing there is in the story is the fault of the early writers. It is not easy to come at the truth about Jamestown. We have usually followed

Smith's *General History of Virginia*, consulting also the accounts of [Christopher] Newport, [Edward] Wingfield, [William] Strachey, and Smith's *True Relation*, with [William] Stith's *History of the First Discovery and Settlement of Virginia*, and [Edward] Neill's *History of the Virginia Company of London*, besides many other works of less importance as authorities. Where we could preserve the very words of the old chroniclers we have done so, believing that it would add to the interest of the reader to see the quaint but vigorous English in use at that time. We have also reproduced some [material when possible from] Smith's *General History*.

Elizabeth Eggleston Seelye
Edward Eggleston

❒❒❒❒❒❒❒❒❒❒

Gold and a route to the East Indies were the dominant ideas in the minds of the early discoverers and explorers of the American continent. [Christopher] Columbus believed to the day of his death that the islands which he had discovered were but the outskirts of eastern Asia. He valued his discovery only as a means of opening a profitable traffic with the East. English commercial ambition long sought an easy route to the East Indies. John Cabot, a Venetian, undertook the first voyage of discovery sent to the New World from England. In 1497, only five years after the first West Indian discovery of Columbus, Cabot reached the shores of America, or the territory of the Grand Cham (Vietnam) in Asia, as he supposed, and returned home, the first discoverer of the American continent. In the following year, while the aged Columbus sailed to the mainland of South America, and the daring young Vasco da Gama of Portugal rounded the Cape of Good Hope, and sailed with streamers flying and trumpets sounding into the harbor of Calcutta (India), the Venetian discoverer's son, Sebastian Cabot, a young man barely twenty-one years old, explored the coast of North America from Newfoundland as far south as Chesapeake Bay. Nevertheless he considered his voyage a failure, since he had not discovered the shortest route to Cathay (China) and Japan, which he reasoned would be by way of the far north. For many years after this, while Spain was making rich conquests in Mexico and Central America, England had no connection with the New World except through the fisheries of Newfoundland, which were frequented by her vessels. In the sixteenth century the world's work seem to the men of that day almost accomplished. An English navigator, named Martin Frobisher, deemed the discovery of a northwestern passage to Asia "the only thing in the world that was yet left undone by which a notable mind might be made famous and fortunate." The making of this discovery was the desire of Frobisher's heart. For fifteen years he solicited help for his project in vain. He was at last aided by Dudley, Earl of Warwick, and in 1576, with a fleet of two small barks and a pinnace, he prepared to cross the ocean. Queen Elizabeth sent a message of approbation to Frobisher, and waved her hand as the little fleet dropped down the Thames. The pinnace of but ten tons burden was soon lost in a storm, and the frightened sailors in one of the other vessels turned homeward, leaving Frobisher to pursue his course alone. In his small bark he discovered Labrador, and reached an inlet north of Hudson's Bay. He imagined the land on the north to be Asia, that on the south to be America, and that the strait which he had discovered led into the Pacific.

  Frobisher landed on an arctic island, which he took possession of in the name of Elizabeth, and gathered some stones, with which he returned home. One of these stones was pronounced by the clumsy London refiners of that day to contain gold. Immediately there were men who desired to purchase these northern gold lands from Queen Elizabeth. But Frobisher was provided with a fleet for the purpose of securing the treasure. Volunteers were plenty for this expedition. The queen, who had vouchsafed only royal favor to the voyage of discovery, sent a large ship of her own on the voyage for gold. With "a merry wind" they sailed from England, but they encountered much danger from icebergs before the shores of America were reached. This great fleet did not penetrate so far as Frobisher had in his little bark. They contented themselves with an island where there was heaps of earth, which to their eyes plainly contained gold. More than this, the island abounded in spiders, and "spiders were true signs of a great store of gold." Admiral and men toiled like slaves to lade the vessels with common earth. But the faith of gold dreamers was unshaken. A colony must be planted in this land of frost in order to secure so rich a country to England. Gentlemen's sons volunteered, Elizabeth bore part of the expense, and in 1578 fifteen vessels set sail—three to remain with the settlement and twelve to hasten back with the coveted ore. The fleet became entangled among great icebergs melting in the summer's sun and adorned with waterfalls. One vessel was crushed, though the men were saved. Bewildered among mists and icebergs, Frobisher lost his course and entered Hudson Strait, south of the land of gold. Here the Admiral believed he could sail through to the Pacific. But he pushed on in a search of the golden island, "getting in at one gap and out at another," among many dangers from hidden rocks on an unknown coast. When he reached the Countess of Warwick Sound the enthusiastic colonists were discouraged, and the sailors were ready to mutiny. One vessel containing much of the provision of the expedition deserted and returned home. The disheartened gold seekers discovered an island, however, containing enough of the supposed gold ore "to suffice all the gold gluttons of the world," but no one proposed to colonize it for the benefit of England. The vessels were freighted and returned home. Neither the projectors of the expedition nor the adventurers who embarked upon it tell us how the lading was disposed of.—Thus ended the first attempt of the English to colonize America.—In 1578 Sir Humphrey Gilbert procured from the queen a charter, which made him proprietary lord of whatever land he might discover and colonize within six years.

In 1579 he set sail, accompanied by his half brother, Walter Raleigh. The loss of a vessel and various misfortunes defeated this venture. Sir Humphrey Gilbert's fortune became too much reduced for him to undertake another expedition. He made various grants of land, but none of them resulted in a successful colony. In 1583, before the patent had expired, Gilbert, assisted by Raleigh, fitted another fleet for settlement in America. On the eve of his departure Sir Humphrey Gilbert received from the queen a token in the form of "a golden anchor guided by a lady"—whatever that may mean. Two days after leaving Plymouth, the largest ship of the fleet, which had been furnished by Raleigh, deserted under the excuse of infectious disease. The commander conducted his remaining vessels to the banks of Newfoundland. He took formal possession of the country, summoning the Spanish and Portuguese fishermen to witness the ceremony. The "mineral man" of the fleet pronounced a certain ore to contain silver. Some of this was carried on board with great secrecy, in order that the Spanish and Portuguese might not suspect its value. A further voyage of discovery along the coast was undertaken, but Gilbert's men were unmanageable. Through the carelessness of the sailors the largest vessel struck, and nearly one hundred persons, were lost, with the "mineral man" and the ore. It now seemed necessary to return home. Sir Humphrey Gilbert insisted on remaining in the *Squirrel*, the little bark in which he had sailed, on account of its convenience for exploring the coast. He said he would not desert the little crew with which he had encountered so many dangers. The voyage was rough. "A more outrageous sea" had not been seen by the oldest sailors. Sir Humphrey was seen from the larger vessel sitting on deck with a book in his hand, and when she would approach within hearing he would call out, "Be of good cheer, my friends, it is as near to heaven by sea as by land."

The little vessel labored painfully in the storm, and about midnight her lights suddenly disappeared, never to be seen again. Raleigh was ambitious to be lord over lands in the New World. He now planned a settlement in a pleasanter climate than that of Newfoundland. From the queen he obtained as ample a patent as that of his half-brother. Two vessels were freighted with men and provisions. Under the command of Philip Amadas and Arthur Barlowe they followed the circuitous route of the day—by way of the Canaries and West Indies. When they neared the coast of

North Carolina it was in all its midsummer beauty. The odor which reached them was "as if they had been in the midst of some delicate garden." The smooth sea, dotted with islands, sparkled in the sun—the land was covered with noble trees festooned with vines. This land seemed a paradise to the colonists, who knew nothing of the terrors of the coast at a more unfavorable season. A settlement was made on the island of Woccon (Ocracoke Island), and the time was occupied with excursions of discovery. The result of their observations of the savages were that "the people were most gentle, loving, and faithful, void of all guile and treason, and such as lived after the manner of the golden age" and yet, strange to say, in their wars they were cruel and bloody, entire tribes being sometimes almost exterminated, and they practiced inviting men to a feast and then murdering them—as the English knew, for the Indians had offered them much booty to participate in such a stratagem against their enemies. After a short stay in the pleasant summer months, the expedition returned to England, with glowing accounts of the country. Queen Elizabeth named the new land Virginia, in honor of herself, the Virgin Queen. A fleet of seven vessels with one hundred and eight colonists was next sent out by Sir Walter Raleigh in 1585, under the command of Sir Richard Grenville. The perils of the North Carolina coast were found to be very great. A settlement was made at Roanoke Island.

Almost one of the first acts of the colonists was to destroy an Indian town and standing corn in retaliation for the theft of a silver cup. Sir Richard Grenville sailed away and the colonists began to explore the country. [Ralph] Lane, the governor, wrote, "It is the goodliest soil under the cope of heaven, the most pleasing territory of the world, the continent is of a huge and unknown greatness, and very well peopled, though savagely." The wily Indians soon discovered the white man's twofold passion for gold and a passage to the "South Sea." One of them told the colonists that Roanoke River sprang from a rock so near the Pacific that the waves sometimes dashed into its fountain, that the people who lived there understood refining gold, of which there was in abundance in the country, and that the walls of their city were made of pearls. This fable coincided with the preconceived notions of Europeans in regard to America. Lane and a band of followers undertook the ascent of the Roanoke in search of its wonderful fountain. Meanwhile the Indians, who were jealous of white settlements prepared to attack the divided colony. The gold seekers toiled up the rapid current of the Roanoke. Their provisions were soon exhausted. Still they persevered, killing and eating their dogs. When this resource failed them they returned home, just in time to frustrate the plans of the Indians. The savages now proposed to plant no corn in order to starve out the English, who depended upon trade with them for their provisions. An old chief, however, objected to this plan. The English had been in the New World nearly a year. They grew more and more fearful of the Indians. They believed that they were forming an alliance with intent to massacre them. They desired an audience of the most influential chief, Wingina, and when admitted to his presence they fell upon him and his principal warriors and killed them. The colonists were growing restless and homesick, and they had now indeed good reason to fear the Indians. In hopes of a better harbor they explored toward the north and reached Chesapeake Bay, long after it had been discovered by the Spanish and named Santa Maria Bay.

 One day many sails were seen on the horizon. It was Sir Francis Drake's great fleet of twenty-three vessels returning from a long privateering and exploring cruise. It came to anchor in "the wild road of their bad harbor." Sir Francis Drake readily supplied all the wants of the colonists, giving them vessels—persuading two experienced seamen to remain with them, and furnishing every means for them to make further explorations. A sudden storm nearly wrecked the fleet, which was only saved by standing off from the dangerous coast. After the storm, nothing was to be seen of the vessels set aside for the colonists use. Sir Francis Drake again offered, however, to supply their wants, but with one voice they begged to be taken back to England. Through these colonists, who had learned to smoke in the New World, the use of tobacco was first introduced into England. Sir Walter Raleigh made the practice fashionable. It is related that a servant of his coming into the room with a tankard of ale saw Sir Walter intent on study, with clouds of smoke issuing from his mouth.

The man immediately threw the ale in his master's face and ran downstairs, crying that Sir Walter was on fire. A few days after the colonists left Roanoke Island vessels with provisions landed at the settlement to find it deserted. Grenville left fifteen men to hold the land for its lord. Sir Walter Raleigh now planned to plant an agricultural colony of men with families, to be established at Chesapeake Bay. In 1587 he fitted out a fleet at his own expense, "Queen Elizabeth, the godmother of Virginia," refusing to contribute "to its education." As might have been expected, nothing remained of the little colony at Roanoke Island but bones. The settlement was overgrown with weeds. The commander of the vessels refusing to carry them further, the colony was obliged to plant itself on this sad spot. There was naturally trouble with the Indians. The tribe of Manteo, the chief who had visited England, was friendly, and this Indian, according to the commands of Raleigh, was baptized and made a baron, with the title of Lord of Roanoke. It may be doubted whether he fully appreciated the honor. The colony was ill-fated, a vessel was sent to England to ask for provisions. Raleigh freighted two ships for his colony, but in chasing after prizes, one vessel was boarded and rifled after a bloody battle, and both were forced to return. England was in a state of intense excitement over the threatened invasion of Spain, and Raleigh, Grenville, Lane, and all those who had been most interested in colonization, were now entirely occupied with the prospect of war. Not until three years after the planting of the colony did the expected supplies arrive at Roanoke, which was then a desert. An inscription directed to the island of Croatoan, the home of Manteo and the friendly Indians. No search was made further than the Island of Roanoke by this expedition, and the fate of the colony is unknown. Raleigh sent many expeditions to search for his lost people, but nothing was discovered of them. There is one statement, though not perhaps to be trusted, that after twenty-one years of life among the savages they were murdered by Powhatan, at the instigation of his priests or medicine men. (See Additional Notes on page 257 for more info on this specific statement by Chief Powhatan.)

In 1602 a direct voyage across the Atlantic was made by Bartholomew Gosnold in a small bark. He discovered Cape Cod and Buzzard's Bay, which he called Gosnold's Hope. On a beautiful island covered with grand forests, wild fruits, and sweet flowers a settlement was planned. On the island is a pond, in which is a little island. On this romantic spot the colonists built their fort, but the road before them appeared too dangerous, fearing starvation and dreading the Indians they resolved to return with Gosnold. They brought back from the New World a load of sassafras root, which was highly valued in the pharmacy of the day. A second expedition was undertaken by Martin Pring in 1603. He explored much of the coast of North Virginia, as New England was then called, and traded trinkets with the Indians for sassafras. Still another voyage under command of George Weymouth was made to the shores of North Virginia.

All the early voyagers agreed in praising the fertility of the soil and the beauty of the scenery in the new land, and it was to the imagination of people in Europe (England) like a land of romance and dreams—a "new world" indeed, as they called it.

☐☐☐☐☐☐☐☐☐☐

It is now nearly three hundred years ago that the first successful colony set out from Blackwall, a suburb of London, to effect a settlement in the "Newfoundland of Virginia," as the whole coast of North America was at that time called. The failure of the colony on Roanoke Island had for many years damped the ardor of English adventurers, but the success of the Spaniards, their great rivals and enemies, piqued the pride of the English, as the wealth won by Spanish gold seekers excited their cupidity. So that at the beginning of the reign of James I, it was resolved to have an English settlement in America, to win territory, and to freight ships with the precious metals.—Sir Walter Raleigh, the founder of the unhappy colony on Roanoke Island, and the lifelong advocate of colonization, was at this time shut up in a dreary cell in the Tower of London, engaged in writing his *History of the World* to while away the hours of a long imprisonment. But Gosnold, whose voyage to the New England coast is related in the previous chapter, had been very active in promoting the present undertaking. In this he had been joined by John Smith, a soldier of fortune who had voyaged about the world, getting out of one daring adventure into another, and who now, having returned from single combats and captivities among the Saracens (Saudi Arabians), could find nothing to satisfy his appetite for danger and hardship so well as a colony in the wilds of America. A third promoter of the scheme was a London merchant named [Edward] Wingfield, and a fourth was a clergyman, Mr. [Robert] Hunt. The latter desired to plant Christianity, Wingfield no doubt represented the commercial desire for gain, while Gosnold and Smith were voyagers and adventurers pure and simple, loving a hard task for the very hardness of it and the honor of overcoming difficulties. The traveler of our time feels some trepidation when he sails across the ocean in a staunch steamer of several thousand tons burden. But the little colony that left Blackwall and dropped down the Thames in the rough December of 1606 had for their largest ships, the *Sarah (Susan) Constant*, of one hundred tons, which ship carried seventy persons, and was commanded by Captain [Christopher] Newport. The second ship, the *Godspeed*, was commanded by the experienced Captain Gosnold, and was of forty tons, carrying fifty-two persons, while the smallest vessel of all, the *Discovery*, was of but twenty tons, a mere sailboat, carrying twenty people on this long voyage, through little known seas, into unknown lands. The seeds of a great nation were here compressed into a small space and entrusted to a frail craft.

    The people of England were very much interested in the little company that left Blackwall on the 19th of December, 1606. There was a clergyman, the Reverend Richard Hakluyt, who when he was a schoolboy had been shown one day some books of travel and a map of the world. He then and there resolved to devote himself to geographical studies, and he became in time better informed on all such matters than any man in England in his day. The great trading companies were accustomed to consult him about their undertakings. He, with other "hearty lovers of colonization," had petitioned for permission to send out this colony, and he was one of the incorporators of it. James I was a pedantic (annoying) man, priding himself on his learning, which was not so great, as his vanity. It is said that when George Buchannan, his preceptor, was censured for having made the king a pedant, he answered that it was the best he could make out of such a prince as he. King James was of a meddling disposition, full of overweening self-confidence, and he unfortunately took great interest in the little colony now setting forth, and had something to do with the mischievous regulations and directions by which the enterprise was well-nigh brought to destruction. There are still extant poems, sermons, and plays that show the general interest of all classes of people in the colony on its setting out, and during the early years of its history. Michael Drayton, a famous poet of the time, who wrote abundantly about a great many things, gave utterance to the popular feeling in an ode full of fire. He begins, "You brave heroic minds, worthy our country's name, that honor still pursue whilst loitering hinds lurk here at home with shame, go and subdue. Britons, you stay too long—quickly aboard bestow you and with a merry gale swell your stretched sail with vows as strong as the winds that blow you." He does not think that these voyagers in little ships need be afraid of shoals, "Your course securely steer, west and by south forth keep, rocks, lee shores, nor shoals where Eolus scowls, you need not fear, so absolute the deep." The dominant idea of the time was to find gold, and this finds place also in Drayton's verses, "And cheerfully at sea success you still entice to get the pearl and gold, and ours to hold Virginia, earth's only paradise."

He seems to have a premonition that the English race will come to greatness in the New World, for he sings of the heroes that shall be brought forth like "those from whom we came," and lastly he describes "industrious Hakluyt" as waiting to record their voyages. But it was especially the finding of gold mines that most concerned the English public. In a play, written the year before the colony sailed, while all England was agitated about it, there is a conversation between two characters who bore the significant names of 'Scapethrift' and 'Seagull.' The general expectation of gold from Virginia is shown up in the extravagant speech of the enthusiastic 'Seagull,' who declares that all their dripping pans are pure gold in Virginia, "and all the chains with which they chain up their streets are massie gold, all the prisoners they take are fettered in gold, and for rubies and diamonds they go forth in holy days and gather them by the seashore, to hang on their children's coats, and stick in their children's caps, as commonly as our children wear saffron gilt broaches, and groats (grain) with holes in them." Not only in the poetry and the plays of the time, but in the sermons and prayers of the people, Virginia is remembered. One prayer of a few years later ends with the petition that God "may vouchsafe to go with us, and we with him into Virginia. Amen and Amen. Be thou the Alpha and Omega of England's plantation in Virginia, O God."—The colony was to be governed under a charter, drawn up, no doubt, under the eye of the fussy and foolish King James.—It abounded in all guarantees for loyalty, but neglected many very important matters.

There were also explicit directions about the manner of settlement and their mode of dealing with the "naturals"—that is, the natives of Virginia. These directions were good enough in their way, but the better policy would have been to have given military authority to someone competent (able) man. This, the projectors of the colony failed to do. The authority at sea was vested not in Gosnold, as we would have expected, but in Captain Newport, who was an experienced mariner, and who had, had the wisdom the year before to make the king a present of two living young alligators and a wild boar, brought from the West Indies. Such trifles delighted James greatly. From the beginning the little colony was beset with difficulties. Scarcely were they out of the Thames when they were met by rough weather, and were long beaten upon by the rough seas of the [English] Channel. It was six weeks before they lost sight of the English coast. But something worse than bad weather overtook them in the jealousy and discord which immediately broke out among the leading spirits of the colony. One would have supposed that while King James and the rest were busy over charters and directions, they would have been at some pains to see that the colony should be made up of such as were suitable to the work in hand. But of the hundred or more who were first settled in Virginia, fifty-three ranked as "gentlemen," many of whom were dissipated young men sent off by friends who wished to be rid of them. Smith says they were afterward dissatisfied because they did not find "any of their accustomed dainties, with feather beds and down pillows, taverns and alehouses in every breathing place, neither such plenty of gold and silver and dissolute liberty as they expected." We do not wonder that "the country was to them a misery, a ruin, a death, a hell." With all these gentlemen there was a small allowance of four carpenters. Twelve men are set down as laborers, but whether they were farm hands or personal servants we are not told. There was one bricklayer, one mason, one blacksmith, and one sailor. But there were also a barber and a tailor and a drummer, while there were four boys, and some others whose manner of life is not set down. From the beginning, as we have said, this ill-assorted crowd divided into factions. Such skillful and vigorous spirits as Bartholomew Gosnold and John Smith were no doubt outspoken against the ascendancy of incompetents among the emigrants. Such men the brusque and brave Captain John calls "merely projecting, verbal, and idle contemplators." No doubt Smith was himself more of a soldier than a diplomatist, and that he stirred up a good deal of anger by his blunt speeches. But there was one patient and peacemaking man in the ships, and that was Mr. Robert Hunt, "Preacher," as he is set down in the list. This good clergyman was so sick at the beginning of the voyage that his life was despaired of, and though the vessels lay for weeks off the downs, in sight of his home, yet he never once proposed to give over his enterprise. "With the water of patience, and his godly exhortations (but chiefly by his true devoted examples), he quenched those flames of envy and dissension." The ships loitered at the Canaries and in the West Indies, consuming their provisions, which were scant at the beginning, and losing the opportunity for spring planting. So high a pitch did their dissensions reach that at one of the islands it was even proposed to hang the impetuous and restless Captain Smith, who probably showed much discontent at this waste of five months in a voyage for which two would have been sufficient. The accounts are conflicting, but there seems no doubt that a mutiny was intended, and that Smith was suspected of a share in it. After the ships had three days passed their reckoning, without finding land, Captain Ratcliffe, of the smallest vessel, seriously proposed that they should turn about and sail back again, probably on the supposition that the continent was lost. While this proposition was under advisement there came up a lucky storm, which drove the ships to the mouth of the James River, and settled in the minds of the navigators any doubts concerning the whereabouts of Virginia. The first cape which they saw was named, for the Prince of Wales, Cape Henry.

The "northern cape" they named Cape Charles, for the King's second son, afterward King Charles I. A landing was made on Cape Charles by thirty men, who were suddenly attacked by five Indians. Two of the white men were dangerously wounded in this first encounter with the "naturals." The country within the capes the voyagers found to be what they regarded as the pleasantest land known. "Here are mountains, hills, plains, valleys, rivers, and brooks, all running most pleasantly into a fair bay, compassed but for the mouth with fruitful and delightsome land." We are assured that "heaven and earth never agreed better to frame a place for man's habitation, were it fully manned and inhabited by industrious people." And indeed at the season of their arrival the banks of the James River are magnificent with the blossoms of the redbud and dogwood, so that after their tiresome voyage the land must have been indeed delightful to their eyes. After much debate, the place ever since called Jamestown was selected as the sight of the colony. Gosnold strongly opposed this selection, while Smith favored it. The event has proved the wisdom of Gosnold's judgment. It was on low ground, and never wholesome. The inroads of the water have since turned the peninsula into an island, and there is now only a ruined church tower to mark the site of the first permanent colony in the United States. As soon as they had landed they opened the box that contained the names of the members of the council, which up to that time had been kept secret from everybody. Captain Smith, who had been under arrest on suspicion for the last three months of the voyage, was among those named, but he was formally excluded by the other members, on what pretext we are not told. Wingfield was chosen president by the council, and this tempest-tossed band of unlucky, unsuitable, and quarrelsome adventurers planted the germs of a great nation at Jamestown. The planting would have proved vain, indeed, had it not been for the one despised and excluded councilor, whose ready tact, valor, and indefatigable zeal (energy) were to save it from the mishaps and destruction which the folly and selfishness of its leaders so often invited.

Rumors of a white people who came from over the sea had reached the Indians of Virginia from time to time. In 1573, a Spanish vessel had sailed into the Chesapeake—the mariners had taken soundings, admired the many rivers and good harbors, and sailed away again. The inhabitants, doubtless, heard also of the unsuccessful settlements of the English on Woccon [Ocracoke] and Roanoke Islands. At first these strangers, who were not known to be sick, and who had no women with them, were believed to be immortals that had not been horn of women, the Indians of the region, indeed, attributed all their ailments to wounds inflicted by the English with invisible bullets. Perhaps [Thomas] Hariot, one of the members of the first colony at Roanoke, had entered some of Powhatan's towns on those journeys in which he was accustomed to show and explain the Bible to the Indians, who would kiss the book and press it to their heads and breasts as an amulet, or "great medicine." The dress of the Indians in the mild climate of Virginia was rather scanty. The aristocracy wore little else than moccasins and a mantle of skin, embroidered with beads, which was exchanged for one of fur during the winter. Pretty mantles were also made of turkey's feathers, interwoven with thread in such a manner that only the feathers showed. The women covered themselves with an apron of deerskin. The "common sort" had little but leaves and grass for clothing. In summer, nearly all covering was dispensed with by rich and poor. What the Indians lacked in clothing was made up in paint and ornaments. They colored their heads and shoulders, a brilliant red, with a mixture made of powdered puccoon root and oil. Women tattooed their skin with figures of beasts and serpents. But ear pendants were their most important ornaments. They had usually three large holes in each ear from which they would hang chains, "bracelets," and copper.

Indian women were seen with strings of pearls hanging from the ear to the waist. A man would sometimes wear as an ear pendant a small green and yellow snake "crawling and lapping itself about his neck." He was "the most gallant that was the most monstrous to behold." What little beard the Indians had was grated away with oyster shells by the women. An Indian beau would spend hours plucking his whiskers out by the roots.

The weapons, tools, and utensils of the aborigines were such as we do not see among the Indians of today who trade with a civilized people. Tomahawks were made of a deer's horn, or of a long sharpened stone set into a handle somewhat like a pickaxe. Arrows were stone-pointed and winged with turkey feathers, which were fastened with glue made from deer's horns. Their only armor was a shield made of sticks or bark, woven together with thread. The women made thread either of bark, deer's sinews, or of a kind of grass. Knives were made of stone, and sometimes shells and reeds were sharpened for this purpose.

A file was made of the tooth of a beaver set in a stick. The Indians kindled a fire by chafing a dry pointed stick in a hole made in a piece of wood. Mortars were hollowed from stone, and in these, corn was pounded into meal. An extensive quarry in which stone vessels and implements were made has recently been discovered in Amelia County, Virginia, and the method of work is shown to have been very ingenious. Corn bread was the staple food among the Indians. Bread was also made of wild oats and of sunflower seed. Fish, deer, turkeys, and other game were their meats. Grubs, locusts, and snakes were also included in the bill of fare. Potatoes and the tuckahoe root were eaten. Tobacco and corn were planted by the Indians. The manner of planting Indian corn was something new and strange to the English, and is thus described, "The greatest labor they take is in planting their corn, for the country naturally is overgrown with wood. To prepare the ground they bruise the bark of the trees near the root—then do they scorch the roots with fire that they grow no more. The next year, with a crooked piece of wood, they beat up the weeds by the roots, and in that mold they plant their corn. Their manner is this, they make a hole in the earth with a stick, and into it they put four grains of wheat (Indian corn) and two of beans. These holes they make four foot one from another, their women and children do continually keep it with weeding, and when it is grown middle high, they hill it about like a hop yard."

The corn harvest was celebrated by the festival of the green corn dance. The Indians delighted in roasted ears of corn. They made a drink of dried hickory nuts, pounded in a mortar and mixed with water. This liquor was called pawcohicora.

From the Indian cookery Americans have borrowed hominy, barbecued meat, and the Southern dish called "prone." The Indians dwelt mostly on the river banks, and always in villages. Their cabins, or wigwams, were framed of saplings tied together and covered very handsomely with reeds, bark, or mats. Across the entrance a mat was sometimes hung for a door.

In the center of the cabins a fire was built, and, says Captain Smith, they were very warm, but also very smoky, notwithstanding the hole in the top to let out smoke. Indian towns were fortified with palisades ten or twelve feet in height. The Virginia Indians worshipped an idol, or Okee, which represented an evil spirit.—They had also, like all of their race, some vague idea of a superior spirit or creator.—Their priests or medicine men controlled them through their superstition by means of divinations and conjurations, by which they professed to cure the sick, and thus lived a life of indolence themselves. The savages seldom dared steal from one another, fearing that their priests might reveal the thief through divination. The rude temple in which they kept their Okee was surrounded with posts on which hideous faces were roughly carved or painted. The Indians divided their year into five seasons—budding time, roasting ear time, summer, the fall of the leaf, and winter. Their rather unmusical instruments were a reed on which they piped, a rude drum, and rattles made of gourds or pumpkins. "These, mingled with their voices," says Captain Smith, "make such a terrible noise as would rather affright than delight any man." The Indians amused themselves with "sham fights," or war dances, accompanied with the war whoop, which seemed quite infernal to the English. Captain Smith says that "all their actions, voices, and gestures, both in charging and retreating, were so strained to the height of their quality and nature that the strangeness thereof made it seems very delightful." When the Indians had a distinguished visitor "they spread a mat, as the Turks do a carpet, for him to sit upon. Upon another right opposite they sit themselves. Then do all with a tunable voice of shouting bid him welcome. After this two or more of their chiefest men make an oration, testifying their love." The English invested savage life with all the dignity of European courts. Powhatan was styled "King," or "Emperor," his principal warriors were lords of the kingdom, his wives were queens, his daughter was a "princess" and his cabins were his various seats of residence. The extent of his conquests, his unlimited power over his subjects, and the pomp which he maintained, invest Powhatan with no little savage dignity. He was a "tall, well-proportioned man, with a sour look, his head somewhat gray—his beard so thin that it seemeth none at all, his age near sixty, of a very able and hardy body, to endure any labor." In his younger days Powhatan had been a great warrior. Hereditarily, he was the chief or *werowance* of eight tribes, through conquest his dominions had been extended until they reached from the James River to the Potomac, from the sea to the falls in the principal rivers, and included thirty of the forty tribes in Virginia. It is estimated that his subjects numbered eight thousand. The name of his nation and the Indian appellation of the James River was Powhatan. He himself possessed several names. His proper personal appellation (title) was said to have been Wahunsonacock. His enemies were two neighboring confederacies (tribes), the Mannahoacs, situated between the Rappahannock and York Rivers, and the Monacans, between the York and James Rivers, above the falls. Powhatan lived sometimes at a village of his name, near where Richmond now stands, and sometimes at Werowocomoco, on the York River.

He had in each of his hereditary villages, if we may believe the stories of early explorers, a house built like a long arbor for his especial reception. When Powhatan visited one of these villages a feast was already spread in the long house or arbor. He had a hunting town in the wilderness called Orapax. A mile from this place, deep in the woods, he had another arbor-like house, where he kept furs, copper, pearls, and beads, treasures which he was saving against his burial. Powhatan was attended by a bodyguard of forty or fifty tall warriors, while, says Captain Smith, "every night upon the four quarters of his house are four sentinels, each from other a slight shoot, and at every half hour one from the corps on guard doth hollow, shaking his lips with his finger between them, unto whom every sentinel doth answer round from his stand, if any fail, they presently send forth an officer that beateth him extremely." The war whoop thus described by Captain Smith is still in use among certain tribes of Indians.

Powhatan was proud of his fleet. It consisted of a large number of the canoes called "dugouts," which are common among some tribes of Indians. The making of these boats was a laborious process. Trees were felled by fire, and from the trunks a boat was shaped by means of burning and scraping with shells and tomahawks. Powhatan had twenty sons and eleven daughters living. We know nothing of his sons except Nantaguas, "the manliest, comeliest, boldest spirit" ever seen in "a savage." Pocahontas was Powhatan's favorite daughter. She was born in 1594 or 1595. Of her mother nothing is known. Powhatan had many wives, when he tired of them he would present them to those of his subjects, whom he considered the most deserving. Indians are frequently known by several names. It is a disappointment to learn that the name which the romantic story of this Indian princess has made so famous was not her real name. She was called in childhood, Matoaka. Concealing this from the English, because of a superstitious notion that if these pale-faced strangers knew her true name they could do her some harm, the Indians gave her name as Pocahontas. Powhatan's authority, like that of all Indian chiefs, was held in check by the severity of custom. "The laws whereby he ruleth," says Captain Smith "is custom. Yet when he listeth, his will is a law, and must be obeyed—not only as a king, but as half a god they esteem him." Each village and tribe had its respective chief, or "werowance," as they were called among the Powhatan Indians. The affairs of the tribe were settled in a council of the chiefs and warriors of the several villages. Every town possessed its council house, just as the villages of New England have a town hall.

Here the chiefs and old men assembled for consultation on any important matter. Powhatan was the great werowance over all, "unto whom," says Captain Smith, "They pay tribute of skins, beads, copper, pearl, deer, turkeys, wild beasts, and corn. What he commandeth they dare not disobey in the least thing. It is strange to see with what care and adoration all these people do obey this Powhatan. For at his feet they present whatsoever he commandeth, and at the least frown of his brow, their greatest spirits will tremble and no marvel, for he is very terrible and tyrannous in punishing such as offend him." It was a barbarous life in which the little Pocahontas was bred. Her people always washed their young babies in the river on the coldest mornings to harden them. She was accustomed to see her old father sitting at the door of his cabin regarding with grim pleasure a string of his enemy's scalps, suspended from tree to tree, and waving in the breeze. Men in England in her time idealized her into a princess and fine lady, in our time historians have been surprised and indignant at finding that she was not a heroine of romance, but simply an Indian maiden. Such as her life made her she was—in her manners an untrained savage. But she was also the steadfast friend and helper of the feeble colony and that is why her (Pocahontas) life is so full of interest to us (United States).

❑❑❑❑❑❑❑❑❑❑❑

The colonists's hearts were buoyant with hopes of a bright future in this lovely land to which they had come in its loveliest season. All set to work in a holiday spirit. The council planned fortifications, the rest cleared the ground of trees, made nets, and prepared the "clapboards"—which in their speech probably meant cask staves—with which the ships were to be laden for their return voyage. Savages frequently visited them with friendly curiosity. Cheerful activity had somewhat stilled the wrangles of the voyages. Captain Smith, through a domineering will and the reputation which he enjoyed for his adventures, excited the jealousy of those who were ambitious of leading. Smith, as an experienced soldier, although not admitted to the council, probably gave advice freely as to the necessity of drilling the colonists and building a strong fort. The president, who was a merchant, did nothing further than to fortify the new town with "boughs of trees cast together in the form of a half moon." Captain Smith's bold spirit was too useful to be neglected.

He and Captain [Christopher] Newport, with twenty others, were sent to discover the source of the James River. They ascended the river as far as the rapids, and planted a cross at the end of their explorations. They visited an Indian chief at the village named Powhatan, which was composed of about twelve cabins pleasantly situated on a hill surrounded by cornfields, and fronted by three fertile islands. Captain Newport presented the chief with a hatchet, with which he was much delighted. The Indians complained at the intrusion of the English into their country.—The chief, concealing his own apprehensions, said, "They hurt you not, they take but a little waste land."—When, however, the exploring party had returned to within twenty miles of Jamestown, they began to suspect treachery. On reaching the colony they found that their suspicions were well-founded.

The colonists, while securely at work and unarmed, had been attacked by the Indians, and were for some time in danger of destruction. A crossbar shot from the vessel struck off the bough of a tree in the midst of the savages, and so frightened them that they fled in every direction. Had it not been for this timely shot, attributed by some authority to the presence of mind of the president, [Edward] Wingfield, the colonists would all have been massacred by the savages. As it was, seventeen men were wounded and one boy killed, while Wingfield had a narrow escape, an arrow passing through his beard. Warned by this attack of the savages, the president now had the town fortified with palisades, the guns mounted, and the men armed and drilled. The Indians hung continually around the white settlement, either making covert attacks, or in ambuscade awaiting an opportunity. Stragglers from the fort—and there were many such—were often hurt, while the Indians always escaped "by the nimbleness of their heels." Captain Newport, who had been hired only to transport the colony, remained six weeks. During this time the labor of the colonists was severe.

With all the work which the immediate needs of the settlers called for, and the loading of the vessels for their return voyage, the settlers were obliged with their small force to watch at night and to guard the workmen by day. Captain Newport at last prepared to set sail. Captain Smith had been for thirteen weeks under suspicion, awaiting a trial. His natural leadership had already asserted itself, while his earnestness and straightforward energy had gained him friends and respect.—His enemies, probably fearing for the success of their plans, proposed, out of charity, to refer him to the council in England rather than to subject him to a public trial at Jamestown.—Captain Smith "scorned" their kindness, and demanded a trial, which resulted very honorably to him. His accusers's witnesses confessed that they had been suborned, Smith was acquitted, and his chief enemy, the president, was condemned to pay Smith two hundred pounds. Captain Smith turned the money into the public store.

The good minister came forward and made peace on all sides, and through his influence and that of Captain Newport, Smith was admitted to his seat in the council. The next day all received the communion together, on the day following the Indians presented themselves to desire peace, and Captain Newport set sail for England with good news from Virginia.

Left thus to their "fortunes, it fortuned" that within a few days the colonists were nearly all sick. The site of Jamestown had been poorly chosen. The adjacent swamps of the Chickahominy made it very unhealthy. The colonists had not become acclimated and unusual toil in a summer's heat, to which they were not accustomed, with a scarcity of provisions, were the causes of this sickness. The council in London believed that they had plentifully provided the colonists with provisions, supposing that the voyage would be made in two months, and that they would reach Virginia in time to plant for themselves. They had, however, been five months on the way, and had thus missed the chance of raising a corn harvest. While the ships remained, the settlers had traded sassafras, furs, and money for biscuits, which the sailors would pilfer from the ship's store.—Now their food consisted of a half pint of wheat and as much barley to each man, boiled in a common kettle.—This grain had lain so long in the ship's hold that it was full of worms, and could not have been very appetizing to the sick colonists, who had no drink but water, and no "lodgings" but "castles in the air." Still, as their narrative says, the council in England was not to be blamed, since "the fault of our going was our own." Every day during the month of August fresh graves were dug. One day the cannons boomed in honor of the burial of Captain Bartholomew Gosnold, the explorer, and one of the first movers of the expedition. To his loss no doubt some of the later misfortunes of the colony were due. At the end of the summer about fifty of the one hundred and five colonists had died. There was naturally much murmuring and discontent in the smitten and hungry colony. "Had we been as free from all sins as gluttony and drunkenness," says their story, "we might have been canonized for saints." They were evidently, however, not free from other sins.—After the death of Captain Gosnold contentions increased.—John Kendall was deposed from his seat in the council, and imprisoned for making trouble between the president and the other members of the council. Wingfield himself, accused of engrossing for his private benefit what delicacies there were, was also suspected of a project to flee to England with their little vessel. The "dead spirits" of the sick colonists were "so moved" that the president was deposed and confined upon the pinnace. He denied the charges against him in a statement written to the council in England, and it cannot be certainly known whether, as Captain Smith believed, there was truth in them or not. There is little doubt, however, that Wingfield was ill-fitted to fill the difficult office to which he had been elected. Captain John Ratcliffe was appointed in his place.

Those men who had survived during the summer had lived mostly on sturgeon and sea crabs. As autumn came on the sturgeon failed them, and their supply of provisions had come to an end. In their weakened condition they expected every day to be attacked by the savages. In this extremity the Indians, however, proved friendly, bringing them plenty of fruit and provisions. Captain Smith's natural gift for leadership had asserted itself through the trials and dangers of the colony.

From this time the real management of affairs fell into his hands. The new president, and [John] Martin, the remaining member of the council, were content to stay at home. By dint of good words, promises, and his own example, Smith got the men to work to build Jamestown. Some cut, others bound thatch, some built cottages, and others thatched them. Among them all worked Captain Smith, taking always the most difficult task as his share. In a short time they all had homes except Smith himself. The superfluity of the Indian harvests in the neighborhood of Jamestown was being used up. Captain Smith resolved to go on a trading expedition into the Indian country. The colonists had no knowledge of the Indian language, their force was small, they knew little about managing a boat without sails, and the men needed clothing and other necessaries. All these were difficulties in the way of the expedition, "yet no discouragement" to the bold spirit of Captain Smith, with five or six men in a shallop they started down the river. They stopped at the Indian village of Kecoughtan, where Hampton now stands. The inhabitants scorned them as starving men. They would offer them a handful of corn in exchange for their swords, or a piece of bread for their clothes. These were Indian jokes. Captain Smith, soldier that he was, finding that "courtesy" had no effect, tried force, though contrary to his commission. He suddenly "let fly his muskets," and ran his boat ashore. The Indians immediately fled for the woods while this company of six or seven men marched into their town. Here were great heaps of corn, and Smith had "much ado" to prevent the hungry soldiers from helping themselves.

    He kept his men in readiness, expecting an attack on the part of the Indians. In a short time there was "a most hideous noise," and sixty or seventy Indians, formed in square order, came dancing and singing out of the woods. They were all painted either black—red, white, or party colored, and bore their Okee before them, made of skin, stuffed with moss, painted and decorated with beads and copper. They charged upon the English, armed with clubs, shields, bows and arrows. They were "so kindly received," however, with a volley of musketry, "that down, fell their god, and divers lay sprawling on the ground."

    The rest of the Indians had disappeared again in the woods. They soon sent a priest with offers for peace and the restoration of their idol. Smith made answer that if they would send six unarmed men to load his boat he would not only return the Okee—but give them beads, copper, and hatchets—and be their friend. Accordingly they brought him venison, turkey, wild fowls, and bread, and were so pleased with the trinkets that he gave them in exchange that the last that the English saw of them they were dancing and singing in token of friendship, though they were no doubt glad when the English were gone. The sickly season had passed, and the colonists were all recovered by the time of the return of the expedition. Captain Smith now fitted up the pinnace for a voyage in search of provisions for the following year. Meanwhile he made several short trips into the country. On one of these journeys he discovered the people of Chickahominy living on the river of that name. The president was a weak man, Martin was in ill-health, and when Captain Smith was absent all was confusion among the colonists. During one of his trips Wingfield and [George] Kendall plotted with some others to sail for England in the pinnace. Captain Smith returned unexpectedly, the plot was revealed to him, and he forced them to "stay or sink" after a skirmish which cost the life of Captain Kendall (unless, indeed, Kendall was executed after a trial, as in some accounts). The president and Captain [Gabriel] Archer entertained a similar project for abandoning the country not long after this, but Smith detained them also. It is said of Smith that—"the Spaniard never more greedily desired gold than he victual, nor his soldiers more to abandon the country than he to keep it."—He had found an abundance of corn on the Chickahominy River. He made an excursion there, and was received by hundreds of Indians with baskets of corn. Times of plenty had now come to the country.

As winter approached, the rivers were covered with swans, ducks, and geese. With these and an abundance of other game, fish, and fruit, the colonists were so feasted that Captain Smith no longer had to threaten the sinking of the little vessel to keep them in Virginia. But their "comedies never endured long without a tragedy." The tragedy was soon to follow.

□□□□□□□□□□

We come now to consider the adventures and explorations of the chief hero of the Virginia colony, Captain John Smith. In an age when romantic adventures were in vogue he was the rarest of adventurers. From boyhood he led a roving life, wandering through Europe, fighting the Turks, enduring captivities, encountering pirates and shipwreck, and at last distinguishing himself by the ready stratagems and unfailing presence of mind with which he managed the savages in Virginia and delivered the colony from destruction. At the early age of thirteen—like many another boy—he was "set upon brave adventures," as he says. But he did not, like the usual boy of modern story books, achieve a brave career in an incredibly short time, and without any previous training. This remarkable man had already attained great renown as an adventurer and soldier when he sailed for Virginia, being then under twenty-eight years of age. He was born at Willoughby, in Lincolnshire, in 1579. Never did a hero of romantic adventure come into possession of a more commonplace name than that of John Smith. His father came, it would seem from an old and well-known family of Smiths, and was a man of some means. John Smith attended the free schools of Alford and Louth. To him, as to all boys of a roving tendency, the sea seemed the only road to "brave adventures." At the age of thirteen he sold his school books and satchel, and planned to run away to sea. The death of his parents at this time, however, checked his adventurous spirit for the moment. His father left him plenty of means, but his guardians cared more for the boy's estate than for the boy. Smith had liberty enough to do as he pleased, but lacked money. When he was fifteen years old his guardians apprenticed him to a merchant of Lynn. Because this merchant would not send him to sea, as Smith quaintly remarks, he saw no more of his master for eight years. John Smith had found a chance to attend the son of Lord Willoughby, who was going with his tutor to France. His guardians had found Smith a troublesome charge, and they gave him ten shillings, from his own estate, "to be rid of him." At Orleans the young nobleman met his brother, and having no more use for Smith, he was dismissed. He had probably engaged to attend him for his passage, but the young gentleman gave him money to pay his fare back to his home. John Smith had no notion of returning to England, however. At Paris he became acquainted with a Scotch gentleman named David Hume, who, if we rightly identify him, was a Protestant minister, the author of several famous books in

English and Latin. He seems to have taken a great fancy to the adventurous boy, for he gave him money and letters to friends in Scotland, who would refer him to King James VI, at that time reigning in Scotland, afterward James I of England.

Arriving at Rouen on his way to Scotland, and finding his money nearly gone, "he better bethought himself," and "down the river he went to Havre de Grace." Here he became a soldier. When peace was concluded in France, he went over into the Low Countries, where he served for three or four years under Captain Joseph Duxbury. He probably belonged to a corps of English auxiliaries who aided the Netherlands in the struggle in which they gained their independence. He next resolved to deliver his letters. On the voyage, with his usual hard fortune, he suffered shipwreck and sickness. He at last arrived in Scotland, where he was most kindly treated, but he had not the means to make a courtier, nor indeed was of the kind of men that dwell in kings's houses. John Smith returned to his native town, where he was soon glutted with a society which was not to his taste.

This young gentleman of nineteen resolved to become a hermit. He selected "a little woody pasture" surrounded by hundreds of acres of other woods, where he built him a "pavilion of bows." Here he studied Machiavelli's *Art of War* and the writings of Marcus Aurelius, while he exercised himself with a good horse, his lance, and ring, after the manner of that time. Like Shakespeare, he was guilty of breaking the game law, for he slyly remarks that "his food was thought to be more of venison than anything else." This romantic hermit was much wondered at. An Italian gentleman, Signor Theodora Polaloga, rider to the Earl of Lincoln, visited Smith, and by his fine horsemanship and "good discourse" persuaded him to return to the outside world again. He stayed for a time with his Italian friend, but could not long be content with such tame pleasures as this life afforded.

He had served his apprenticeship in the wars of France and the Netherlands. He now desired to see more of the world, and "lamenting and repenting to have seen so many Christians slaughter one another," he was ambitious to "try his fortunes" against those about killing whom he would have no compunction—namely, the infidel Turks. Smith first set out for the Low Countries. Here he met four French adventurers, one of whom gave himself out as a nobleman, Lord Dapreau, while the rest were his attendants. They formed a friendship with the young Englishman, and proposed to Smith to go into France, where they might procure letters from the Duchess of Mercoeur to the Duke, her husband, who was a general in the Turkish War. They embarked for France, and on a dark night arrived at St. Valery in Picardy. The Frenchmen planned with the captain to put them ashore with their own and Smith's baggage, while he was to wait for the return of the boat. The captain did not return until the next night, saying that the sea was so high that he could not come, and that Lord Dapreau had gone to Amiens, where he would await the arrival of Smith. This young gentleman was now left without clothes except what he wore, and without money except one small piece. The passengers were indignant at the villainy of the captain, and with the lawlessness of the times would have killed him, and seized the ship had they known how to manage it. When Smith came to shore he was obliged to sell his cloak in order to pay for his passage. One of the passengers, a solider named Curzianvere, informed Smith that this great lord who had disappeared with his baggage and money was but the son of a lawyer in Brittany, that his gentlemen were three young citizens, and that they were all "arrant cheats." Curzianvere promised to go with Smith to their home, in order that he might get some redress. They journeyed through Normandy, stopping to visit the "ruinous tomb of William the Conqueror," and arrived in Brittany, where they found the rascals. Curzianvere, however, could not help him, for he was a banished man, and dared not be seen by any but his friends. Smith was unable to recover his property, but his story became known, and some of the nobility supplied his wants and entertained him kindly. This life did not suit the young man's independent spirit. He wandered on, from seaport to seaport, in search of a man-of-war (warship). His money was at last all gone, and he lay down in a forest by a "fair fountain," "near dead with grief and cold." Here he was found by a rich farmer and relieved of his wants. Walking through the woods one day, he met one of the French robbers in a still more miserable condition than himself. Without a word they both drew their swords and fought until the Frenchman fell. He confessed his robbery, in the presence of the inhabitants, of "an old ruinated tower" nearby. Smith got his revenge, but that was all.

He now traveled to the castle of the Earl of Ployer, under whom he had fought in the French wars. This nobleman refitted him, and showed him the sights of the country. Turning out of his road many times to see places of interest, Smith at last reached Marseilles, where he embarked for Italy. The vessel was crowded with Catholic pilgrims of all nations bound for Rome.

They "cursed" Smith for a Huguenot, his nation for pirates, and "railed on" his sovereign, Queen Elizabeth. Smith was always a good churchman, and a loyal subject, and being neither a very meek nor patient man, it is probable that he answered them in the same fashion. Stormy weather forced the vessel to put into the harbor of Toulon, and again to anchor off the Isle of St. Mary, near Nice, in Savoy. The pilgrims concluded that they would never have fair weather so long as Smith was with them, so, like a second Jonah, he was thrown overboard.

◻◻◻◻◻◻◻◻◻◻◻

Smith swam ashore to St. Mary's Isle, which he found inhabited only by a few cattle and goats. But he was not long destined to play *Robinson Crusoe*. The next morning he espied two other ships which had been forced in by the storm. He was taken on board a vessel, commanded by Captain La Roche, a neighbor of the Earl of Ployer. "For the love" of this nobleman Smith was well-entertained. The French vessel sailed to Alexandria, delivered her freight, and coasted the Levant (Middle East) "rather to view what ships were in the road than anything else." In those days sailors were always on the watch for plunder. They met a Venetian argosy, richly laden. The French vessel attempted to bespeak her, but the captain answered them with a broadside, probably expecting no better treatment from such as he met. Captain La Roche immediately gave chase, giving her his broadside, then his stern, and then his other broadside, until the Venetian's sails and rigging were so torn that she was obliged to stand and give battle "shot for shot." Twice in an hour Captain La Roche boarded her, and once the argosy fired him, with much danger to both vessels. The fire was quenched, however, and the battle continued until the Venetian yielded. The rich vessel, loaded with silks, velvets, cloth of gold, and gold and silver money, was rifled of the least bulky part of her cargo. Smith was set ashore in Piedmont (region in Italy) with his share of the spoils, five hundred sequins, and "a little box, probably containing jewels, worth twice as much more." Having now both the means and opportunity, he was glad "to better his experience by the view of Italy." At Rome he saw Pope Clement VIII and his cardinals "creep up the holy stairs." Having "satisfied his eyes with the rarities" of the principal cities of Italy, he started from Venice for the seat of the Turkish war. In 1601, Smith, then but twenty-two years of age, reached Graz, in Styria. The feeble Rudolph II, Emperor of Germany, was at this time waging war against the Turks, who had invaded Hungary and given the Emperor much trouble. Smith met two of his countrymen, who introduced him to Lord Eberspaught. This officer examined him, and presented him to Baron Khissl, general of the artillery, who placed him in the regiment of the Earl of Meldritch.

  The Christians had lost the strong fortress of Canisia, or Kaniska, in Hungary, and the Turks were ravaging the neighboring country. They now laid siege with twenty thousand men to Olympach, which was commanded by Lord Eberspaught. All intelligence and supplies were entirely cut off from the beleaguered garrison. Baron Khissl had come to the assistance of Olympach, and wished to send a communication to the commander. It was impossible for a messenger to pass the Turkish ranks. At this juncture John Smith appeared before the Baron, and told him that he had previously explained a method of telegraphy to Lord Eberspaught, and that if he would take him to some place where a torch might be seen from the town, he would undertake to communicate with him. He explained his plan to the Baron, who allowed him guides to take him on a dark night to the top of a mountain seven miles from Olympach. From this point Smith showed three torches at an equal distance from one another. After waiting a while he saw that Lord Eberspaught had guessed the meaning of this, for three answering lights appeared from the town. Smith's plan was to show one torch a corresponding number of times to the place in the alphabet of the letter which he wished to designate. By this means he spelled out the words, "On Thursday, at night, I will charge on the east, at the alarm sally you." The answer came from the town, "I will."

This mode of telegraphy is ancient, and Smith had probably found it in his reading. Smith also proposed that on the night of the attack several thousand matches should be fastened to strings, stretched suddenly upon a line on the plain, and fired, an instant before the alarm, in order to deceive the enemy as to the place of attack. The night arrived. The Turks hearing the report of the matches, supposed it to be the firing of musketry, and their force was immediately directed to that quarter. So great was the confusion produced by the false alarm, the real attack in another quarter from Baron Khissl, and the sally of Lord Eberspaught, that the Baron put two thousand good soldiers into the town before morning, and the besieged succeeded in procuring an abundance of provisions from the Turkish encampment. The result was that the Turks abandoned the siege. As a reward for these services, Smith was given the command of a body of two hundred and fifty horses. Duke Mercury, as Smith calls him—more properly, the Duke de Mercoeur, under whom Smith served, now undertook the siege of Alba Regalis, in Hungary, with a force of thirty thousand men. Smith, with characteristic readiness of resource, had invented a sort of bomb made of earthen pots filled with an explosive mixture, and thrown from slings. These were put in use at the siege of Alba Regalis, doing much execution, and firing the suburbs several times. One suburb of the city was strongly defended by a muddy lake, and thought to be impregnable. Earl Roswarine, however, provided every man on a dark night with a bundle of sedge and reeds, which they threw before them, and thus crossed this lake, so surprising the Turks that they fled into the city. The inhabitants of the other suburb, not understanding the cause of panic, followed suit, so that it was readily taken by the Duke. The city, not being as strong as the suburbs, was battered with the ordnance which had been captured. The inhabitants were put to the sword after the barbarous custom prevailing in warfare between Turks and Christians. The Sultan had raised an army of sixty thousand men under the command of Hasan Pasha to march to the relief of Alba Regalis. Hearing that the city was lost, he still continued his march, hoping to retake it. He was met by the Christians, twenty thousand strong, on the plains of Girke. A fierce battle was fought, in which the Earl of Meldritch and his men were so surrounded by the semi-circular Turkish regiments that they were thought to be lost, but were relieved by other brave leaders in the Christian army. Captain Smith was severely wounded, and had his horse shot from under him, but he was not long unmounted among so many riderless horses. Night closed the contest, and another action followed, in which the Turks were defeated with a loss of six thousand men.—The Duke de Mercoeur now divided his army into three parts, that under the Earl of Meldritch being sent into Transylvania, whose Prince, Sigismund Bathory, was both contending with the Emperor of Germany, and, like the Emperor, was waging war against Turkey.—The Earl of Meldritch was to join the Emperor's army against Sigismund. This service was distasteful to him, since he was himself a Transylvanian, and probably sympathized more with the Prince than with the Emperor. His men were mostly adventurers who had entered the service to fight the Turks, and were anxious to serve where the most booty might be obtained. Their pay had been poor in the Emperor's service, and they were easily persuaded to follow their leader, who offered himself to Prince Sigismund to fight the Turks, then holding that part of Transylvania where the estates of his family were situated. Earl Meldritch made incursions into the mountain regions infested with Turks, Tartars (also spelled Tatars), robbers, and renegades. These were forced into the city of Regal, which was so surrounded by mountains that it was entered only by difficult passes and seemed impregnable.

Meldritch with eight thousand men began the siege of the city, or, as Smith poetically states it, "The earth no sooner put on her green habit than the Earl overspread her with his armed troops." The Turks were so well-fortified and garrisoned that they scorned this army. The Christian forces were soon augmented, however, by the arrival of Prince Moyses with nine thousand men. The strong fortress was so well-situated that they could neither frighten nor hurt the Turks, who grew insolent while the Christians were preparing to plant their ordnance, saying they were at pawn, and grew fat for want of exercise.

☐☐☐☐☐☐☐☐☐☐☐

This challenge was one day received in the Christian camp from Regal, "That to delight the ladies, who did long to see some court-like pastime, the Lord Turbishaw did defy any captain that had the command of a company who durst combat with him for his head." So many [soldiers] were ambitious of fighting the Turkish lord that it was necessary to draw lots. The name of Captain Smith was drawn. The day of the contest came. The ramparts of the town were "all beset with fair dames" and armed men. With the sound of hautboys (musicians), the Lord Turbishaw entered the field finely mounted, splendidly armed, and with a great pair of wings fastened upon his shoulders, "compacted of eagles feathers within a ridge of silver, richly garnished with gold and precious stones." Before him went a janissary (infantry) bearing his lance, while one went on either side leading his horse. Captain Smith entered the lists with a flourish of trumpets—attended only by a page—who bore his lance. He passed his antagonist with a courteous salute. At the sound of the trumpet the combatants met at full speed, and the Christian's lance pierced the visor of the Turk, who fell dead. Smith alighted and cut off the Lord Turbishaw's head, leaving the body to his friends. The victor was received with triumphant joy in the Christian camp. The death of this champion brought great chagrin into the Turkish fortress. His vowed friend, Grualgo, challenged Smith to single combat, to regain the head of his friend or to lose his own. The challenge was accepted, and the next day appointed. At the sound of trumpets the combatants met, their lances were shivered, and they passed each other unhurt, although the Turk was nearly unhorsed. They next met with pistols. Smith's armor was dinted, but they again passed unharmed. At the third encounter Captain Smith wounded his antagonist in the left arm. Unable both to manage his horse and defend himself, the Turk was thrown to the ground, where he quickly lost his head. According to the terms of the challenge, horse and armor went to the victor, while the body and rich apparel were returned to the town. The works of the besiegers progressed slowly. A few unimportant skirmishes only took place. Smith now procured leave to send a challenge into the town on his part. The message was to this effect, that he was not so "enamored" of the heads of the ladies's servants that he would not afford any Turkish knight a chance to redeem them and secure his own if he could win it. This challenge was accepted by a Turk named Bonny Mulgro, who, having the choice of weapons, avoided the lance, in the use of which Smith had proved himself so skillful—and chose pistols, battleaxes, and swords. On the following day the champions entered the lists as before, and discharged their pistols at the first encounter without effect. Such heavy blows from the battleaxe followed as to nearly stun both Turk and Christian. Smith was not, however, so skillful with this weapon, and the Turk dealt him a blow that forced him to drop his battleaxe, and he came near following it to the ground. A great shout of triumph arose from the ramparts of Regal. But the battle was not yet won. The Turk followed up his advantage with heavy blows, which Smith, however, avoided by dexterous horsemanship, and, contrary to the expectations of the witnesses, he succeeded in piercing the body of his enemy with his sword. The head of Bonny Mulgro followed those of his friends. After this Smith was conducted to the pavilion of Prince Moyses with a guard of six thousand men—preceded by the three heads upon lances—and the horses of the conquered Turks. Captain Smith presented his trophies to the Prince, who received him with an embrace and presented him a richly caparisoned horse, and a scimitar and belt worth three hundred ducats, while the Earl of Meldritch made him major of his regiment. The siege of Regal continued, and the place was at last taken after a fierce assault. The garrison was put to the sword in retaliation for the massacre of the Christian garrison from whom the Turks had taken the place. Prince Sigismund, when he came to review his army, was informed of Captain Smith's valor and services, for which he gave him his picture set in gold, and a pension of three hundred ducats. He gave Captain Smith a patent of nobility, with three Turks's heads in his coat of arms. This patent was afterward accepted, and recorded in the College of Arms in England.

☐☐☐☐☐☐☐☐☐☐

Prince Sigismund at last gave up his unequal struggle with the Emperor. Transylvania became a German province, and Sigismund retired to the life of a private nobleman in Prague with an ample pension. By this means the allegiance of Sigismund's armies was transferred to the Emperor, a master to whom they were so little attached that it became necessary to occupy them. The opportunity was not long wanting in those troubled times. Wallachia was then in possession of the Turks. The inhabitants revolted against the tyranny of the vaivode, or prince, of this province, and applied for assistance to the Emperor. Lord Rodoll was appointed vaivode in place of the Turk, whose name was Jeremy. The Earl of Meldritch, with an army of thirty thousand men, was sent to support the new ruler. Jeremy met him with forty thousand Turks, Tartars, and Moldavians. A bloody battle ensued between the two pretenders to the principality, which resulted in establishing Rodoll as vaivode. Jeremy had, however, gathered together another army in Moldavia, and threatened trouble. The Earl of Meldritch, with thirteen thousand men, was sent against him. They were successful in several skirmishes, in one of which he was assisted by Smith's inventive genius.—The latter manufactured fireworks, which were carried upon the tops of lances in a night attack, and so frightened horse and man that the victory was an easy matter.—The end was disastrous, however. The Earl of Meldritch was attacked by an army of forty thousand Turks in a mountain pass. He ordered his eleven thousand remaining men as best he could—planted sharpened stakes with their heads toward the enemy, with holes dug among them, as his defense, and bravely encountered the multitudes of the foe. When numbers became too much for them, the Christians retired behind their defense, and Captain Smith says "it was a wonder to see how horse and man came to the ground among the stakes." The Christians could not, however, long prevail. The Earl of Meldritch made one last effort. He formed all his men into a column, and attempted to cut his way through the enemies's ranks. In this he succeeded for a time, but was at last overwhelmed, night came on, and the Earl escaped with some thirteen hundred horsemen by swimming the river. On this terrible battlefield nearly thirty thousand men lay dead or wounded, among them Captain Smith. "Most of the dearest friends of the noble Prince Sigismund" perished in the battle. Smith tenderly recorded in his history the names of some nine of his own countrymen who fell on this forgotten battlefield.

Searching among the dead, the pillagers discovered Captain Smith, and judging by his rich armor and dress that he was a person of some importance, they saved him, hoping to get a good ransom. His wounds were healed, and he was taken with numbers of other prisoners to Axiopolis to be sold as a slave. Here, "like beasts in a marketplace," they were viewed by the merchants, their limbs and their wounds carefully examined, and finally they were made to struggle together to try their strength. Captain Smith was purchased by the Bashaw, or, as we should say, Pasha, Bogall. A number of slaves were chained by the necks in groups of twenty and marched to Constantinople, where they were delivered to their several masters. Smith was presented by the Bashaw to his fair young mistress, Charatza Tragabigzanda. He wrote her that this slave was a Bohemian nobleman whom he had captured in battle. The young lady immediately became interested in her fine-looking young slave. She understood Italian, and would make opportunities to speak with him. She inquired if he were indeed a Bohemian noble conquered by her lord. Captain Smith protested that he had never seen Bashaw Bogall until they had met in the slave market. She had him examined by those who could speak English, to whom he told his story. Convinced of the truth of it, she took the more interest in him, and treated him with the greatest kindness. Charatza Tragabigzanda had formed a romantic attachment for her Christian slave. She had, however, no use for him, and fearing lest her mother, who may have suspected her love for him—should cause him to be sold—she resolved to send him to her brother Timor, Bashaw of Nalbrits in Tartary. With him she sent a letter to this lord, requesting him to use her slave well, since she intended him but to sojourn in Nalbrits to learn the language and become a Turk until she became her own mistress. At the end of his journey Captain Smith was brought before Timor in his "vast stony castle." The proud Bashaw read his sister's letter, and was incensed that she should look with favor on a Christian slave. He immediately ordered that his head should be shaven, a great iron collar riveted upon his neck, and that he should be dressed in a rough haircloth garment. Among hundreds of slaves he was slave to them all, though he said "there was no great choice, for the best was so bad that a dog could hardly have lived to endure."

 Captain Smith now had a tyrant for a master, who took delight in beating and abusing the Christian slave. In all his hopeless misery Smith noted the manners and customs, religion and government, of the Tartars. Of their disgusting style of living he speaks in the strongest terms, but he praises their skillful horsemanship and endurance of hardship in war. "All the hope he had ever to be delivered from this thraldom," said Smith, "was only the love of Tragabigzanda, who surely was ignorant of his bad usage, for although he had often debated the matter with some Christians that had been there a long time, slaves, they could not find how to make an escape by any reason or possibility. But God, beyond man's expectation or imagination, helpeth his servants when they least think of help as it happened to him." Captain Smith was put to thresh grain at a farm more than a league from the castle of the Bashaw. Timor was accustomed often to visit his various granges. One day he visited Smith at his work, and beat and reviled him so unmercifully that Captain Smith, "forgetting all reason," rose in defense and beat out the Bashaw's brains with the bat which the Tartars used for threshing. There was now no hope for him in remaining where he was, his condition could not be altered for the worse. He quickly hid the Bashaw's body under the straw, dressed himself in his clothes, and filling his knapsack with grain, closed the doors of the barn, and mounting his master's horse, fled into the desert. Here he wandered for several days, not knowing the way, and yet thankful that he met no one of whom he might ask it, since the Bashaw's clothes could not conceal the slave's iron collar, stamped with his master's sign. He at last came upon a great road on whose crossings were signposts marked with a crescent for Tartary, a black man with white spots for Persia, a picture of the sun for China, and a cross for Christian lands. Captain Smith followed the grateful sign of the cross for sixteen days in fear and trembling lest he should meet a Turk. He at last reached Ecopolis, a Russian fortress on the River Don. The governor listened to his story, relieved him of his irons, and treated him so kindly that "he thought himself newly raised from death." Here he was a second time befriended by a lady, for he says "the good Lady Callamatta largely supplied all his wants." The kindly governor furnished him with letters of recommendation, and he journeyed under the protection of convoys to Hermannstadt, in Transylvania.

The countries through which he traveled were so desolate that he says "it is a wonder any should make wars for them."

Nevertheless, "in all his life he seldom met with more respect, mirth, content, and entertainment, and not any governor where he came but gave him somewhat as a present, beside his charges, seeing themselves as subject to the like calamity." We do not know how long Captain Smith was in captivity, but it could not have been many months, for he was captured in 1602, and we find him again in Christendom in 1603. When he arrived in Transylvania he was received with joy by his friends as one raised from the grave. He says he was so "glutted with content and near drowned with joy" that he would never have left his friends here had it not been for his desire "to rejoice himself after all these encounters in his native country." It may be doubted, however, if his roving disposition would have suffered him long to remain content in any quiet life. He next went to Leipsic, where he found the Earl of Meldritch with Prince Sigismund, who gave him a patent of the nobility which he had previously bestowed upon him, and fifteen hundred ducats to repair his losses. Possessed of more money, Smith seems to have forgotten his great desire to return to England, for with this means he set out to see many of the "fair cities" of Germany, France, and Spain.—"Being thus satisfied," as he says, "with Europe and Asia," and hearing of wars in Barbary, he set sail in a French man of war for Africa.—He went to Morocco, inquired into the causes of the murderous civil wars, and unable to decide which side was the most in the wrong, he refused to join either. He noted the manners and customs of the people, and returned to the vessel in which he had come, resolved to "try some other conclusions (adventures) at sea." Captain Smith added to his adventures yet one more, for the French vessel sustained a desperate battle with two Spanish men-of-wars, who boarded her and fired her. They fought thus for two nights and a day, the Spaniards once asking a truce to parley with the captain, but the desperate Frenchman, knowing there was but one way, "would have none but the report of his ordnance." They at last succeeded in beating off the Spanish vessels and making port. Captain Smith returned to England about the year 1604. His restless temperament at last found an enterprise worthy of it. Captain Bartholomew Gosnold was endeavoring to awaken an interest in the colonization of Virginia. Captain Smith entered heartily into his projects, and these gentlemen, with Mr. [Edward] Wingfield and the Reverend Mr. [Robert] Hunt, by persistent agitation, at last succeeded in interesting men of influence, who formed a company, and obtained a patent from the king. In two years more the energetic Captain Smith was on the way to a country with which he had not as yet satisfied his eyes—a land of promise to all bold spirits, a field for the bravest of adventures and the greatest self-denial.

□□□□□□□□□□□

Let us now return to the colony at Jamestown, where the adventurous Smith was rapidly rising into prominence. But there were murmurings against him. He had not yet discovered the source of the Chickahominy. This river flows from the northwest, and the colonists had received directions from the council in England to explore such a river, since it was supposed that its head might be near the South Sea or Pacific Ocean, and a passage to the East Indies might thus be discovered.—So little did the early settlers of America know of the extent of their continent.—Even the colony's council reprehended Smith for being "too slow in so worthy an attempt." Accordingly, in early winter Captain Smith and his men began the ascent of the Chickahominy. In a rude barge they penetrated to where fallen trees obstructed the passage. The discoverers only proceeded by dint of chopping away the obstacles. When at last the barge could penetrate no farther, Captain Smith moored her in a wide bay out of danger, and commanded his men not to go ashore.

Taking with him two Englishmen, and as many native guides, he pushed twenty miles higher up the narrow stream in a canoe. The river's head was found in swampy meadows, or "slashes," as they are called in Virginia, but the surges of the Pacific did not roll into it as in the fabled fountain of the Roanoke. Captain Smith was the only man in the colony who did not look for an ocean over the next hill, and a gold mine at every step. On reaching the source of the Chickahominy his first thought was of the present necessity for food instead of a chimerical opening for future commercial wealth. Leaving his two men, [John] Robinson and [Thomas] Emry, with their matchlock guns lighted, in charge of the canoe, he went with an Indian guide in search of game.

Meanwhile the men in the barge made a tour of discovery on shore, and succeeded in discovering some three hundred Indian bowmen, under the command of Opechancanough, chief of the Pamunkey Indians, a tribe of Powhatan's confederacy.

The savages attacked them—captured one of their number—George Cassen, and nearly succeeded in cutting off the other men with their barge. They drew the whereabouts of Captain Smith from their prisoner, and afterward executed him in a most barbarous manner. (See page 257 for details on Cassen's fate.) The Indians then divided themselves into parties and searched the river banks. They crept upon Robinson and Emry, off their guard, or possibly asleep by their fire, and shot them through and through with arrows. Captain Smith himself was suddenly beset by the Indians. With a garter he quickly bound his Indian guide to his left arm as a shield, and bent a pistol at his breast to enforce submission. Thus with one of their race between him and their arrows he defended himself with his musket. In the skirmish which ensued he killed three Indians and wounded several others. Their superstitious awe of firearms was increased, and they retired to a safe distance. Captain Smith had received but one wound, though his clothes were full of arrows. With his eyes upon the enemy he started for his canoe. He naturally watched the wily Indians more closely than his own footsteps, and he had not gone far before he sank with his guide to the waist in a treacherous marsh. Still the Indians dared not approach their entrapped enemy until, almost dead with cold Smith threw away the dreaded weapons and surrendered. According to an agreement between them, they drew him out of the water and led him to the fire where his men had been shot. While they chafed his benumbed limbs Captain Smith turned over in his mind plans for appeasing his captors. He asked for their captain. They pointed out Opechancanough. With quick presence of mind, Captain Smith drew forth the only trinket (ornament) in his possession—a round ivory double dialed compass—and presented it to the Indian chieftain. The savages all crowded around with eager curiosity. They wondered at the motions of the little instrument, and were still more astonished when they put forth their hands to touch the trembling needle and were checked by the glass. Glad of a chance to astonish them and divert their minds, Captain Smith, aided by gestures and the globe-like toy, proceeded to demonstrate "the roundness of the earth and skies, the sphere of the sun, moon, and stars, and how the sun did chase the night around the world continually, the greatness of the land and sea, the diversity of nations, variety of complexions, and how we were to them antipodes, and many other such like matters." It may be doubted whether much of his lecture was suitable to savage comprehension. Captain Smith's theory of the solar system which was that commonly held in his day was hardly nearer the truth than their own ideas as to the lights of the day and night. The Indians, however, stood "as amazed with admiration." Nevertheless, within an hour preparations had all been made for his execution. He was tied to a tree, and as many as could stand within range took aim at him. But the chief at this moment held up the ivory compass, and the Indians threw down their bows and arrows. Captain Smith was next to figure in the triumphal procession so common among the Indians. The warriors formed in Indian file. In the center of the line came the chief with the captured swords and firearms borne before him, and followed by the prisoner, held by three great Indians and surrounded by a guard of warriors with arrows drawn. Captain Smith was conducted thus to the Indian village of Orapax. On nearing the town they were met by all the women and children, "staring to behold" the first white man they had ever seen. The Indians immediately made preparations for a dance. Their heads and shoulders were painted a "scarlet-like color," which "made an exceeding handsome show." Everyone wore his ornament, a bird's skin dried, with wings spread, pieces of copper, white shells, a long feather, or "a small rattle growing at the tails of their snakes," says Captain Smith. Each Indian was armed with quiver, club, and bow. They "cast themselves into a ring" around the guarded prisoner, and their chief "dancing in such several postures," and singing, yelling, and screeching so wildly that Captain Smith must have felt that he was indeed among demons. Three such dances had been performed when the prisoner was taken to the long house for refreshment.

He was guarded by thirty or forty Indians, and enough bread and venison was brought him to have supplied twenty men. His captors probably felt the same interest that people in a menagerie have in seeing the animals feed. The English, however, knew little of the practices of the North American Indian, and Smith had a strong suspicion that he was to be fattened for a cannibal meal. In spite of the long fast and tempting food, he says that he thinks "his stomach at that time was not very good." What he left was put in two baskets, tied up over his head, and served to him again about midnight.

In the morning fresh food was brought, while the Indians who had refused to eat with him heretofore ate what had been left from his previous meals. The weather was extremely cold, and an Indian named Maocassater presented Captain Smith with a mantle in return for some beads and toys which he had given him on the arrival of the colony in Virginia. Two days after this an Indian, whose son was dying with a wound Smith had inflicted in his skirmish with the savages, would have killed the Captain had not the guard defended him. Captain Smith was believed to be a wonder worker far superior to their priests or medicine men. He was taken to the bedside of the dying savage to affect a cure. He told the Indians that he would go to Jamestown and get water which would heal the man, but the savages were not to be thus outwitted. Captain Smith trembled to hear the Indians discuss plans for the destruction of Jamestown. Preparations were being made for this purpose, and the Indians consulted Smith about it. If he would assist them he was offered life, liberty, and wives. Captain Smith, however, romanced about the dangers they would meet with in attacking Jamestown, dilating upon the great guns, secret mines, and other engines of death. He asked permission to send messengers to Jamestown, who might confirm his story. His request was complied with, and tearing a leaf from his memorandum book, he wrote a note to the colonists informing them of the danger of an attack, giving them directions as to how they should terrify the bearers of the note, and instructing them to send him some articles of which he gave a list. He entrusted this note for deliverance to the messengers who were not suspicious that it could betray their own plans, and told them just what the colonists would do, what would happen to them, and what articles they would send. The messengers were much frightened by his description of the engines of death in possession of the whites. Still they undertook the journey in the bitter cold of an unusual winter. In Jamestown Captain Smith was believed to be dead. The men with the barge returning home had told the story of their attack, and of the probable death of Captain Smith and his two companions. This intrepid soldier was mourned as heartily as he had been detested. When the Indian messengers neared Jamestown they saw men sally out to meet them as Smith had told them. This fulfillment of the first item in his prophecy so frightened them that, dreading the explosive nature of the ground in the neighborhood of Jamestown, and fearing the supernatural weapons [guns] of the English, they were panic-stricken, and fled, leaving their note behind them.

    When night came on, however, they crept cautiously to the spot where Captain Smith had told them they would find an answer. There were the very articles he had promised them. Taking them, they returned home "with no small expedition." At the account of their adventures, and the sight of the promised trinkets, the Indians were all wonderstruck, concluding "that he could either be divine or the paper could speak." They now gave up all idea of attacking Jamestown, and led Smith from village to village in a triumphal procession. Having thus traversed the dominions of a number of tribes, he was brought back to the seat of the chief of Pamunkey. Here he was put through a ceremony intended to discover whether he meant them good or evil.

    Early in the morning a great fire was built in a "long house," probably the council house. Two mats were spread upon the ground, upon one of which the prisoner was seated, his guard retired, and he was left alone. "Presently came skipping in a great grim fellow, all painted over with coal mingled with oil."

He was adorned with "many snake and weasel skins stuffed with moss, and all their tails tied together, so as they met on the crown of his head in a tassel, and round about the tassel was a coronet of feathers, the skins hanging round about his head, back, and shoulders, and in a manner covering his face, with a hellish voice, and a rattle in his hand." This man was a priest. He began a weird invocation, accompanied by "most strange gestures," and concluded by surrounding the fire with a circle of meal. Immediately three more "such like devils," painted half red, half black, adorned with red strokes to imitate moustaches, and with eyes colored white, rushed in and went through with "the like antic tricks." These grotesque figures had danced "a pretty while," when, in came three more "as ugly as the rest, with red eyes, and white strokes over their black faces."

Captain Smith saw a strong resemblance in these "fiends" to Satan, and he must have felt anything but comfortable during their strange ceremony. They at last sat down on the mat opposite to him, three upon either side of the first-comer, who was the chief priest. They sang a song, accompanied by their rattles. When this was done the chief priest made, with the greatest efforts of gesticulation, a short oration, at the close of which the priests all groaned (moaned) and the orator laid down five grains of corn.—Then followed another song, another strained oration, and a groan, when five more grains were placed upon the ground.—This ceremony was kept up until the fire had been twice encircled with corn, then in the same manner sticks were placed between the divisions of corn. All day long neither priests nor prisoner ate or drank, but at night they "feasted merrily" upon the best of provisions.—Three days was this ceremony celebrated.—The Indians informed Captain Smith that "the circle of meal signified their country, the circles of corn the bounds of the sea, and the sticks his country. They imagined the world to be flat and round like a trencher (circular piece of wood) and they in the midst." The Indians one day brought Captain Smith a bag of gunpowder which they had captured and were saving until spring in order that they might plant it, as they wished to know the nature of this seed. Captain Smith did not undeceive them, thinking, doubtless, that this was the best use to which they could put gunpowder. The prisoner was invited to the habitation of the chief's brother, Opitchapan, where he was sumptuously feasted upon bread, fowl, and wild beasts.

As heretofore no Indian would eat with him, although they made no objections to eating after him. His fate was at last to be decided. The Indians started with their prisoner for Werowocomoco, where lived the great chief Powhatan.

☐☐☐☐☐☐☐☐☐☐☐

Powhatan was sensible of the pomp and dignity proper to his position as a great warrior, and he particularly desired to impress the English. On arriving at Werowocomoco, Captain Smith was detained until preparations had been made to receive him in state.—While the prisoner waited, more than two hundred "grim courtiers stood wondering at him" as though he were "a monster."—When Powhatan and his train had, had time to deck themselves in all "their greatest braveries," Captain Smith was admitted to the chief's presence. He was seated upon a sort of divan resembling a bedstead. Before him was a fire, and on either hand sat two young women about eighteen years of age. Powhatan, "well-beaten with many cold and stormy winters," wore strings of pearls around his neck, and was covered with a great robe of raccoon skins decorated with the tails. Around the council house was ranged a double row of warriors. Behind these were as many women. The heads and shoulders of the Indians were painted red, many had their hair decorated with white down, and all wore some savage ornament. On the appearance of the prisoner a great shout arose from these primitive courtiers.

An Indian woman—perhaps at sister of the chief, whom Smith styles "the queen of Appomattoc"—was appointed to bring water for the prisoner to wash his hands in. Another woman brought him feathers to dry them, and Captain Smith was then feasted in the "best barbarous manner," and a council was held to decide his fate. This debate lasted a long time, but the conclusion could hardly have been favorable to Captain Smith, since Powhatan was jealous of a white colony which already encroached upon his seclusion at Werowocomoco. During this solemn debate Captain Smith must have felt anything but comfortable. He did not know his doom until two stones were brought in and placed before Powhatan, and as many as could lay hands on him dragged him to the feet of the chief and laid his head upon the stones. The executioners raised their clubs to beat out his brains. Such a scene was not uncommon in this forest court. From childhood these savage men and women were accustomed to exult in the most barbarous tortures and executions. It is then the more wonderful that the heart of a little Indian maiden should have been touched with pity for the doomed white man. Pocahontas, a child of ten or twelve, and "the king's dearest daughter," pleaded for the life of the captive. But "no entreaty could prevail" with the stern Powhatan. The warriors were ready to strike the blow, when the child flew to the side of Captain Smith, took "his head in her arms and laid her own upon his to save him from death, whereat," says the quaint narrative "the Emperor was contented he should live to make him hatchets and her beads and copper," thinking he was accustomed to follow all occupations. "For," says the story, "the king himself will make his own robes, shoes, bows, arrows, and pots," while he would "plant, hunt, or do anything so well as the rest." Powhatan did not long detain Captain Smith for such trivial uses as making trinkets for Pocahontas. It had become the desire of his heart to possess the powerful weapons and tools of the English. He saw that a friend in Jamestown would be a good thing, and he perhaps hoped from friendly commerce with the colony to acquire ascendancy over other Indian tribes. He took occasion to express his wishes to Captain Smith in a curious manner. Two days after his rescue from death he had the captive taken to one of his arbor-like buildings in the woods, and left alone upon a mat by the fire. The house was curtained off in the center with a mat. Soon a most doleful noise came from behind the mat—and Powhatan—disguised in "the most fearfullest manner," and looking "more like a devil than a man," entered, with some two hundred Indians, painted black. The outcome of this impressive ceremony was that Powhatan told Captain Smith that they were now friends, and that he would presently send him home, and that when he arrived at Jamestown he must send him two great guns and a grindstone. In return he said he would give him the country of Cappahosic, and would always consider him his son. Captain Smith was accordingly sent to Jamestown with twelve guides. The Indians delayed on their journey, though the distance was short. They camped in the woods one night, and feasted sumptuously, but Captain Smith was in constant fear of his life still, "expecting every hour to be put to one death or another."

He was, however, led in safety to the fort. Here he treated his savage guides with great hospitality, and showed Rawhunt, a trusty servant of Powhatan, two demi-culverins (long cannons carrying a nine-pound shot), and a millstone to carry to his chief. The Indians, however, "found them somewhat too heavy." For their benefit, Captain Smith had the guns loaded with stones, and discharged among the boughs of trees covered with icicles.—The crashing fall of the ice-laden limbs so frightened the Indians that they fled, "half dead with fear," and it was some time before they could be induced to return.—Presents of various toys were given them for Powhatan and his family, and they went away satisfied. Captain Smith found Jamestown "all in combustion" (disarray) and the strongest faction again about to desert with the little vessel. He affirms that for the third time he forced them with cannon and musket shot "to stay or sink." At the same time he was tried under the Levitical law for the death of Robinson and Emry, who had been killed on his Pamunkey expedition.

On this trumped-up charge the president and some others sought to put him to death. The matter was ended, however, by the arrival of Captain Newport. Such were the miserable squabbles of the forty surviving colonists. Among these homesick, suffering, and desperate men one cannot pretend to judge.—It is natural that their statements should vary greatly, and one now finds it hard to decide what were the facts.—But it is certain that to John Smith must be ascribed the credit of enforcing order with the rough hand of a soldier, while good Mr. [Robert] Hunt strove to smooth the ruffled waters, and there were those in the colony who deserve a better fame than to be associated with this story of mutinies and disputes.

Meanwhile the despairing spirits of the colonists were revived by Captain Smith's account of the state and bounty of Powhatan, and above all by the "love of Pocahontas."

The story of her rescue of Smith may be doubted, but there can be no doubt that she saved the colony from starvation. Every four or five days this Indian child, with her attendants, would cross the river and come to the fort with provisions.

□□□□□□□□□□

Captain Smith had endeavored to impress Powhatan with the greatness of Captain [Christopher] Newport. The Indians already regarded Smith as an oracle. The God of the white man they called Captain Smith's God, and their respect for him was increased when Newport arrived at the time he had predicted. After leaving the little colony, Captain Newport had taken the more direct route across the Atlantic, and arrived at home in safety. It was noted with evident disappointment in England that he had brought back neither gold, nor silver. Two vessels were, however, immediately fitted out with all necessary provisions, and one hundred and twenty new adventurers. On the 8th of January, 1608, the vessel under the command of Newport arrived in Jamestown. The second vessel, commanded by Captain [Francis] Nelson, had been lost from sight, and was supposed to have been wrecked. Jamestown forgot its misery and its squabbles, and all was joy over this supply of men and provisions, with news from home. The colonists were so "overjoyed" that they gave the sailors permission to trade freely with the Indians. Thus the market was glutted, and it soon came about that what could formerly be bought for an ounce of copper could not now be obtained with a pound of that metal. This "cut the throat" of their trade, but it confirmed Powhatan's opinion of the greatness of Captain Newport, who also sent him presents from time to time. The chief became very desirous of meeting Newport, who accordingly resolved to make him a visit. He fitted out the pinnace, and accompanied by Captain Smith and Mr. [Matthew] Scrivener, a gentleman who had newly arrived, and had been admitted to the council, Captain Newport sailed for Werowocomoco. On nearing this place he began to fear treachery on the part of Powhatan. Captain Smith therefore offered first to visit the chief. He landed with twenty men, and marched for the chief's hamlet. They were obliged to cross a creek spanned by a miserable bridge. The English had some suspicion that it was a mere trap, and for this reason Smith prudently sent several savages ahead while he detained others as hostages until enough men had passed over to guard the rest.

They were conducted by several hundred Indians in safety to the town. Here "Powhatan strained himself to the utmost of his greatness to entertain them, with great shouts of joy, orations of protestations, and with the most plenty of victuals he could provide to feast them." He was seated upon his bed of mats with a leathern pillow embroidered in Indian fashion with pearls and beads, dressed in "a fair robe of skins as large as an Irish mantle." A "handsome young woman" sat on either hand, while twenty of his wives, with heads and shoulders painted red, and necks adorned with chains of beads, were ranged on either side of the house. In front of these sat Powhatan's chief men, and on either side of the door stood a file of twenty Indians with platters of bread. Behind them were some five hundred people. Orations were made, and old acquaintance renewed. The day closed with singing, dancing, and feasting. Captain Smith and his companions spent the night at Werowocomoco. The next day Captain Newport came ashore and was received with savage pomp, Smith taking the part of interpreter. Newport presented Powhatan with a boy named Thomas Savage. In return the chief presented him with a servant of his named Namontack. Three or four days were spent in "feasting, dancing, and trading."

The demeanor of Powhatan was so "proud" yet "discreet" that the Englishmen admired "his natural gifts, considering his education." The chief and the sea captain endeavored to outdo each other in magnificence. Powhatan pretended that he scorned to trade as his subjects did. "Captain Newport," said he, "it is not agreeable to my greatness, in this peddling manner to trade for trifles, and I esteem you also a great werowance. Therefore lay me down all your commodities together, what I like I will take, and in recompense give you what I think fitting their value." Smith interpreted this flattering speech to Newport, and at the same time expressed an opinion that Powhatan intended to make a sharp bargain. But Captain Newport, with the reckless open-handedness of a sailor was sure that he could so astonish the chief with ostentation of generosity that he might get all he desired from him. Copper, beads, toys, and some cloth "very much moth-eaten," which the London Company had purchased from the East India Company for this purpose, was accordingly displayed, and Powhatan made an ample selection, valuing his corn so high that the English did not get four bushels where they had expected twenty hog heads. Words followed between the two Captains, Newport desiring to please the "insatiable savage," and "Smith to cause the savage to please him." Captain Smith, however, "smothered his distaste" of these proceedings, and began "glancing" many trinkets "in the eyes of Powhatan."

The chief's eye was attracted by some blue beads. But Smith seemed unwilling to part with them. Powhatan became importunate. Still Smith did not wish to sell them, for he said they were "composed of a most rare substance of the color of the skies, and not to be worn but by the greatest kings in the world." Powhatan immediately became "half mad" to own "such strange jewels." It ended in Captain Smith securing two or three hundred bushels of corn for a pound or two of blue beads. They parted with Powhatan on the most friendly terms, and visited the chief of Pamunkey, Opechancanough, before their return. Captain

Smith "fitted" this chief with blue beads on the same terms. Blue beads had now become so highly esteemed that no one but the greatest chiefs and their wives and children dared wear them.

The winter of 1607-1608 was remarkably cold, both in Europe and America. In the midst of its severity an accident resulted in a fire which destroyed many of the reed-thatched cottages, the palisades, and much of the provisions of the colonists. Among the greatest sufferers was the good minister, who had nothing left but the clothes he wore, having lost all his books, the consolation of his hours of exile. What greater testimony can there be to this man's brave character than the simple words that "none ever heard him repine at his loss!"

The colonists would still have had enough provisions had not the vessel remained so long as to consume much of the store of grain. The sailors assisted in building a storehouse and a church of logs, roofed with sedge and earth. This building was soon almost washed away by rain. The vessel was loaded with iron ore, sassafras, cedar posts, walnut boards, and what was supposed to be gold ore. The colonists had been attacked by a dangerous gold fever. Among those who had come over with Newport were two goldsmiths, two refiners, and a jeweler. It was absolutely necessary to return with some news of gold, since all England was expecting such an issue. During the months in which Captain Newport had been absent, the colonists—men who had neither experience nor taste for frontier life and its hardships—had taxed their indolence too severely in the struggle for life, and had devoted their thoughts too much to the momentous disputes of the small world contained within the palisades of Jamestown to make any considerable explorations, pick in hand, in search of gold. Captain Smith, the only leader who had made any excursions into the neighboring country, was a skeptic about the easy discovery of gold, and desired only something more precious to the little colony—namely, corn. The indolent colonists now became fired with the desire to send precious metal to England. In the sands of a little stream near Jamestown glittering particles were found resembling gold. It is now surmised that these particles were minute pieces of mica (silicate mineral), which abound in the soil of Virginia. No man was to be found idle after that. The largest share of work was the most desirable. The whole colony turned out to lade the vessel. In the words of their chronicler, "there was no talk, no hope, no work, but dig gold, wash gold, refine gold, load gold." There was so much talk of gold that a "mad fellow" requested "to be buried in the sands lest they should, by their art, make gold of his bones." Among all these happy dreamers of riches, Captain Smith must have been a most unwelcome croaker (complainer). The process of trying the gold was carried on in some secrecy. Captain Smith, being admitted to the trial, told Captain [John] Martin, the discoverer of the mine, that unless "he could show him a more substantial trial—he was not enamored with their dirty skill." Rude and rough this sturdy Captain undoubtedly was with his obtrusive common sense.

In the narrative contained in his own *History*, it is said that "never did anything more torment him than to see all necessary business neglected to fraught such a drunken ship with so much gilded dirt." The vessel stayed fourteen weeks at Jamestown, consuming provisions, and leaving to the colony the legacy of ship rats. On the 10th of April, 1608, Captain Newport sailed from Jamestown (on the *Phoenix*), taking with him the troublesome President [Edward] Wingfield and Captain [Gabriel] Archer.

☐☐☐☐☐☐☐☐☐☐

Meantime the vessel commanded by Captain Nelson, and containing seventy of the one hundred and twenty colonists sent out from England in "the second supply," as they called it, had come within sight of the headlands of Cape Henry, but a storm had forced her so far to sea, that the next land which she sighted was in the West Indies. Here Captain Nelson put in for wood, water, and repairs. He made a long stay, but was able to feed his men well on the natural products of the tropics. Meanwhile, immediately on the departure of Captain Newport, Mr. Scrivener and Captain Smith had set to work with the colonists to rebuild the burnt Jamestown. The labor was divided between building cottages, repairing palisades, cutting down trees, preparing and planting cornfields, and replacing the church and storehouse.

While all were thus busy, Captain Nelson's ship arrived. The unexpected appearance of the lost vessel, the addition of seventy fresh adventurers with supplies, and the reloading of the ship for her return voyage, filled Jamestown with a new bustle of activity. Captain Nelson himself seems to have been a favorite among the colonists, for, says their narrative in Smith's *History*, "he had not anything but he freely imparted us, which honest dealing (being a mariner) caused us to admire him." What should be returned to England in this vessel? Nothing seemed good enough. The authorities disagreed. Captain Martin desired that the vessel be loaded with his "fantastical gold," the president wished to "reload" her with "some good tidings" of discovery and common sense. Captain Smith said that she ought to be freighted with cedar, which was at least sure to be of some value.

To carry out his plan the president ordered Captain Smith to discover the commodities of the Monacan Indians, beyond the falls. Sixty men were selected for this expedition, and Captain Smith began training them. There was, however, more than enough work to be done at Jamestown, and this plan was abandoned for the time. The colonists seem to have begun to feel doubts of their gold mine, and the ship was finally loaded with cedar. Captain Martin, who had never lost faith in the gold of his own discovery, returned with Captain Nelson to England to enjoy the glory of it. In July, 1608, the vessel, which had long been given up as lost, arrived in England. It was noted with disappointment that she brought no "novelties" or commodities from Virginia except "a sweet wood." Powhatan looked with covetous eyes upon the glittering swords, the ponderous muskets, and the serviceable pistols of the English. So long as the white man used supernatural bullets and sharp-edged swords, and the red man possessed only tomahawks of stone and stone—pointed arrows and javelins—so long were the English safe from Indian attacks.

It was now the ambition of Powhatan's life to obtain a goodly store of English weapons, instead of the rude wooden swords used by the Indians. Savage-like, he went about his purpose in the most crafty way with the most innocent air. Just before Newport's departure, Powhatan sent him twenty turkeys "to express his love," with the request that the Captain would return the compliment with a present of twenty swords.

The good-natured sailor immediately complied with this demand. Powhatan then proceeded to try a similar experiment upon Smith, who received a present of "the like luggage" on condition of the same return. But Smith refused, knowing it would cut the throat of the colony to put such weapons into the hands of the crafty chief. Powhatan was not to be thus outdone. If he could not procure the swords in one way he would in another. "He caused his people with twenty devices to obtain" as many swords. The Indians became "insolent." They surprised the colonists at their work. They would lay in ambuscade at the very gates of Jamestown and procure the weapons of stragglers by force. The council in England had deemed it the only wise policy to keep peace with the savages at all hazards, and a wise policy it was if it were not carried too far. The orders from this body had been very strict—the colonists were in no way to offend the Indians. This accounts in part for the obliging disposition of Captain Newport, and the patience of the colonists under these annoyances.—Thus a "charitable humor prevailed" until it happened one day that Captain Smith was the man they "meddled" with.—This fiery soldier did not wait for deliberation. He hunted the miscreants, and those whom he captured he "terrified" with whipping and imprisonment. In return, the Indians captured two straggling Englishmen, and came in force to the very gates of Jamestown, demanding seven Indians, whom, "for their villainies," Smith had detained. The irrepressible Captain immediately headed a sally in which he forced the Indians to surrender the Englishmen unconditionally. He then examined his prisoners, but they were faithful to their chief, and he could get nothing from them. He made six of them believe, by "several volleys of shot," that he had caused one of their number to be killed. They immediately confessed, in separate examinations, to a plot on the part of Powhatan to procure the weapons, and then to cut the throats of the colonists. Captain Smith still detained the Indians, resolving to give them a wholesome fright. Pocahontas presently came to Jamestown, accompanied by Indian messengers. Her father had sent them with presents, and a message excusing "the injuries done by some rash, untoward captains, his subjects, desiring their liberties for this time with the assurance of his love forever." When Captain Smith had punished his seven prisoners as he thought fit, he "used them well" for a few days, and delivered them to Pocahontas, pretending that he saved their lives only for the sake of the little Indian girl.

□□□□□□□□□□□

On the second day of June, 1608, as Captain Nelson dropped down the James River, he was accompanied by an open barge of less than three tons burden. She possessed but a single mast and sail, and was also propelled by oars. This little boat was bound on a voyage of discovery. The grand bay which the colonists had entered more than a year ago was yet entirely unknown to them. There seemed a possibility that this arm of the sea might stretch into the western ocean so much sought after.

The frail little craft, poorly provisioned, manned with but fifteen "gentlemen" and "soldiers," was to be the first vessel to explore the shores of the great Chesapeake Bay, to enter her many rivers, and to anchor off her islands. The discoverers were gay with hope as they left Jamestown. They even feared that their commander, Captain Smith, would make "too much haste" to return. They took leave of the homeward bound ship at Cape Henry, and crossed the bay to the eastern shore. They discovered Smith's Islands, and named them for their leader. Upon Cape Charles they saw two "grim, stout" Indians, carrying javelins headed with bone. These savages "boldly demanded" of the discoverers what they were, and what they wanted. After some parley they showed kindly intentions, and invited the voyagers to visit their chief at his village at Accomac. The English landed at this place, and were treated with hospitality. They were struck with the appearance of the chief. He is pronounced the "comeliest, proper, civil savage" that they met on the voyage.

Captain Smith easily conversed with these Indians, as they spoke the language of Powhatan's people. They gave their visitors some descriptions of the bay, with its islands and rivers. From here the discoverers sailed, coasting for some distance in and out of the smaller bays and inlets of the shore, while they could see many islands out in the great bay. They "bore up for" a group of islands, but before reaching them they were caught in an "extreme gust of wind, rain, thunder, and lightning." Only with great danger to their small boat did they escape the "unmerciful raging of the ocean-like water." The voyagers named these uninhabited islands for one of their number, Walter Russell, "doctor of physic" but they are now called Tangier Islands. The discoverers traversed them in search of fresh water, but found none. Still seeking water, they came to the river now known as the Pocomoke. Here the Indians attacked them at first "with great fury," but they soon became reconciled to the white strangers, whom they received with "songs, dances, and much mirth." The English searched the Indian villages for fresh water, but could only find enough to fill three casks, and this was described in their narrative as "such puddle" that for the first time they knew what it was to want good water. They dug and sought everywhere for it, but could find none. In two days they would have refused two casks of gold for one cask of even the "puddle water" of the Pocomoke River. They continued their voyage past many low islands to a promontory which was named Point Ployer in honor of the nobleman who had relieved Captain Smith "in an extreme extremity." Here they found a pond of hot water.

Crossing from the mainland to islands out in the bay, they were again caught in a storm. Their one mast and sail was blown overboard, and the barge was nearly swamped with water, which the voyagers worked hard to bail out. They landed on one of these islands, which, from the "extremity of gusts, thunder, rain, storms, and ill weather," the discoverers named Limbo. It is one of a group now called Watts Islands. The plucky voyagers repaired the sail with their shirts, and again set out. Their next discovery was a river on the eastern shore now called Wicomico. As they approached the shore, the astonished people ran in troops from place to place. How strange indeed this great floating boat with its flapping sail must have seemed to the Indians, who had never seen anything larger than a canoe cross the waters of Chesapeake Bay! Their first impulse was always to resist the incursion of this frightful thing with its pale, strangely dressed inhabitants. At this place the Indians got into the tops of trees and used their arrows without stint. The boat, however, rode safely at anchor out of reach of arrows, while the English constantly made signs of friendship. For a long time the Indians kept up their one-sided warfare. On the following day they tried new tactics, appearing unarmed, and dancing in a ring with baskets in their hands. The English were too wise in Indian warfare to be drawn on shore by baskets. They believed that "there was nothing in them but villainy," and accordingly discharged their muskets at the Indians, who were all instantly seen "tumbling on the ground" without regard to whether they were hurt or not. They crept into the reeds, where they had previously put their warriors in ambuscade. Toward evening the barge approached the shore. The discoverers landed, but could find nothing of the Indians except their baskets. Seeing smoke on the other side of the river, they crossed over and found several cabins with fires in them, but no inhabitants. The whites deposited in each cabin pieces of copper, beads, bells, and looking glasses. Early in the morning four savages, who had been out in the bay fishing, and knew nothing of the events of the past two days, came to the barge. The Englishmen treated them so kindly that the Indians told them to wait for them and they would soon return. This they did, bringing with them some twenty of their friends, and seeing that the strangers had kindly intentions, hundreds soon surrounded the boat, each Indian with some present. They considered one bead ample return for all they did. The English and Indians soon became such good friends that the savages would contend among themselves as to who should bring the strangers water, stay with them as hostages, or conduct such of the men as wished to go ashore. These people made mention of a great nation of Indians called the Massawomeck. Finding the eastern shore low and mostly destitute of fresh water, the voyagers crossed "by Limbo" to the western side, which was hilly, thickly wooded, with plenty of fresh water, and abounding in wolves and bears. The first navigable stream they came to they called Bolus, from a peculiar clay which they found in its banks. This stream is known to us as the Patapsco.

Fifteen adventurers had now been confined to this open barge on the rough waters of the bay for two weeks. These gentlemen, unused to such severe exercise, had become tired at the oar, and their bread had been so frequently rained upon that it was quite rotten, though the salt air and hard work had given them such "good stomachs" that they could still digest it.

The disheartened voyagers began to despair of an end to the great body of water on which they floated. They begged Captain Smith to return. "Gentlemen," said the Captain, "if you remember the memorable history of Sir Ralph Lane, how his company importuned him to proceed in the discovery of Morattico (the source of the Roanoke), alleging they had as yet a dog that, being boiled with sassafras leaves, would richly feed them in their returns, then what a shame it would be for you, that have been so suspicious of my tenderness, to force me to return, with so much provisions as we have, and scarce able to say where we have been, or yet heard of that we were sent to seek! You cannot say but I have shared with you in the worst which is past, and for what is to come of lodging, diet, or whatsoever, I am contented you allot the worst part to myself. As for your fears that I will lose myself in these unknown large waters or be swallowed up in some stormy gust, abandon these childish fears, for worse than is past is not likely to happen, and there is as much danger to return as to proceed. Regain, therefore, your old spirits, for return I will not, if God please, till I have seen the Massawomecks, found Potomac, or the head of this water you conceit to be endless." Two or three days more of adverse weather so added to the disheartenment of the voyagers that three or four of them fell sick. Their piteous complaints caused Captain Smith to turn about. The adventurers had not gone far on their homeward journey, however, before they discovered the wide Potomac. The sight of this "seven mile broad river" encouraged the discoverers, the sick speedily recovered, and all were willing "to take some pains" to know its name. They sailed up the river for thirty miles before they saw inhabitants. They were met by two savages, who conducted them up a little creek. On the banks of this creek numbers of Indians were in ambuscade, strangely "painted and grimed," and giving fearful war whoops. Captain Smith prepared with apparent willingness to encounter them in their attack. The whites shot so that their bullets grazed the water. This and the echoing woods so startled the Indians that they hastily dropped bows and arrows.

Hostages were exchanged, and the Indians became very friendly, saying that their attack had been ordered by Powhatan. Ascending the Potomac further, the adventurers received various treatments at the hands of the Indians of different tribes, and what seemed important, they dug the ground in several places, and discovered "yellow spangles." The Indians of Virginia were seen to use a substance in painting themselves black which gave them the appearance of being dusted over with silver. Captain Newport, supposing this to contain precious metal, had carried some little bags of it to England. The English knew there was a mine where this substance was procured, somewhere in the neighborhood of the Potomac. The adventurers now inquired for this mine among the Indians. Japazaws, the chief of the Potomacs, gave Smith guides to conduct him to this mine, situated on a creek supposed to be Potomac Creek. The Captain ascended this stream as far as the boat could penetrate. Leaving the barge with several of his men, he made hostages of some of the savages, whom he led by a chain, which he promised them for their trouble. They saw no indignity in this, and were "proud to be so richly adorned." The mine was found to be on a rocky mountain, and was a great hole dug by the Indians with shells and hatchets. The savages put this substance into little bags and sold it everywhere, it being a toilet article with the Indians.

The English took away as much of the useless stuff as they could carry. Smith afterward found that this precious something was the ore that we know as sulfide of antimony, which may be pounded to a black powder. In ancient times fine ladies used this same substance to color their eyelashes. Several times on this voyage the discoverers entered great schools of fish, so thick that, in default of nets, they attempted to catch them with a frying pan "but," says their narrative, "we found it a bad instrument to catch fish with. Neither better fish, more plenty, nor more variety for small fish, had any of us ever seen in any place swimming in the water, but they are not to be caught with frying pans." The adventurers had many "quarrels, treacheries, and encounters" among the Indians. On first meeting a new party of savages, Captain Smith, an admirable manager of savages, always demanded a surrender of their arms and a child or two as hostages to test their friendship. In their own words, the voyagers, in all encounters with the Indians, had "curbed their insolences," and "lost not a man." Having finished the exploration of the Potomac, and the provisions running low, the adventurers sailed toward home. Smith had some intention of stopping to visit his old "imprisonment acquaintances" on the Rappahannock. The barge ran aground at the mouth of this river at low tide.

The men on the boat could see many fish near the reedy bottom. To while away the time as they waited for the tide to come in, Captain Smith began "nailing" these fish "to the ground with his sword." Instantly all hands were at work, and more fish were "speared" in an hour than they could eat in a day. Smith, however, in taking a stingray from his sword, was stung in the wrist. At first nothing could be seen but a little blue spot, but instant torment ensued, his arm and shoulder swelled, and the voyagers "all with much sorrow concluded his funeral." A man seldom superintends the digging of his own grave. Captain Smith, however, had his grave dug according to his own directions on an island nearby. Meanwhile Doctor Russell used his probe and an ointment with such good success that the commander recovered, and was able to revenge himself by eating a part of the fish for supper. In memory of this incident the island was named for the fish, and is still called Stingray Island (Point). From this point the discoverers sailed for home. When they reached Kecoughtan, now Hampton—the Indians met them with wonder. Their boat was loaded with bows, arrows, mantles, and furs. Captain Smith's arm was still bandages, and another man had an injured shin. This was evidence enough to the Indians that the English had been at war, and they were importunate to know "with whom." The whites, humoring their fancy, and with an eye to the Indians's respect for those who conquer, told the savages that they had gained these spoils from the Massawomecks. As they neared Jamestown, on the twenty-first of July, the voyagers, in gay spirits, trimmed their bark with bright streamers, and so disguised her that they frightened the colonists, who supposed a Spanish boat was upon them.

□□□□□□□□□□

In spite of their spoiled bread, their mishaps, and their discomforts, the explorers had been happier than those who remained at Jamestown. Here all was misery and discontent. Those who had recently arrived in America were sick, while most of the others had some ailment, and none were able to work. The president was accused of appropriating the public store of provisions to his own private ends, and had caused much discontent by building himself a pleasure house in the woods, in which unwelcome work some of the colonists seem to have got lame and others bruised. The news of their discoveries, and especially the "good hope" which the voyagers derived from the stories of the Indians that their bay "stretched into the South Sea, or somewhat near it," acted as a tonic. [John] Ratcliffe was deposed from the Presidency, and Smith was elected in his place. He, however, substituted Mr. [Matthew] Scrivener, and prepared to finish his explorations. The heat of the summer was so great that the colonists could not work, and the captain left them "to recover their health." All his business was affected within three days, and on the twenty-fourth of July, Smith set out with twelve men. The wind was contrary, and the barge was forced to stop at Kecoughtan, where she remained for several days. They were feasted here "with much mirth" by the chief, who was sure another expedition against the Massawomecks was on foot.

For while the Indians beguiled the whites with stories of an easy road to the Pacific, the whites duped the savages with lies of another kind, so that each party heard that which they most desired.—The English terrified the natives in the evening by a display of rockets. The Indians concluded that nothing was impossible with these strange people. The first night out was spent at Stingray Island. Seven of the voyagers upon the present expedition had but recently arrived in Virginia, and not being acclimated, they were all sick. But six men, including the Captain, remained to toil at the oars. They passed the mouth of the great Potomac and sailed directly for the head of Chesapeake Bay.

While crossing the bay they saw seven or eight canoes of the dreaded Massawomecks approaching them. The Indians instantly prepared for an attack. The English dropped their oars and mustered their force of five well men. The Captain, ever quick with expedients, shut the sick under a tarpaulin, made their hats placed upon sticks do duty in place of them. These sticks were ranged on the barge's side. Between every two sticks a man was placed armed with two muskets. Having thus made themselves "seem many," the adventurers sailed down upon the Indians. This display of hats, with the strange nature of the boat, seems to have entirely demoralized the Indians, for they fled to the shore, and there stood staring at the barge's sail until she anchored right against them. It was a long time before the Indians could be coaxed to approach them.—At last two of their number (group) ventured out unarmed in a canoe.—They were closely followed by the others as reinforcement in case of hostilities. These two Indians were presented with a bell apiece. Immediately the others came aboard with presents of venison, bear meat, bows, arrows, clubs, shields, and bear skins. The English could not understand their speech. By signs they managed to communicate to the voyagers the fact that they had been at war with the Tockwogh Indians. The English understood them to say that they would meet them again in the morning, but no more was seen of them. The discoverers entered the Tockwogh River, now known as the Sassafras. Here they were met and surrounded by Indian canoes. On inquiry, it was found that one of their number (group) could speak the language of the Powhatan Indians. Through his mediation a friendly parley was brought about. They saw the weapons of the Massawomecks, and the English, pretending that they had fought these Indians, were immediately well-received. The Indians conducted the white men to their village, which was fortified with palisades. Here they spread mats for the strangers to sit upon, while men and women welcomed them with dances and songs. These people possessed hatchets, knives, and pieces of brass and copper, which they said they had obtained from the Susquehannock (Susquehanna), a mighty people who dwelt upon the river of this name, two days's journey above the falls.

These people were also mortal enemies of the Massawomecks. Being desirous of discovering the commodities of different Indian nations, the Englishmen persuaded these Indians to send to the Susquehannocks and invite them to come and meet the white strangers. In four days the messengers returned with sixty of these people. They are described in Smith's *History* as being a "giant-like" race, but this must have been one of those exaggerations for which travelers are famous, and from which Captain Smith is certainly not free. It was customary with Captain Smith, who was as staunch in his loyalty to his religion as in his loyalty to the king, to have prayers and a psalm read every day. The solemnity of this devotion impressed the savages.

They watched until the service was over, and then "began in a most passionate manner to hold up their hands to the sun with a most fearful song." They may have thought that the devotion was in some way connected with Captain Smith, for they embraced him, went through more ceremonies, and closed with an oration expressive of friendship. They "robed" him in a painted bear skin, placed an immense chain of white beads around his neck, and lay at his feet eighteen mantles made of different skins. The outcome of all this flattery was that they desired him to remain with them and assist them in their wars with the Massawomecks. The voyagers understood the Susquehannock Indians to say that they lived on some great water which, with their ignorance of geography, they took to be either some lake or the St. Lawrence River, where the French had settled. To the sorrow of those Indians the whites insisted on leaving them, but promised to return the following year. In this voyage Captain Smith and his men explored the extreme limits of Chesapeake Bay, all her important rivers and inlets, and named many capes and headlands after the members of the party.

At the limit of their explorations up the rivers, the discoverers cut crosses on the trees, and sometimes left crosses of brass. The voyagers found the Rappahannock River inhabited by a people called the Moraughtacunds. Among these they found an old friend of their previous voyage on the Potomac called Mosco. This savage possessed that rare thing among Indians, a full beard. The English accounted for this by supposing him to be the son of some Frenchman. He was very proud of his beard, and called the English his countrymen. Mosco was delighted to see them now, would fetch them wood and water, and with his friends would tow their boat "against wind and tide." Mosco endeavored to dissuade Captain Smith from visiting the Rappahannocks, enemies of the Moraughtacunds, who had recently stolen three of their chief's women. Mosco represented that they would kill the English on account of their friendship with the Moraughtacunds. Believing that Mosco was anxious to secure all their trade to his friends, Captain Smith ascended the Rappahannock. The discoverers at first found some sixteen Indians standing on the shore who showed them a good landing and pointed to several canoes full of commodities. The English, however, demanded an exchange of hostages. After a little consultation, several Indians waded out into the water, left one of their number (group), and took in exchange an Englishman named Anas Todkill. This man made sharp use of his eyes, being suspicious of ambuscades. He asked to be allowed to go across the plain to get some wood, but the savages would not let him. He managed, however, by degrees, to move back some two stones's throws. He thought he could see several hundred savages behind the trees, and tried to return to the boat. The Indians caught him up, and were going to carry him away, when he called out to his companions in the barge that they were betrayed. That instant their hostage jumped overboard, but he was followed as quickly by the man who had been set to watch him. They had a struggle in the water, which resulted in the death of the Indian. A volley of musketry enabled Todkill to regain his freedom, but he was so closely pursued with Indian arrows that he fell flat on the ground. The English fought from behind a fortification made like a forecastle upon the forepart of their boat of the Massawomeck shields. This had been done at the suggestion of Mosco. Indian arrows rained around the barge for a short time, but the savages soon fled into the woods.

  Armed with these wicker shields, the whites sallied ashore and rescued Todkill, whose clothes were bloody with the wounds of those who had held him captive. The English captured the canoes, broke all the arrows they could find, except some that they saved for their friend Mosco. They then returned down the river to the village of the Moraughtacunds, where they presented Mosco with the captured canoes and arrows, and he in his turn received them with great rejoicings and a triumphal march.

  The next day the voyagers spent in securing poles to the barge's side, and hanging wicker shields upon them. They thus encircled the deck of their boat with an impenetrable curtain. On the following day the voyagers again set sail for the country of the Rappahannocks. They were followed along the shore by Mosco with a wistful face. He at last mustered courage to ask if he might not go with them. He was taken on the barge. She sailed up the river past three Indian villages situated on high cliffs. They were suddenly attacked by thirty or forty savages, who had "so accommodated themselves with branches" that the adventurers took them for bushes, until their arrows began to strike the curtain of shields, dropping into the water. Instantly Mosco fell on his face crying, "Rappahannocks! Rappahannocks!" It was some time before the English could make out that what seemed to be bushes were disguised enemies, but the bushes fell among the reeds at the first volley of shot from the barge. Sailing on up the river, the white men were well-entertained at several villages of smaller tribes. While on the Rappahannock one of the company, Mr. [Richard] Featherstone, an "honest, valiant, and industrious" gentleman, died, and was buried with military honors in a little bay which his companions named Featherstone's Bay. The other new arrivals in Virginia, in spite of being huddled together in a small boat with poor diet, had recovered.

□□□□□□□□□□

The day after the burial of their companion the adventurers sailed as high as their boat could go up the river. They then landed, set up crosses, and cut their names on trees, leaving one man to watch. The sentinel saw an arrow fall near him, gave the alarm, and all grasped their arms. Looking sharply, they could see about a hundred "nimble Indians" slipping from tree to tree. Arrows now fell thick and fast, but the English found that they also could dodge behind trees. Mosco was most active in the service of his friends. He shot away a quiver full of arrows, and ran to the boat for more. He made so much noise, and slipped from one point to another so constantly, that he impressed the enemy with the idea that the whites had quite a company of Indian allies. This dodging warfare continued for about half an hour, when the Indians disappeared as suddenly as they had come. Mosco slipped after them to be sure they were gone. On his return an Indian was discovered apparently dead. He was turned over, and was found to be shot in the knee and still living. Instantly Mosco wanted to beat out his brains.—"Never was dog more furious against a bear" than this savage against his enemy.—The wounded man, however, was taken to the boat, where he was treated by a surgeon who had accompanied the expedition to dress Captain Smith's stingray wound. Mosco's disappointment was alleviated by the Englishmen turning out to help him gather up the arrows which had been scattered in the battle. He soon got an armful, over which "he gloried not a little." Meanwhile, the prisoner's wound being dressed, within an hour he began to look "somewhat cheerfully," and could eat and speak. Mosco was persuaded to act as interpreter. The savage said his name was Amoroleck, and gave some description of his own and neighboring tribes. "Why did you come in this manner to betray us that came to you in peace and to seek your love?" demanded the whites through their interpreter. "We heard," answered Amoroleck, "that you were a people come from under the world to take our world from us." "How many worlds do you know?" queried the English. "I know no more," said the savage, "but that which is under the sky that covers us, that is the Powhatans, the Monacans, and the Massawomecks, that are higher up in the mountains." "What is beyond the mountains?" asked the whites. "The sun," answered Amoroleck. "Of anything else I know nothing, because the woods are not burnt."

The English presented Amoroleck with various toys, and tried to persuade him to go with them. He, however, desired them to await the coming of his people. He would tell them, he said, all about their kind usage of him, and they would then be good friends, for he was a chief's brother. Mosco, however, advised the whites "to be gone, for they were all naught." They said they would remain till evening, however. The English occupied the time in preparing for the reception of what Indians might come, while Mosco sat sharpening his arrows. At nightfall they all embarked, for the river was here so narrow, and the banks so high, that the savages might do them much damage if they were caught here in daylight. Meanwhile the Indian chief had been gathering his men and holding a council of war, when his spies informed him that the boat was gone. The Indians immediately set out to follow her, and presently arrows were heard dropping on every side of the boat in the darkness.

The Indians ran along the shore with wild war whoops. The English could not make their voices heard through the din, but now and then a musket was fired, aimed where the greatest noise was heard. The savages followed the boat more than twelve miles, keeping up this running warfare. Daylight appeared, and the voyagers found themselves in a wide bay out of danger. Here they anchored and "fell to breakfast." They took no notice of the Indians until the sun had risen when they cleared away their covering of shields, and appeared, each man with shield and sword. Amoroleck made a long speech to his countrymen, telling them how kindly he had been used by the whites, that they had a Potomac Indian with them who loved them "as his life," and who would have killed him had not the whites protected him, that he might have his liberty if they would but be friendly, and as for hurting the whites, "it was impossible." When the Indians heard this speech they hung their bows and arrows upon the trees.

Two Indians swam out to the boat, one with a bow, and the other with a quiver of arrows tied upon his head. These they presented to Captain Smith, who received them kindly and told them that if the three other chiefs among them would also give up their bows and arrows in token of friendship that the great king of his world, whose men he and his companions were, would be their friend. This was immediately agreed to. The English landed on a low point of land. The four chiefs received Amoroleck, and were ready to give the white men whatever they had. They were much astonished at the commodities of the English, and supposed their pistols to be pipes. They desired some of these, but the voyagers contented them with more harmless toys. These Indians, who were Manahoac, parted with the English on the most friendly terms. In their return down the river they revisited the villages of the various minor tribes. They were all pleased to hear of the victory over the Mannahoacs, and desired the English to make peace with the Rappahannocks. "They have twice," answered the Captain, "assaulted me that came only in love to do them good, and therefore I will now burn all their houses, destroy their corn, and forever hold them enemies till they make me satisfaction." The Indians desired to know what satisfaction he would require. "They shall present me," said Captain Smith, "the king's bows and arrows, and not offer to come armed where I am, they shall be friends with the Moraughtacunds, my friends, and give me their king's son in pledge to perform it, and then all King James's men shall be their friends." These Indians sent to the Rappahannocks to meet the English. This tribe was now ready to agree to all the conditions, but the chief did not want to give up his son, for, "having no more but him, he could not live without him." In place of his son he said Smith might have the three women the Moraughtacund Indians had stolen from him. The Captain, wishing to make peace, accepted this questionable favor in this wise. He sent for the women. Then he made the chief of Moraughtacund, the chief of Rappahannock, and Mosco stand up before him. He told the Rappahannock chieftain to choose the woman of the three that he loved best. To the Moraughtacund chief he gave the second choice, and the third woman was allotted to Mosco. This manner of dealing out justice so struck the Indians that their canoes were instantly speeding across the water and those who had no canoes swam across. They all returned in a short time with presents of venison and provisions. A friendly intercourse was carried on until, in the words of the quaint narrative, "the dark commanded us to rest." The occasion was celebrated on the following day by hundreds of Indians, who danced and sang, while neither bow nor arrows could be seen among them. After the manner of the Indians, Mosco showed his friendship by changing his name to Uttasautasough, the name by which the Indians called the whites. At parting, the Indians promised ever to be friendly, and to plant corn especially for the strangers, who on their part promised to provide hatchets, beads, and copper for the Indians. The boat pushed off with a volley of shot, while the Indians gave a great shout. They next sailed up the Piankatank River as far as it was navigable. The inhabitants were nearly all absent on a hunting expedition. The voyagers saw only a few old men, women, and children tending corn. Like all other Indians whom they had met on their voyages, these people promised them corn when they should choose to come for it. The barge was caught in a dead calm. The voyagers were obliged to make their way by rowing toward Point Comfort. They anchored for the night in Gosnold's Bay. Suddenly, in the night, they were struck by a thunderstorm. Their cable broke, and they drove before the wind. Only by "the flashes of fire from heaven" could they keep off of the "splitting shore." They "never thought more to have seen Jamestown."

But by the assistance of the lightning they succeeded in finding Point Comfort in safety. After "refreshing" themselves, the voyagers resolved to complete their discoveries by seeking their nearer neighbors, the Chesapeake and Nansemond Indians. They sailed up the Chesapeake, now Elizabeth, River, a tributary of the James River. After proceeding six or seven miles they saw some cornfields and cabins, but no inhabitants. The river was very narrow, and the discoverers returned to the James River, hoping to find some of the natives. They coasted the shore until they came to the Nansemond River. At the mouth of this stream six or seven savages were busy making weirs for fishing. They fled when they saw the barge. The voyagers landed, and laid some toys where the Indians had been at work. They pushed off again, but they had not gone far before the Indians returned, and seeing the toys, began to dance and sing, endeavoring to recall the whites. Thus friendly intercourse began. One Indian desired that the Englishmen should visit his cabin up the Nansemond River. He voluntarily boarded the barge to direct them, while the others ran along the shore. After sailing seven or eight miles they came to an island on which was the Indian's cabin, surrounded by cornfields. The savage said that the people were all gone hunting. The English gave him and his family various presents, with which they seemed much delighted. The other Indians now asked the whites to go a little further up the river and see their homes. To this they consented, the first Indian leaving them here, and the others accompanying the barge in a canoe. They passed on up the river by the island, and to where the stream was very narrow. The English now became a little suspicious. They asked the

Indians to come on board the barge. They answered that they would when they had got their bows and arrows. They got ashore, and arming themselves, tried to persuade the whites to proceed up the river. The whites, on the other hand, tried to persuade the Indians either to enter their own canoe or to come on to the barge. They refused, and the adventurers begin "to prepare for the worst." They started on up the river, and had not gone far when they found themselves followed by seven or eight canoes. Presently from each bank of the narrow stream came arrows thick and fast. The English immediately turned about to sail for a wider part of the stream. The Indians in the canoes had also been shooting their arrows, but the white men "bestowed so many shot amongst them" that the Indians all leaped overboard and swam ashore, with the exception of two or three, who escaped by swift rowing. The English soon reached a more open spot, and the Indians found that shot could reach farther than arrows. They speedily disappeared in the woods. Having thus escaped an Indian "trap," laid and baited with Indian treachery, the English seized the deserted canoes for booty, and examined their own injuries. They were not serious, Anthony Bagnall having been wounded in the hat, and another man in the sleeve.

    There were evidently many Indians concerned in this attack, and it was rightly concluded that the Chesapeakes and Nansemonds were banded together. A council of war was held on board the barge "to bethink" whether it were better to burn the cornfields on the island, or to try to make some peace with the Indians. The conclusion was to set fire to the island when night came. Meanwhile the English began to cut the canoes in pieces, and the Indians speedily began to lay down their bows and arrows. The savages made signs of peace. The English told them that they would make peace if they would deliver up the chief's bow and arrows, present them with a string of pearls, and give them four hundred baskets of corn when they came again.

    The Indians expressed their willingness to comply if they had but a canoe. One was set adrift. Savages swam to get it, and the whites said they would keep on cutting up the other boats until the Indians performed their promise. The Indians cried to them not to do this, for they would keep their promise, which they did. Basket after basket was brought, until the barge was well loaded for the good of the colony. On the seventh of September the discoverers arrived safely at Jamestown. They estimated that in these two expeditions they had traveled about three thousand miles, though it is quite likely that the weary men naturally overestimated the distance they had traversed. From what he learned on this voyage, Captain Smith prepared a wonderfully good map of Chesapeake Bay and the tributary rivers. The narratives of these two voyages given in Smith's *History* are signed by men who were members of the expedition. One cannot refrain from admiring in these brave men and their captain the fortitude and persistence that they showed, and the wonderful tact with which they managed the natives.

☐☐☐☐☐☐☐☐☐☐☐

The discoverers found on their return that many of the colonists had died, some had recovered, and others were still sick. The late president, Captain [John] Ratcliffe, had been imprisoned for "mutiny," while Mr. [Matthew] Scrivener had fulfilled his trust faithfully. Under his direction the corn harvest had been gathered, though much of the colony's provision was spoiled by the leakage of their poor storehouse. On the tenth of September Captain Smith was installed as president. He governed the colony wisely. His measures were doubtless severe, but severity was necessary among these men, totally unqualified for a frontier life, with an unwise management in England, and endless discontent and jealousy at Jamestown. Into the merits of the childish squabbles of the colonists, which have perpetuated themselves in their writings, and broken out afresh among historians in our time, we cannot enter. Doubtless there was some wrong on all sides. Men shut up together in hard circumstances are sure to fall out. Captain Smith went energetically to work to better the condition of the colony. Jamestown was once more the scene of busy activity. Church and storehouse were repaired, new houses built for more supplies, and the fort altered in form. The soldiers were drilled every day upon a plain called Smithfield. Here crowds of Indians would gather to watch with wonder the Englishmen shoot at a mark. It was now the season to trade for corn with the Indians.

  The boats were prepared, and George Percy was sent on a trading expedition. They had not gone far, however, before they met Captain [Christopher] Newport with the second supply from England. He brought Percy's company back to Jamestown with him, as he had planned a voyage of discovery. Captain Newport had undertaken to return to England with either a lump of gold, the discovery of a passage to the South Sea, or one of the lost colony of Roanoke. The folly of the council in their management of a far distant colony was made very manifest in this second supply. A crown was sent over with which Powhatan was to be crowned, and a basin and ewer, bed, bedstead, and suit of scarlet clothes, as presents to the American king. Captain Newport also brought a great cumbersome boat, which the colonists were to carry across the Blue Ridge and launch in the South Sea.

  As heretofore, most of the newly arrived adventurers were white-handed gentlemen. The first women of the colony, Mrs. [Margaret Foxe] Forrest and her maid Anne Burras came in this vessel. Among the seventy adventurers of this supply were eight Poles and Germans, sent out to make tar, glass, and soap ashes. For the members of the London Company were determined to have some kind of immediate return from the struggling infant colony for the money which had been laid out upon it.—As most of the colonists who had gone to Virginia were in expectation of immediately stumbling on wealth, so most of those who had joined the London Company expected an immediate return for their investment.—Newport brought a severe letter from the disappointed council to those who might be in power in Virginia. The president probably wished this supply, with the great boat, basin, ewer, bed, bedstead, scarlet clothes, and crown, safely home again. He spoke his mind freely in the colony's council, which had now two new members, Captain Peter Wynne and

Captain Richard Waldo, "ancient soldiers and valiant gentlemen." He considered it folly to make these presents to an Indian who would be as well-pleased with a few beads and some copper. In his opinion, it was unwise to undertake the discovery of the South Sea when it was the proper time to procure food for the winter. Captain Newport, however, promised to procure corn of the Indians for them, and thought that Smith was only trying to hinder his journey of discovery. The council overruled the president, supplies for the winter were neglected, and a hundred and twenty picked men were allotted to Newport for his discovery. The latter was apprehensive that the Indians might take revenge on him for what he considered the cruelty of Captain Smith in his previous dealings with the Indians.

The president, to quiet all fears, and to show his willingness to assist in the business on hand, as well as to hasten an affair which would consume so much valuable time, undertook with four companions a journey to Werowocomoco, to ask Powhatan to come to Jamestown and receive his presents.

◻◻◻◻◻◻◻◻◻◻◻

When the Englishmen reached the home (village) of Powhatan, they found that he was some thirty miles away. They were received by the steadfast friend of all white men, Pocahontas. She sent messengers for her father, and undertook to entertain her friends while they waited. The Englishmen were left in an open space, seated on a mat by the fire. Suddenly they heard a "hideous noise" in the woods. Supposing that Powhatan and his warriors were upon them, they sprang to their feet, grasped their arms, and seized two or three old Indians who were near them. Pocahontas came to them, however, with her apology, saying that they might kill her "if any hurt were intended." All who stood near, men, women, and children, assured the white men that all was right. Presently thirty young women came rushing out of the woods. Their only covering was a cincture or apron of green leaves, they were gaily painted, some one color and some another. Every girl wore a pair of deer's horns on her head, while from her girdle and upon one arm hung an otter's skin. The leader wore a quiver of arrows, and carried a bow and arrow in her hands. The others followed with swords, clubs, and pot sticks. "These fiends, with most hellish shouts and cries," says the ungallant narrator, "cast themselves in a ring about the fire, singing and dancing with most excellent ill variety." This masquerade (show) lasted about half an hour, when the Indian girls disappeared as they had come. They again reappeared in their ordinary costume. Pocahontas invited Captain Smith to a dinner which had been spread for him with "all the savage dainties" which they could procure. They tormented the Captain by pressing around him, saying, "Love you not me? Love you not me?" While he feasted they danced, and ended by conducting him to his lodging with firebrands for torches. Powhatan arrived the next day, and Captain Smith delivered his message. "If your king has sent me presents," said Powhatan, "I also am a king, and this is my land, eight days I will stay to receive them. Your Father (Captain Newport) is to come to me, not I to him, nor yet to your fort, neither will I bite at such a bait." He drew rude maps on the ground and described the countries through which Captain Newport intended to pass. "But for any saltwater beyond the mountains," said Powhatan, "the stories you have had from my people are false." Some complimentary courtesy (kind words) passed between the chief and the president, but Captain Smith was obliged to carry this dignified answer to Jamestown.

□□□□□□□□□□

    The presents were accordingly sent around by water in the boats to the haughty chief. Captains Newport and Smith with fifty men crossed over by land, and met them at Werowocomoco. The day following their arrival was appointed for the ceremony of Powhatan's coronation. The basin and ewer were presented to him, his bedstead was set up, and the English endeavored to persuade him to put on the scarlet suit and cloak. The chief, however, looked upon them with suspicion, and would not consent to wear them until Namontack, the boy whom he had given to Captain Newport, and who had been in England, assured him that they would not hurt him. The coronation, however, caused more ado. Powhatan had no appreciation of the honor these people intended to do him, and he could on no account be persuaded to kneel. Long the English coaxed him, instructing him by word and action how he should bow. We can imagine these English gentlemen dropping on their knees by way of example before the stubborn savage. It was all of no avail. Powhatan would not even bend the knee. His instructors were at last tired out. They contented themselves with bearing very hard upon his shoulders until he stooped a little. The crown was then hastily placed upon his head by three men, a signal was given, a volley of shot was fired from the boats, and Powhatan sprang up in consternation. This part of the ceremony was explained to him, and he became quiet. He now thought it fitting that he should make a suitable return for all these honors. This he did by graciously presenting Captain Newport with his old moccasins and mantle. It had been calculated that all this display would induce the great chief to aid Captain Newport in his imposing expedition in search of the South Sea. The making of these ostentatious presents to a mere savage chief may be attributed to the ever meddling folly of King James, with his belief in the divine rights of royalty. The wisdom of the policy is shown by the fact that Powhatan now refused to give Newport either men or guides for his journey, and tried to divert him from his purpose.

His return for the costly gifts was but some seven or eight bushels of corn. The narrative of these events in Smith's *History* says that the presents "had been much better spared than so ill spent, for we had Powhatan's favor much better only for a plain piece of copper, till this stately kind of soliciting made him so much overvalue himself that he respected us as much as nothing at all." Newport now set out on his voyage to the Pacific Ocean with one hundred and twenty men led by Captain Waldo, Lieutenant Percy, Captain Wynne, Mr. West, a brother of Lord Delaware, and Mr. Scrivener. They arrived at the falls of the James River, where Richmond now stands, and started by land with their boat. They marched some forty miles in two days and a half, discovered two Indian villages, where we are not surprised to hear that the Indians remained entirely neutral, seized a chief or "king" as they styled him, and led him bound as a guide. They returned on their own path, searching in many places where they thought they had discovered mines. They "spent some time in refining," having "a refiner fitted for that purpose," and returned to the falls, where the Indians, who were anxious to get well rid of their visitors, told them that ships were coming into the bay to attack Jamestown. The Indians refused to trade, and thus ended the great expedition for the discovery of a passage to the South Sea. Let us not smile too much at the ignorance of the London Company. The Spaniards had found the Pacific Ocean near to the Atlantic at the Isthmus (Panama), and the London geographers had no means of guessing at the width of the continent.

□□□□□□□□□□

Immediately on the return of the explorers, Smith set every well man to work to hasten the reloading of the vessel. Parties were sent out to make glass, tar, pitch, and soap ashes, while the president went with thirty gentlemen some five miles into the woods to fell trees and make clapboards. The work was undertaken with a cheerful spirit. Sleeping in the woods was a pleasant novelty, and these gentlemen "made it their delight to hear the trees thunder as they fell." The president lodged, ate, drank, worked, and played with the rest. These amateur woodmen had one trouble. Axes would blister their tender hands, and it often happened that "every third blow had an oath to drown the echo." Captain Smith undertook to cure this "sin."

He had every man's oaths counted and recorded. At night a can of water was poured down the sinner's sleeve for every oath which had escaped him during the day. It is recorded that in consequence of this rather sharp method, profanity became rare among the wood choppers. These gentlemen were anxious not to be considered "common wood haggers," and wished to have it understood that after they became inured to it they considered it but "pleasure and recreation." It was said that thirty or forty voluntary gentlemen laborers could do more than one hundred of the indolent gentlemen of Jamestown would do when forced to it, but still twenty good workmen would have "been better than them all." When Captain Smith had returned from his wood choppers camp, he resolved to make an expedition in search of corn. Taking with him two barges, he went to the country of the Chickahominy Indians. This "dogged nation," however, knowing all too well the wants of the colony, answered all overtures for friendly trade with scorn and insolence. Captain Smith saw that it was the policy of the much-honored Powhatan to starve the English. He told the Indians that their corn had not been so much the object of his journey, but that he had come to revenge his imprisonment and the death of his men. He landed, and prepared for a charge, but the Indians fled. They soon sent ambassadors with presents of corn, fish, and game, and a desire to make peace. The result was that the boats were laden with corn, and they parted good friends. It is alleged that the sailors while at Jamestown made use of many indirect means for trading with the colonists, getting in this way valuable furs to sell in England.

Captain Newport's vessel is called "our old tavern" in the account given in Smith's *History*. Meantime Mr. Scrivener went on a trading expedition to Werowocomoco. The savages were at first disposed to fight, but Mr. Scrivener managed them so wisely that he procured three or four hogsheads of corn. Captain Newport was now ready to sail with samples of the various commodities which the colonists had undertaken to make, and the president, Smith, wrote a very plain letter in answer to the London Company's letter. This was America's first impudence to the mother country, a defiance that began in her very babyhood. "I received your letter," wrote Captain Smith, "wherein you write that our minds are so set upon faction and idle conceits in dividing the country without your consents, and that we feed you with ifs and ands, hopes and some few proofs, as if we could keep the mystery of the business to ourselves, and that we must expressly follow your instructions sent by Captain Newport, the charge of whose voyage amounts to near two thousand pounds, the which if we cannot defray by the ship's return we are alike to remain as banished men. To these particulars I humbly entreat your pardons if I offend you with my rude answer. For our factions, unless you would have me run away and leave the country, I cannot prevent them, because I do make many stay that would else fly any whither. For the idle letter sent to my Lord of Salisbury by the president and his confederates for dividing the country, etc. What it was I know not, for you saw no hand of mind to it nor ever dreamt I of any such matter. That we feed you with hopes, etc. Though I be no scholar, I am past a schoolboy, and I desire but to know what either you and these here do know, but I have learned to tell you by the continual hazard of my life. I have not concealed from you anything I know—but I fear some cause you to believe much more than is true. Expressly to follow your directions by Captain Newport.—Though they be performed, I was directly against it, but, according to your commission, I was content to be overruled by the major part of the council, I fear greatly to the hazard of us all, which is now generally confessed when it is too late. Only Captain Wynne and Captain Waldo I have sworn of the council, and crowned Powhatan according to your instructions. For the charge of this voyage of two or three thousand pounds, we have not received the value of an hundred pounds. And for the quartered boat to be borne by the soldiers over the falls, Newport had one hundred and twenty of the best men he could choose. If he had burnt her to ashes one might have carried her in a bag, but as she is, five hundred cannot, to a navigable place above the falls. And for him at that time to find the South Sea, a mine of gold, or any of them sent out by Sir Walter Raleigh, at our consultation I told them was as likely as the rest. But during this great discovery of thirty miles (which might as well have been done by one man and much more for the value of a pound of copper at a seasonable time) they had the pinnace and all the boats with them but one that remained with me to serve the fort. In their absence I followed the new begun works of pitch and tar, glass, soap ashes, clapboard, whereof some small quantities we have sent you. But if you rightly consider what an infinite toil it is in Russia and Swethland, where the woods are proper for naught else, and though there be the help both of man and beasts in these ancient commonwealths which many an hundred years have used it, yet thousands of those poor people can scarce get necessaries to live but from hand to mouth.

And though your factors there can buy as much in a week as will fraught you a ship or as much as you please, you must not expect from us any such matter, which are but as many of ignorant, miserable souls that are scarce able to get wherewith to live and defend ourselves against the inconstant savages, finding but here and there a tree fit for the purpose, and want all things else the Russians have. For the coronation of Powhatan, by whose advice you sent him such presents, I know not, but this give me leave to tell you, I fear they will be the confusion of us all ere we hear from you again. At your ships's arrival, the savages harvest was newly gathered, and we going to buy it, our own not being sufficient for so great a number. As for the two ships's loading of corn Captain Newport promised to provide us from Powhatan, he brought us but fourteen bushels, and from the Monacans nothing but the most of the men sick and near famished. From your ship we had not provision in victuals worth twenty pounds, and we are more than two hundred to live upon this, the one half sick and the other little better. For the sailors, I confess they daily made good cheer, but our diet is a little meal and water, and not sufficient of that. Though there be fish in the sea, fowls in the air, and beasts in the woods, their bounds are so large, they so wild, and we so weak and ignorant, we cannot much trouble them. Captain Newport we much suspect to be the author of those inventions. Now, that you should know I have made you as great a discovery as he for less charge than he spendeth you every meal, I have sent you this map of the bays and rivers, with an annexed relation of the countries and nations that inhabit them, as you may see at large. Also two barrels of stones and such as I take to be good iron ore at the least, so divided as by their notes you may see in what places I found them. The soldiers say many of your officers maintain their families out of what you sent us, and that Captain Newport hath an hundred pounds a year for carrying news. For every master you have yet sent can find the way as well as he, so that an hundred pounds might be spared, which is more than we have all that helps to pay him wages. Captain Ratcliffe is now called [John] Sicklemore, a poor counterfeited imposture. I have sent him home lest the company should cut his throat. What he is, now everyone can tell you. If he and [Gabriel] Archer return again, they are sufficient to keep us always in factions. When you send again, I entreat you rather send but thirty carpenters, husbandmen, gardeners, fishermen, blacksmiths, masons, and diggers up of trees's roots, well-provided, than a thousand of such as we have, for except we be able to both lodge and feed them, the most will consume with want of necessaries before they can be made good for anything. Thus, if you please to consider this account and the unnecessary wages to Captain Newport or his ships so long lingering and staying here (for notwithstanding his boasting to leave us victuals for twelve months, though we, eighty-nine, by this discovery lame and sick, and but a pint of corn a day for a man, we were constrained to give him three hogsheads of that to victual him homeward), or yet to send into Germany or Poland for glass men, and the rest till we are able to sustain ourselves and relieve them when they come. It were better to give five hundred pound a ton for those gross commodities in Denmark than send for them hither till more necessary things be provided. For in over toiling our weak and unskillful bodies to satisfy this desire of present profit, we can scarce ever recover ourselves from one supply to another.

    And I humbly entreat you hereafter let us know what we should receive and not stand to the sailors's courtesy to leave us what they please, else you may charge us what you will, but we not you with anything. These are the causes that have kept us in Virginia from laying such a foundation that ere this might have given much better content and satisfaction, but as yet you must not look for any profitable returns, so I humbly rest."

Marvelous good common sense is this! It is the fashion of late years to revile Smith for a boaster. But where can we find prudence and sound sense in all this miserable management but from him? No wonder that he esteemed his service highly. common sense was so scarce in Jamestown and in London.

Cold weather had come, and famine began to stare the colonists in the face. Taking with him Captain Wynne and Mr. Scrivener with three boats, the president set out for the country of the Nansemond Indians. These people refused not only to provide the four hundred bushels of corn which they had promised in their treaty with the colonists on their previous visit, but they refused to trade at all. Their excuse was that they had used up the most that they had, and that they were under commands from Powhatan neither to trade with the English nor to allow them to enter their river. The English had recourse to force, and the Indians fled at the first volley of musketry without shooting a single arrow. The first cabin the white men discovered they set on fire. The Indians immediately desired peace, and promised the English half that they had. Before night all the boats were loaded with corn, and the English sailed some four miles down the river. Here they camped out for the night in the open woods on frozen ground covered with snow. The manner in which these adventurers of nearly three hundred years ago made themselves comfortable is interesting. They would dig away the snow and build a great fire, which would serve to dry and warm the ground. They would then scrape away the fire, spread a mat on the place where it had been, and here they would sleep with another mat hung up as a shield against the wind. In the night, as the wind shifted, they would change their hanging mat, and when the ground grew cold they would again remove their fire and take its place. Their story says that many "a cold winter night" did the adventurers sleep thus, and yet those who went on these expeditions "were always in health, lusty, and fat." About this time the first marriage in Virginia took place. The one single woman in Jamestown would naturally not remain long unmarried. Anne Burras was married to John Laydon, a laborer, and one of the earliest colonists. Almost immediately after his return, Captain Smith started on another expedition in search of corn. As they sailed the Indians fled from them until they discovered the Appomattox, a tributary of James River. The natives had not much corn, but they divided what they had, for which they were amply requited with copper and trinkets.

☐☐☐☐☐☐☐☐☐☐

Finding that the old Indian chief had determined to starve the colony out of existence by a refusal to trade with the white men, Captain Smith, appreciating the desperate extremity, resolved to take, as usual, the boldest plan out of the difficulty. He meditated a plan for surprising and entrapping Powhatan into his power. Smith saw no other chance to procure food, and starving men do not stop to debate whether a course is right or wrong. About this time Powhatan sent a message to Smith inviting him to visit him, and saying that if he would but build him a house, give him a grindstone, fifty swords, some firearms, a hen and rooster, and much beads and copper, he would fill the ship with corn. Captain Smith made haste to accept this offer. He sent some of the Dutchmen and some Englishmen ahead to begin the building of Powhatan's house. The barge and pinnace were fitted up for this expedition. The president with twelve men sailed in the barge, while fifteen men, among whom were Lieutenant [George] Percy and Mr. [Francis] West, brother of Lord Delaware [Thomas West], sailed in the pinnace. This party started from Jamestown in December, 1608. They stopped for the first night at the village of Warrasqueake. They were treated very kindly by the chief of this town, who advised them not to visit Powhatan. Smith, however, was determined to go. "Captain Smith," said the chief, "you shall find Powhatan to use you kindly, but trust him not, and be sure he has no opportunity to seize on your arms, for he hath sent for you only to cut your throats." The captain thanked him for his advice, and resolved to follow it. He asked this chief for guides to the Chowanoc Indians. The chief immediately complied with his request, and Captain Smith sent Mr. Michael Sicklemore, a "valiant soldier, with the guides to this place in search of Sir Walter Raleigh's lost company, and silk grass or peminaw." What is said of the people of the lost colony by different writers is quite hard to understand. Sometimes they seem (assumed) to have been all exterminated—again we hear rumors that some of them are alive. When Captain Smith parted with the friendly chief, he left him his page to learn the language. The next night the English lodged at Kecoughtan. Here they were storm bound for about a week. They were thus obliged to keep Christmas at this Indian village, and a merry time they had of it. They feasted upon fish, venison, wild fowl, with the sweet corn bread of the country, and enjoyed themselves around great fires in the warm, smoky cabins of the Indians. Traveling on from here the English were forced, when they could find no cabins, to sleep in the woods as we have described. During the journey Captain Smith, Anthony Bagnall, and Sergeant [Edward] Pising shot a hundred and forty-eight wild fowl at one time. At the Indian village of Kiskiack, now corrupted to Chescake, and pronounced Cheesecake, the English were again forced by the cold and contrary winds to spend several days in Indian cabins.

These Indians were not friendly, and the whites were obliged to guard their barge with care. On the twelfth of January the English neared Werowocomoco. The ice extended nearly half a mile from shore in the York River. Captain Smith pushed as near the shore as he could in the barge, by breaking the ice. Impatient of remaining in an open boat in the freezing cold, he jumped into the half-frozen marsh, and waded ashore. His example was followed by eighteen of his men, among whom was a Mr. [John] Russell, who could not be persuaded to stay behind, although he was a very heavy man, and "somewhat ill." This gentleman "so over-toiled himself" that it was with difficulty that his comrades got him ashore and restored warmth to his benumbed body. The English quartered at the first cabins they reached, and announced their arrival in a message to Powhatan, requesting provision. The chief sent them plenty of bread, venison, and turkeys, and feasted them according to his custom. The following day, however, he desired to know when they "would be gone," pretending that he had not sent for the English. He made the astonishing statement that he himself had no corn, and his people had much less, but that he would furnish them forty baskets of this grain for as many swords. Captain Smith quickly confronted him with the men who had brought Powhatan's message to Jamestown, and asked the chief "how it chanced he became so forgetful." Powhatan answered with "a merry laughter," and invited the English to show their commodities. But the crafty chief was not suited with anything, unless it was guns or swords. He would value a basket of corn higher than a basket of copper. "Powhatan," said Captain Smith, "though I had many courses to have made my provision, yet believing your promises to supply my wants, I neglected all to satisfy your desire, and to testify my love I sent you my men for your building, neglecting mine own. What your people had you have engrossed, forbidding them our trade, and now you think by consuming the time we shall consume for want, not having to fulfill your strange demands. As for swords and guns, I told you long ago I had none to spare, and you must know those I have can keep me from want. Yet steal or wrong you I will not, nor dissolve that friendship we have mutually promised, except you constrain me by your bad usage." Powhatan listened attentively to this speech, and promised that he would spare them what he could, which he would deliver to them in two days. "Yet, Captain Smith," said the chief, "I have some doubt of your coming hither that makes me not so kindly seek to relieve you as I would, for many do inform me your coming hither is not for trade, but to invade my people and possess my country, who dare not bring you corn, seeing you thus armed with your men. To free us of this fear, leave aboard your weapons, for here they are needless, we being all friends."

But Captain Smith was not to be cajoled into a council without weapons. That night was spent at Werowocomoco, and the following day the building of Powhatan's house went forward. The Dutchmen seeing the plenty of Powhatan and his power, and thinking the colony could not long withstand the wily chief, had betrayed the English, though this was not discovered until some six months afterward. Meanwhile the English managed "to wrangle" some ten bushels of corn out of the chief for a copper kettle. Powhatan then made a speech setting forth the advantages of remaining at peace with the colony. "Captain Smith," said he, "you may understand that I, having seen the death of my people thrice, and not anyone living of those three generations but myself, I know the difference of peace and war better than any in my country. But now I am old, and ere long must die, my brethren, namely Opitchapan, Opechancanough, and Kekataugh, my two sisters and their two daughters, are each others's successors. I wish their experience no less than mine and your love to them no less than mine to you. But this brute from Nansemond, that you are come to destroy my country, affrighted all my people as they dare not visit you. What will it avail you to take that by force you may quickly have by love, or to destroy them that provide you food? What can you get by war when we can hide our provisions and fly to the woods, whereby you must family by wronging us, your friends? And why are you thus jealous of our loves, seeing us unarmed and both do and are willing still to feed you with that you cannot get but by our labors? Think you I am so simple not to know it is better to eat good meat, lie well, and sleep quietly with my women and children, laugh and be merry with you, have copper, hatchets, or what I want being your friend, than be forced to fly from all, to lie cold in the woods, feed upon acorns, roots, and such trash, and be so hunted by you that I can neither rest, eat, nor sleep, but my tired men must watch, and if a twig but break everyone crieth, there cometh Captain Smith! Then must I fly I know not whither, and thus with miserable fear end my miserable life, leaving my pleasures to such youths as you, which through your rash unadvisedness may quickly as miserably end for want of that you never know where to find. Let this therefore assure you of our loves, and every year our friendly trade shall furnish you with corn, and now also, if you would come in a friendly manner to see us, and not thus with your guns and swords as to invade your foes." "Seeing you will not rightly conceive of our words," answered Captain Smith, "we strive to make you know our thoughts by our deeds. The vow I made you of my love both myself and my men have kept. As for your promise, I find it every day violated by some of your subjects, yet we, finding your love and kindness, our custom is so far from being ungrateful that for your sake only we have curbed our thirsting desire of revenge, else had they known as well the cruelty we use to our enemies as our true love and courtesy to our friends. And I think your judgment sufficient to conceive, as well by the adventures we have undertaken as by the advantage we have by our arms of yours, that had we intended you any hurt, long ere this we would have affected it. Your people coming to Jamestown are entertained with their bows and arrows without any exceptions, we esteeming it with you, as it is with us, to wear our arms as our apparel. As for the danger of our enemies, in such wars consist our chiefest pleasure, for your riches we have no use, as for the hiding your provision, or by your flying to the woods, we shall not so unadvisedly starve as you conclude, your friendly care in that behalf is needless, for we have a rule to find beyond your knowledge." Certainly the word fencers were a match in subtle insinuation, and neither one was to be caught off his guard.

Some trading was again begun. The chief was dissatisfied that he could not have his way. "Captain Smith," said Powhatan with a sigh, "I never used any werowance so kindly as yourself, yet from you I receive the least kindness of any. Captain Newport gave me swords, copper, clothes, a bed, towels, or what I desired, ever taking what I offered him, and would send away his guns when I entreated him, none doth deny to lie at my feet or refuse to do what I desire but only you, of whom I can have nothing but what you regard not, and yet you will have whatsoever you demand. Captain Newport you call father, and so you call me, but I see for all us both you will do what you list, and we must both seek to content you. But if you intend so friendly as you say, send hence your arms, that I may believe you, for you see the love I bear you doth cause me thus nakedly to forget myself."

The wily old chief was right. Captain Smith was determined to have his own way. He saw that nothing could be gained thus. Powhatan was watching with lynx eyes for a chance to get the white men into his power while he delivered those eloquent and persuasive speeches which are so characteristic of Indians. Captain Smith asked the savages to break the ice for him that his boat might reach the shore, to take him and the corn. He intended, when the boat came, to land more men and surprise the chief. Meanwhile, to entertain Powhatan and keep him from suspecting anything, he made the following reply to his last speech, "Powhatan, you must know as I have but one God I honor but one king, and I live not here as your subject, but as your friend, to pleasure you with what I can. By the gifts you bestow on me you gain more than by trade, yet would you visit me as I do you, you should know it is not our custom to sell our courtesies as a vendable commodity. Bring all your country with you for your guard I will not dislike it as being over jealous. But to content you, tomorrow I will leave my arms and trust to your promise. I call you father, indeed and as a father you shall see I will love you, but the small care you have for such a child caused my men to persuade me to look to myself." But Powhatan was not to be fooled. His mind was on the fast disappearing ice. He managed to disengage himself from the Captain's conversation, and secretly fled with his women, children, and luggage. To avoid any suspicion, two or three women were left to engage Captain Smith in talk while the Powhatan warriors beset the house where they were. When Captain Smith discovered what they were doing, he and John Russell went about making their way out with the help of their pistols, swords, and Indian shields. At the first shot, the savages tumbled "one over another" and quickly fled in every direction and the two men reached their companions in safety.

Powhatan saw that his stratagem had failed. He immediately tried to remove the unfavorable impression which this event and the sudden appearance of so many warriors might make on the minds of the English. He sent an "ancient orator" to Captain Smith with presents of a great bracelet and chain of pearls. "Captain Smith," said the Indian, "our werowance has fled, fearing your guns, and knowing when the ice was broken there would come more men—he sent these numbers but to guard his corn from stealing—that might happen without your knowledge. Now, though some be hurt by your misprision, yet Powhatan is your friend and so will forever continue. Now since the ice is open, he would have you send away your corn, and if you would have his company, send away also your guns, which so affrighteth his people that they dare not come to you as he promised they should." The Indians provided baskets that the English might carry their corn to the boat. They were very officious in tendering their services to guard the colonists's arms while they were thus occupied, lest anyone should steal them. There were crowds of these grim, sturdy savages about, but the sight of the white men cocking their matchlock guns rendered them exceedingly meek. They were easily persuaded by this sight to leave their bows and arrows in charge of the Englishmen, while they themselves carried the corn down to the boats on their own backs. This they did with wonderful dispatch. Ebb tide left the boat stuck in the marsh, and the adventurers were obliged to remain at Werowocomoco until high water. They returned to the cabins where they were at first quartered. The savages entertained them until night with "merry sports," and then left them. Powhatan was gathering his forces and planning the certain destruction of his visitors. The English were alone in the Indian cabins. Suddenly Pocahontas, Powhatan's "dearest jewel and daughter," as she is styled in the quaint narrative, appeared before Captain Smith. She had come this dark night through the "irksome woods" alone from her father's cabin. "Captain Smith," said she, "great cheer will be sent you by and by, but Powhatan and all the power he can make will after come and kill you all, if they that bring you the cheer do not kill you with your own weapons when you are at supper. Therefore, if you would live, I wish you presently to begone." Captain Smith wished to give Pocahontas presents of those trifles dear to the heart of an Indian, and such as Pocahontas most delighted in. "I dare not," said the girl, with tears running down her cheeks, "be seen to have any, for if Powhatan should know it, I am but dead."

She then ran away into the woods as she had come. Within less than an hour, eight or ten "lusty" savages came, bringing great platters of venison and other food. They begged the Englishmen to put out the matches to their guns, for the "smoke made them sick," and to sit down to eat. But the Captain was vigilant. He made the Indians first taste of every dish, and he then sent them back to Powhatan, asking him "to make haste," for he was awaiting his arrival. Soon after more messengers came, "to see what news," in the words of the story, and they were followed in a short time by still more. Thus the night was spent by both parties with the utmost vigilance, though to all appearances they were on very friendly terms. When high water came the English prepared to depart. At Powhatan's request they left a man named Edward Brinton (Brynton) to hunt for him, while the Dutchmen remained to finish his house. On an eminence near where Werowocomoco must have been, still stands a stone chimney which is known to this day as "Powhatan's Chimney" (located at Wicomico in present-day Gloucester County, Virginia), and according to tradition is the chimney of the house which the colonists erected for this chief. The English pushed on to Pamunkey in search of corn, hoping that upon their return the frost would be gone, and if Powhatan still gave occasion, a better opportunity might then be found to subdue his pride. If the actions of Smith seem sometimes lacking in good faith, we must remember the desperate position of the little colony (circa 1607) entrusted to his care, and the extreme difficulty of dealing with Indians in such circumstances.

In two or three days the barge and pinnace arrived at Pamunkey. The chief entertained them with "feasting and much mirth." The day appointed for trade came. Captain Smith, accompanied by fifteen men, among whom were Lieutenant [George] Percy, Mr. [Francis] West, and Mr. [John] Russell, marched a quarter of a mile to the cabin of Opechancanough. There was no one to be seen but a lame Indian and a boy. The English waited, and the chief soon came, followed by a guard of his people fairly laden with bows and arrows, but with "pinching commodities," upon which they put an enormous price.

"Opechancanough," said Captain Smith, "the great love you profess with your tongue seems mere deceit by your actions. Last year you kindly freighted our ship, but now you have invited me to starve with hunger, you know my want and I your plenty, of which by some means I must have part, remember it is fit for kings to keep their promise. Here are my commodities, whereof take your choice, the rest I will proportion fit bargains for your people." The chief accepted this offer with seeming kindness, and sold what his people had brought at a fair price. He promised to meet the English the next day with a larger company better provided with commodities. On the following day the captain and his fifteen comrades again started for the chief's cabin, leaving the boats in charge of Mr. [William] Phettiplace, captain of the pinnace. Arrived at the place of meeting, they found four or five Indians who had just come.—Soon after the chief entered with "strained cheerfulness."—He began a long-winded conversation on how much trouble he had taken to keep his promise, with which he took up the time until Mr. Russell stepped up to Captain Smith and said, "We are all betrayed, for at least seven hundred savages, well-armed, have environed the house and beset the fields." Opechancanough guessed what Mr. Russell said from the expression of his face. Captain Smith turned to his comrades and discussed the difficulties of the situation. "Worthy countrymen," said he, "were the mischief of my seeming friends no more than the danger of these enemies, I little cared, were they as many more, if you dare do but as I. But this is my torment, that if I escape them our malicious council, with their open-mouthed minions, will make me such a peace breaker in their opinions in England as will break my neck. I could wish those here that make these (the Indians) seem saints and me an oppressor. But this is the worst of all wherein I pray you aid me with your opinions. Should we begin with them and surprise the king, we cannot keep him and defend well ourselves. If we should each kill our man, and so proceed with all in the house, the rest will all fly—then shall we get no more than the bodies that are slain and so starve for victual. As for their fury, it is the least danger, for well you know being alone assaulted with two or three hundred of them, I made them by the help of God compound to save my life. And we are sixteen and they but seven hundred at the most, and assure yourselves God will so assist us that if you dare stand but to discharge your pieces, the very smoke will be sufficient to affright them. Yet, howsoever, let us fight like men and not die like sheep, for by that means you know God hath oft delivered me, and so I trust will now. But first I will deal with them to bring it to pass we may fight for something, and draw them to it by conditions. If you like this motion, promise me you will be valiant." There was no time for argument, these men, who were the very pick of the colonists, vowed to "execute whatsoever he attempted or die." The Captain turned to the chief and challenged him thus, "I see, Opechancanough, your plot to murder me, but I fear it not. As yet your men and mine have done no harm but by our direction. Take therefore your arms, you see mine, my body shall be as naked as yours, the isle in your river is a fit place, if you be contented, and the conqueror of us two shall be lord and master over all our men. If you have not enough, take time to fetch more, and bring what number you will, so everyone bring a basket of corn, against all which I will stake the value in copper, you see I have but fifteen, and our game shall be this, *the conqueror take all.*" The chief, who was surrounded by some forty or fifty warriors as a guard, tried to quiet Captain Smith's suspicions. He told the Captain that a great present awaited him at the door, and he entreated him to go and receive it.

This was but a bait to draw the Captain outside, where the present was backed up by some two hundred warriors, while thirty more were in ambush under a great tree with bows ready drawn. The president commanded one of his men to "go and see what kind of deceit" this might be. The man refused, and Captain Smith was so vexed at his cowardice, that though all the other gentlemen of the party desired importunately to go in his place, the Captain would not let them. Captain Smith ordered Lieutenant Percy, Mr. West, and the others to guard the entrances to the cabin, and suddenly turning he grasped the chief's long lock of hair and put his pistol to his breast.

In this manner he led Opechancanough, trembling and "near dead with fear," out among his people. The chief delivered his bow and arrows to Captain Smith. "I see, you Pamunkeys," said the Captain, still holding the chief by the hair, "the great desire you have to kill me, and my long suffering your injuries hath emboldened you to this presumption. The cause I have forborne your insolences is the promise I made you before the God I serve to be your friend till you give me just cause to be your enemy. If I keep this vow, my God will keep me, you cannot hurt me, but if I break it, he will destroy me. But if you shoot but one arrow to shed one drop of blood of any of my men, or steal the least of these beads or copper I spurn here before you with my foot, you shall see I will not cease revenge, if I once begin, so long as I can hear to find one of your nation that will not deny the name of Pamunkey. I am not now at Rassawek, half drowned with mire, where you took me prisoner, yet then for keeping your promise and your good usage and saving my life, I so affect you, that your denials of your treachery do half persuade me to mistake myself. But if I be the mark you aim at, here I stand, shoot he that dare! You promised to freight my ship ere I departed, and so you shall, or I mean to load her with your dead carcasses, yet if as friends you will come and trade, I once more promise not to trouble you except you give me the first occasion, and your king shall be free and be my friend, for I am not come to hurt him or any of you." At the close of this boastful speech, away went bows and arrows, the chief was released, and trade began in good earnest. Men, women, and children thronged around the Captain with their commodities. After two or three hours of this business the president became weary. He left two gentlemen, Mr. [Robert] Behethland and Mr. [William] Powell, to trade, and went into the council house, where he fell fast asleep. His friends were off their guard, and here was a chance for the treacherous Indians. Forty or fifty warriors, armed with clubs and English swords, crowded into the building. Their haste shook the cabin and aroused the Captain, who, half awake as he was, took to his sword and shield, followed by Mr. Raleigh Croshaw and some others who were present. They charged toward the crowded doorway. But the Indians moved back more hastily than they had pressed forward. Opechancanough with some old men made a long oration, excusing this intrusion. The remainder of the day passed (went) off in friendly trading, the Indians being well-satisfied with the payment they got for their commodities and the English sailed away from Pamunkey with their corn.

☐☐☐☐☐☐☐☐☐☐☐

Meantime two of the "Dutchmen," as they are called, returned to Jamestown, and told Captain [Peter] Wynne, who was in command of the fort, that they had come for some tools which they needed, and a change of clothes. They procured new arms on the pretence that Captain Smith, having need of their arms, had taken them. They also plotted with some men in the fort, and secured various arms, ammunition, and tools—which they conveyed to Indians outside the fort—who carried them away. By aid of these confederates within Jamestown, to whom it was represented that they would be favorites of Powhatan and safe from the miseries of the colony, there was a constant leakage of weapons for months. Meanwhile, the Englishmen who had been left with Powhatan were in constant fear of their lives. While Captain Smith was still away, a sad accident happened at Jamestown. Mr. Scrivener for some reason desired to visit an island in the river where the colonists kept their hogs and which to this day retains its name of Hog Island. The name in Smith's *History* is sometimes given a more poetical sound by calling it the "Isle of Hogs." Mr. Scrivener entered the skiff accompanied by Captain [Richard] Waldo, Mr. Anthony Gosnold, and eight more. It was an "extreme frozen time" there was a violent wind, and the boat was overloaded. She was upset in the tempest, and the Indians were the first to find the bodies. The loss was a great one to the little colony, and the Powhatan Indians were the more encouraged by it. No one could be found to go and tell the sad news to the president until Mr. Richard Wyffin undertook this dangerous mission. When he arrived at Werowocomoco the English were not there, and he could see preparations for war on every side. Mr. Wyffin's life was in danger, but Pocahontas came to his assistance. She hid him while he was at Werowocomoco. When he had gone, the Indians prepared to pursue him, but Pocahontas sent them in the direction opposite to the one in which he had gone. After three days's journey, and by the use of ample bribes among the savages, Mr. Wyffin reached the adventurers. Captain Smith made him swear to keep his sad news a secret for the present, fearing lest his men should become demoralized for the dangers through which they must yet pass. Powhatan seems to have had trouble to persuade his people into any skirmishing with the whites. In the words of the narrative, the Indians hated a fight with them "almost as ill as hanging, such fear had they of bad success." On the morning following the arrival of Mr. Wyffin, the English stopped at an Indian village.

    At sunrise the fields were covered with Indians and their baskets of commodities. They would not trade unless Captain Smith would come ashore, and they would not on any account endure the sight of a gun. The Captain complied with their request, but he managed to arrange some of his men in ambush so that he might be assured of a defense without affecting savage nerves with the sight of firearms. All went on well until the Indians had beset the Captain and his companions with numbers. The Indians drew their arrows even now with trembling hands, and when the ambuscade was suddenly discovered, they fled precipitately, "esteeming" in the words of the history, "their heels for their best advantage." During the night Mr. [Raleigh] Croshaw and Mr. [Robert] Ford were sent to Jamestown with the barge.

This boat, passing down the river in the darkness added to the Indians's fright, for they thought Captain Smith was sending for more men. The chief sent a string of pearls as a conciliatory present, and promised to freight the ship with food. For several days they flocked in from all parts of the country, bearing corn upon their naked backs. A young warrior named Wecuttanow, a son of one of the principal chiefs, brought the English some food which was poisoned. This would have cost the life of Captain Smith and several others had not the dish been overdosed with poison. The young Indian was suspected of knowledge of this affair. Seeing him stand on the defensive, Captain Smith caused a good whipping to be administered to him, and then spurned him as though he thought him too mean for further punishment.

When the English again reached Werowocomoco, they found that Powhatan had deserted the place. He did not relish his proximity to the colony. They sailed with all speed for Jamestown, well-supplied with corn and deer suet.

Those who had been left at the fort had lived upon what provision there was—which was spoiled by rain and eaten by rats and worms—so that it could not have been pleasant diet. The colonists now found that they had good food enough to last until the next corn harvest. Captain Smith appointed six hours a day to be spent at work and the remainder of the day in "pastime and merry exercises." He made his unruly colonists a speech. "Countrymen," said the Captain, "the long experience of our late miseries I hope is sufficient to persuade everyone to a present correction of himself. And think not that either my pains nor the adventurers's purses will ever maintain you in idleness and sloth. I speak not this to you all, for divers of you I know deserve both honor and reward better than is yet here to be had, but the greater part must be more industrious or starve, however you have been heretofore tolerated by the authority of the council from that I have often commanded you. You see now that power resteth wholly in myself. You must obey this now for a law, that he that will not work shall not eat, except by sickness he is disabled, for the labors of thirty or forty honest and industrious men shall not be consumed to maintain an hundred and fifty idle loiterers. And though you presume the authority here is but a shadow, and that I dare not touch the lives of any but my own must answer it, the letters patent shall each week be read to you, whose contents will tell you the contrary. I wish you therefore without contempt to seek to observe these orders set down, for there are now no more councilors to protect you nor curb my endeavors. Therefore, he that offendeth let him assuredly expect his due punishment." The Captain furthermore made a public record of every man's behavior, hoping thus both by encouragement and shame to better the conduct of the colonists. Meanwhile there was a constant leakage in arms, ammunition, and tools, by means of the Dutchmen's confederates within Jamestown, who, though the loss was known, were not caught until it was too late. The Dutchmen remained with Powhatan, instructing him in the use of English arms. Their rendezvous was at a glass house half a mile distant from Jamestown.

    One of the men came here one day disguised as a savage. Captain Smith, hearing of his arrival, went to the glass house with twenty men, hoping to capture him. He was already gone, however, and sending his men in pursuit, Smith undertook to return alone to Jamestown, armed only with a sword.

    On his way he met the chief of Paspahegh, who immediately prepared to shoot the Captain, who, however, sprang forward and grappled with him. The chief was very strong and stout and he picked up the Captain and carried him to the river. Into the river he jumped with his enemy and attempted to drown him. They struggled together in the water until Smith managed to get a good grip of the chief's throat. He drew his sword, and would have cut off his head, but the Indian begged piteously for his life, and Smith led him prisoner to Jamestown, where he had him put into chains. The Dutchman was also brought in prisoner, but he told Captain Wynne a story about how

Powhatan had detained him by force, that he had escaped at the hazard of his life, and meant to have returned immediately to Jamestown, but was only walking in the woods in search of walnuts. He was inadvertently allowed to go with this excuse, though the imprisoned chief confessed to a very different story. Captain Smith told him that if he could procure the return of the Dutchmen he would save his life. The poor Indian did his best to accomplish this, sending messengers daily to Powhatan.

    The answer came back that Powhatan did not detain the Dutchmen, but that they would remain, and he could not send them fifty miles on men's backs. Every day the wives, children, and people of the prisoner would come to Jamestown to visit him, bringing with them presents to appease the anger of the English. His liberty was promised him, but finding his guard negligent one day, he made sure of it. The runaway chief was pursued, and two Indians named Kemps and Tussore were captured in the pursuit. These Indians were said to be the "two most exact villains in all the country." With these for guides, Smith sent Captain Wynne to recapture the escaped chief, in which, however, Wynne failed, though he burnt the chief's house. Captain Smith now set out himself, and attacked the Paspahegh Indians, who, recognizing him, threw down their arms and sent their orator, a young man named Okaning, to him "Captain Smith," said Okaning, "my master is here present in the company, thinking it Captain Wynne and not you, of him he intended to be revenged, having never offended him. If he hath offended you in escaping your imprisonment, the fishes swim, the fowls fly, and the very beasts strive to escape the snare and live. Then blame him not, being a man. He would entreat you remember, you being a prisoner, what pains he took to save your life. If since he has injured you, he was compelled to do it, but howsoever you have revenged it with our too great loss. We perceive and well know you intend to destroy us that are here to entreat and desire your friendship and to enjoy our houses and plant our fields, of whose fruit you shall participate, otherwise you will have the worse by our absence, for we can plant anywhere, though with more labor, and we know you cannot live if you want our harvest, and that relief we bring you. If you promise us peace, we will believe you, if you proceed to revenge, we will abandon the country." Peace was accordingly made. When Captain Smith returned to Jamestown, he found that the Chickahominy Indians had been discovered in various thefts. Among other things a pistol had been stolen. The thief had escaped, but two young Indian brothers, who were known to be his confederates, were captured. One of the brothers was imprisoned, and the other was told to go and get the pistol, and if he did not return with it in twelve hours his brother would be hung. The savage sped away on his errand. Meantime Captain Smith took pity on the poor naked Indian, in his cold dungeon, and sent him food and charcoal for a fire. About midnight the brother returned with the stolen pistol. On entering the dungeon it was found that the prisoner had been smothered with the carbonic acid gas generated by the charcoal fire, and had fallen senseless among the coals—where he was badly burnt.

    The poor brother was heartbroken. He lamented his death with such bitterness that the bystanders were touched. Captain Smith, though he had little hope that the Indian could be brought to, quieted the brother with the assurance that if they would steal no more he would make him alive again. The Englishmen went to work with brandy and vinegar, and the Indian presently came to his senses. His brother, however, was still more distressed to see him quite out of his mind from the effects of the smothering and fright, to say nothing of the brandy. Captain Smith promised to cure him if they would both behave well hereafter. He had the man put by a fire to sleep. He awoke in the morning in his right mind, his wounds were dressed, and the brothers were sent away well-pleased with presents of copper. The story was told among the Indians as a miracle, and they believed that Captain Smith could bring back a man that was dead. Another Indian got possession of a great bag of gunpowder and the back piece of a suit of armor. With a great display of superior knowledge he proceeded to dry the powder over the fire in the piece of armor as he had seen English soldiers do. The Indians crowded around him, peeping over his shoulder, to see this wonderful process. The result was that the powder blew up, killing the Indian and several others, and scorching all so badly that they had no desire to meddle with (gun) powder again. These and "many other such pretty accidents," as the writers wittily call them, gave the superstitious minds of Powhatan and his people a good fright. The Indians came in from all parts desiring peace, bringing presents and returning many stolen things of which the English had, had no suspicion. Any of their people caught in theft after this were sent by Powhatan back to Jamestown for punishment and a savage dared not "wrong an Englishman of a pin."

☐☐☐☐☐☐☐☐☐☐

This peaceful state of affairs enabled the colonists to follow their business quietly and successfully. Tar, pitch, and soap ashes were manufactured, a specimen of glass was made, a well of sweet water, a thing much needed heretofore, was dug within the fort, some twenty cottages were built, the church was covered, and fishing nets were prepared. A block house was built on the neck of the peninsula and garrisoned as a place for trade with the savages, and to prevent the constant thieving and disturbances. As spring came, land was tilled and corn planted.

The colonists had started with some three hogs and a few chickens. They had now "sixty and odd pigs," and it was stated as a great wonder that "five hundred chickens" had "brought up themselves" without feeding. Upon Hog Island, which served as a natural pig pen, another block house was built as a point from which notice of shipping might be given.—The colonists cut down trees and made clapboards and wainscoting for exercise.—They began the building of a fort as a place of retreat in case of extremity. This place was said to be situated near a river, upon a high hill. There stands in Virginia a building called "the Old Stone House," situated twenty-two miles from Jamestown, upon a high, steep bluff overlooking Ware Creek, a tributary of York River, which is in all probability the place of retreat which the colonists built. It is constructed of sandstone from the creek's bank and without mortar. It is a very small structure, being eight and a half feet wide by fifteen in length, and has a basement and one story. The walls and chimney are standing, there is a doorway six feet in width, and it is everywhere pierced with loopholes. This little fort is in a solitary, romantic spot reached only along a narrow ridge, deep in gloomy woods, full of ivy-grown ravines. Tradition has connected this building with legends of Captain Smith, Pocahontas, and the hidden treasures of the pirate Blackbeard. The fortress was never finished. In examining the store of corn one day, it was found to be almost consumed with the rats whose ancestors had been left by the ships, and who had multiplied enormously, while what they had spared was rotten.

The colonists were driven to their wits ends. The Indians, who lay by no store, and were always improvident, had now no corn left. The colonists must either make out to live upon the wild fruits of the country or starve. All other work was abandoned in the search after food. The two Indians, Kemps and Tussore, who were considered such villains, had been retained as prisoners among the English. They had been used to teach the colonists how to plant Indian corn. Having already too many mouths to feed, the English set these Indians at liberty. They had grown so fond of the colonists, however, that they were quite unwilling to go. The natives showed the utmost friendliness in this extremity, bringing in quantities of game and venison. Every exertion was made to supply food. At one time sixty or eighty men were sent down the river with Ensign Saxon to live upon oysters, twenty men to Point Comfort with Lieutenant Percy to fish, and twenty more up the river, but this party could find nothing but acorns to live upon. As usual there were some thirty or forty who provided food for the colony by their own industry, while the others had to be forced to save themselves from starvation. There were then, as now, quantities of sturgeon to be had in the James River. Some of the more industrious colonists dried the meat of this fish and pounded it, mixing it with herbs, so as to make a sort of bread out of it, after the manner of the Indians, while others would gather roots for food. The idlers wished Captain Smith to sell tools, arms, even the very ordnance and houses of Jamestown, to the savages for food. They were very desirous of deserting the country. The government was now entirely in Captain Smith's own hands, he being both council and councilors. The last member of the council, Captain Wynne, had died before the times of plenty were over. Although the council had often hampered him in his management of treacherous Indians abroad and unruly Englishmen at home, he had a most affectionate feeling for all its later members. Captain Smith at last made the followings speech to the colonists, "Fellow soldiers, I did little think any so false to report or so many to be so simple to be persuaded that I either intended to starve you or that Powhatan at this present time hath corn for himself, much less for you, or that I would not have it if I knew where it were to be had. Neither did I think any so malicious as now I see a great many, yet it shall not so passionate me but I will do my best for my most maligner. But dream no longer of this vain hope from Powhatan, nor that I will longer forbear to force you from your idleness and punish you if you rail. But if I find any more runners for Newfoundland with the pinnace, let him assuredly look to arrive at the gallows. You cannot deny but that by the hazard of my life many a time I have saved yours, when, might your own wills have prevailed, you would have starved, and will do still, whether I will or no. But I protest by that God that made me, since necessity hath not power to force you to gather for yourselves those fruits the earth doth yield, you shall not only gather for yourselves, but those that are sick. And this savage trash you so scornfully repine at, being put in your mouths your stomachs can digest, if you would have better, you should have brought it, and therefore I will take a course you shall provide what is to be had. The sick shall not starve, but equally share of all our labors, and he that gathered not every day as much as I do, the next day shall be set beyond the river and be banished from the fort as a drone, till he amend his conditions or starve." Every effort was made to carry the colonists through this period of want. For this purpose some of their number (group) was boarded, so to speak, among the Indians, where they were treated with the utmost kindness. So comfortable were they that several of the colony (colonists) ran away. They sought out the old prisoners, Kemps and Tussore, thinking they would be sure of friendly treatment and an idle life with them. These Indians, however, had no desire to entertain truants. Kemps proceeded to make sport of them for the benefit of the Indians. He dealt with them as the white men had dealt with him when a prisoner. He made fun for the Indians by feeding "the runaway Englishmen with this law, who would not work must not eat." The indolent truants were nearly starved, and constantly threatened with beatings. Nor would this jocular Indian allow them to escape. He at last returned them as prisoners to the authorities at Jamestown. Mr. [Michael] Sicklemore returned about this time from Chowanoc, with accounts of where the silk grass might be found, having discovered nothing of Sir Walter Raleigh's lost colony. Nathaniel Powell and Anas Todkill were also sent in search of the lost colony among the Mangoag Indians, where they could learn nothing but that they were all dead. (See page 257 for more information about the Lost Colony of Roanoke.) The chief of these Indians is honored in the old narrative with numerous adjectives, being an "honest, proper, good, promise keeping king." Though he adhered to the faith of his people, he admitted that the God of the English "as much exceeded his as our guns did his bow and arrows." He would sometimes send presents (trinkets) to Captain Smith, requesting him "to pray to his God for rain, or his corn would perish, for his gods were angry."

☐☐☐☐☐☐☐☐☐☐

One day a vessel arrived in command of Captain Samuel Argall, a relative of Sir Thomas Smith, the treasurer of the London Company. Captain Argall had come with a load of wine and provisions to trade with the colonists, contrary to the company's regulations. The necessities of the colonists were so pressing that they seized upon Argall's provisions, which they returned to him when they received their supply from England. Captain Argall brought with him news of a change in the London Company, of preparations for a large supply of colonists, and of the appointment of Lord Delaware (La Warr or De Le Warr) to the office of Governor General to the colony. A new patent had been granted by King James to the company, which now included many noblemen whose influence and wealth had enriched it to such an extent that the third supply sent to Virginia was undertaken on a large scale. Like all commercial bodies, the company was selfish. It lacked farsightedness, and looked only for immediate enrichment at the hands of an infant colony, caring little whether the colony succeeded in maintaining a foothold or not, if only the projectors might receive some commercial benefit from these men who were sent into the wilderness totally unqualified for the struggle of frontier life.

Hopes were still held out from time to time of the discovery of mines of precious metal or the attainment of sudden riches after the manner of the Spanish. To be sure gold had not been found lying in profusion on the very surface of the earth, and people now saw that it was unreasonable to expect that it should be. Still it was argued that gold certainly must be there. Everything was done in England to encourage the public faith in Virginia's resources. Among other things, [Richard] Hakluyt published a translation from the Portuguese, entitled, *Virginia Richly Valued by the Description of Florida*. In this book the Spaniard's testimony as to the existence of mines of gold and other metals in Florida was taken to prove that Virginia must also if contain precious metal. While the aim of the company at home was commercial wealth, Captain Smith's mind was set upon such commonplace objects as corn and deer suet for hungry mouths looking only to the firm planting of a new England in Virginia. Captain Smith's letter, plain spoken almost to rudeness, was not calculated to conciliate the London Company. He received letters by Captain Argall rebuking (criticism) him for his treatment of the savages, and it seemed to be the company's desire to take the government (colony) from his hands as quickly as possible.

Nine vessels were fitted out for a voyage to Virginia—the *Sea Adventure (Sea Venture)*, the *Diamond*, the *Falcon*, the *Blessing*, the *Unity*, the *Lion*, the *Swallow*, and two smaller boats. Five hundred colonists sailed in these vessels, some of whom were veteran soldiers, though many were dissolute gentlemen, "packed thither by their friends to escape ill destinies." Eight horses were also sent over in this fleet. Sir Thomas Gates was appointed Lieutenant General, Sir George Somers, Admiral of Virginia, and Captain [Christopher] Newport, Vice Admiral. Gates and Somers were to govern the colony in the place of Lord Delaware [Thomas West], and each of these three gentlemen was furnished with a commission to take the government out of Captain Smith's hands immediately on his arrival. But it chanced that they all sailed in the same vessel, the *Sea Adventure (Sea Venture)*. Among the captains of this fleet were the old colonist [John] Martin, and the evil spirits [John] Ratcliffe and [Gabriel] Archer. The ships sailed from Plymouth on the first day of June, 1609. They had a pleasant voyage until the twenty-third of July, when they were caught in a hurricane. The vessels were dispersed, and one of the smaller boats lost. In the early part of August the *Blessing* sailed up the James River. She was soon followed by the *Falcon*, the *Unity*, and the *Lion*.—Shortly after the *Diamond* appeared with her mainmast gone, followed in two or three days by the *Swallow*, in a similar state.—But no *Sea Adventure (Sea Venture)* appeared. No one had the authority to take the government out of Captain Smith's hands, and yet it was not likely that the new colonists, under a fresh charter, which did not look to the rights of the older settlers, and led by Ratcliffe, Martin, and Archer, who certainly had no more friendly feeling for Captain Smith than he had for them, would be likely to submit to his rule. All was confusion—the colony was divided into factions "today the old commission must rule, tomorrow the new, the next day neither." It is stated that Captain Smith would willingly have returned to England [if asked], but there seemed now no hope that the new rulers would arrive, and the colony was in a deplorable condition with no lawful rulers—the old commission withdrawn, none to take its place, and the majority of the colonists newly-arrived, headstrong (obstinate), ambitious, and entirely inexperienced, more determined upon finding gold than anything else. Captain Smith resumed the government. He planned a new settlement to be made under Mr. West at the falls in the James River, and another under Captain Martin at Nansemond. His year had about expired, however. He made Captain Martin president in his place—but this gentlemen knowing his own inefficiency—resigned within three hours in favor of Captain Smith, and proceeded to Nansemond. Here he had ill success, getting into a skirmish with the Indians, in which some of his men were killed and his provisions stolen. Mr. West's company was planted in an unhealthy and inconvenient spot. Captain Smith purchased from Powhatan the site of his hamlet of Powhatan for the use of Mr. West's company. These men, however, being mostly of the new supply, refused to occupy this new situation. The strong-willed Captain went up the river with five men and endeavored to force them to obey. They resisted, and Captain Smith was forced to protect himself by a retreat to his boat. He spent nine days attempting to bring the unruly company into submission and trying to disabuse them of their ideas of gold mines and a South Sea beyond the falls. He at last set sail for Jamestown. Immediately the Indians, who did not relish their proximity and the harsh treatment they had received at their hands, made an attack upon the settlement.

  Meantime Captain Smith's boat had run aground, and the settlers, frightened by the hostile Indians, came to him and gave in their submission. Captain Smith imprisoned some of the ringleaders of the mutiny, and settled the others at Powhatan, which was fortified in Indian manner with boughs of trees, possessed many dry cabins, was in a commanding situation, and surrounded by pleasant cornfields. The delighted colonists, considering it the pleasantest place in Virginia, gave this village the name of Nonesuch. But when West, who had been to Jamestown, returned he—"having bestowed cost to begin a town in another place, misliked it"—and the settlement was removed to its former situation. Returning down the river to Jamestown, an accident happened to Smith. While lying asleep in the boat his powder bag exploded and wounded him severely. The Captain instantly leapt into the water to quench the fire, and was only rescued with difficulty from drowning. It is stated in Smith's *History* that Captain Smith's return to England soon after was to obtain surgical aid, while Captain Ratcliffe wrote in a letter at the time that Smith was sent home to answer some misdemeanors. This may also have been the case, since the colony was involved in constant squabbles upon which it is impossible to pass judgment. Captains Ratcliffe and Archer were imprisoned by Smith for insubordination, their trial was about to take place at the time of Smith's accident, and they in their turn would probably send him to England if they could get the power.

However that may be, Captain Smith left Virginia in the fall of 1609, never to return. He had been in the colony a little over two years. At the time of his departure he says that there were about four hundred and ninety persons in the colony, the corn newly harvested, a good supply of arms, ammunition, and tools, with many domestic animals. Whatever were his faults he had saved the colony from the Indians and from starvation—and had carried it through some of its worst perils. More than any other man he [rightly] deserves the title of founder of Virginia.

Of all its evil accidents, the colony suffered none that so much threatened its existence as Smith's departure.

The admiral's ship was beaten upon by a fearful storm, which is most graphically described by William Strachey, who was on board the doomed vessel. The people began to "look one upon the other with troubled hearts and panting bosoms" but their cries were "drowned in the winds and the winds in thunder." Nothing was "heard that could give comfort, nothing seen that might encourage hope. Such was the tumult of the elements that the sea swelled above the clouds and gave battle unto heaven. It could not be said to rain, the waters like whole rivers did flood in the air," while "winds and seas were as mad as fury could make them." The ship "spewed out her oakum" and sprung leaks in almost every joint. This news, "imparting no less terror than danger ran through the whole ship with much fright and amazement." It was "as a wound given to men that were before dead." There was now a dire fight for life. Sailors and passengers stood up to their waists in water, bailing with buckets, kettles, anything. "The common sort stripped naked, as men in galleys, the easier both to hold out and to shrink from under the salt water which continually leapt in among them, kept their eyes waking, and their thoughts and hands working with tired bodies and wasted spirits, three days and four nights destitute of outward comfort, and desperate of any deliverance, testifying how mutually willing they were, yet by labor to keep each other from drowning, albeit each one drowned while he labored."

Hope was almost gone with the exhausted passengers. Some even drank a farewell to one another, until a speedy meeting in the other world. The aged admiral, Sir George Somers, sat upon the poop directing the vessel's course almost without food or sleep. On the last night of their dreary vigil, he called his men to see the electrical phenomenon known as St. Elmo's light, "an apparition of a little round light, like a faint star, trembling and streaming along with a sparkling blaze, half the height upon the mainmast, and shooting from shroud to shroud, tempting to settle as it were upon any of the four shrouds. Half the night it kept with us—but upon a sudden, towards the morning watch, they lost it, and knew not which way it made." Sir George Somers from his post called out that land was in sight. "This unlooked-for welcome news," says Smith's *History*, "as if it had been a voice from heaven, hurrieth all above hatches to look for that they durst scarce believe, so that improvidently forsaking their task (the bailing of water), which imported no less than their lives, they gave so dangerous advantage to their greedy enemy, the salt water which still entered at the large breaches of their poor wooden castle, as that in gaping after life they had well-nigh swallowed their death." It was not necessary now, however, to urge every man "to do his best." The coast before them was one usually avoided by sailors, but these storm-tossed adventurers spread all sail to reach it. The *Sea Adventure (Sea Venture)* struck first upon a rock, from which the surge of the sea cast her away again, and then upon another. The much-battered vessel at last found safe harbor wedged in an upright position between two rocks on the coast of the Bermuda Islands, as though in a dry dock at home. The adventures of this vessel probably suggested the subject of one of the greatest plays in the English language, the *Tempest* of Shakespeare. The one hundred and fifty colonists upon the *Sea Adventure (Sea Venture)* were thus safely landed upon the Bermudas. These islands had long had a reputation among sailors for being enchanted, a "den of furies and devils, the most dangerous, unfortunate and forlorn place in the world." The delighted adventurers, roaming over their island, found it to be "the richest, health-fullest, and pleasantest they ever saw."

All went busily to work, some taking what could be gotten from the wrecked vessel, some in search of food and water, and others building cabins of palmetto, while old Sir George did not search long before he found "such a fishing" that in the course of half an hour he caught enough fish with a hook and line to feed the whole company. The island was found to abound in wild hogs. In fact the colonists lived in such plenty and so easily upon the game and fruit of the island that many of them desired never to leave it. For about nine months the adventurers dwelt upon the Bermudas, which were then named the Somers Isles, in honor of the admiral, the name was afterwards corrupted to "Summer Islands." In spite of the plenteous fruitfulness of the land, this little colony was not without its jealousies and dissensions.

On the whole, however, the winter passed pleasantly in the occupation of building two pinnaces out of cedar and the remains of the old *Sea Adventure (Sea Venture)*. Two children were born upon the island. The boy was christened Bermudas [possibly Bermuda Eason, son of Edward Eason], and the girl, daughter to a Mr. John Rolfe, was named Bermuda [Bermuda Rolfe]. They had also "a merry English marriage." Sir George

Somers's cook wedded the maid of Mrs. Mary Horton, named Elizabeth Persons. A long boat was sent to Virginia in the spring, but never was heard of [again]. The adventurers were at last ready to embark for Jamestown. The two vessels, the *Deliverance* and the *Patience*, were furnished with what provisions had been saved from the wreck, and the colonists [finally] embarked in May, 1610, for Virginia. A forlorn welcome awaited them.

☐☐☐☐☐☐☐☐☐☐

The winter of 1609-1610 at Jamestown was known as "the starving time." George Percy, who was in poor health, had been elected president, but the unruly colonists had no leader, no indomitable will to force them to something like thrift and forethought. Pigs were eaten, the horses were devoured—not a chicken was left in the colony. Weapons and tools went for food. Trips into the Indian country in search of provision were managed poorly, and resulted disastrously. One supply party of thirty men was cut off by Powhatan, only one man escaped, and a boy named Henry Spelman was saved by the never failing kindness of Pocahontas. He lived for some years afterwards among the Potomac Indians. A company of men deserted in the colony's largest vessel, some of them became pirates, others returned to England with an exaggerated tale of horrors as an excuse for their own conduct. A miserable winter of hunger and crime was followed by a hopeless spring. Things became desperate.

In ten days more the last of the colonists would have been dead. But, says Smith's *History*, God "was not willing that this country should be unplanted." The hopeful little colony from the Summer Islands landed to find left but sixty wretched men out of the four hundred and ninety. Sir Thomas Gates entered the dilapidated and deserted church. The bell was solemnly rung, summoning the survivors. Service was held and a "zealous and sorrowful prayer" was made on the part of Chaplain [Richard] Buck, who had come with the Bermuda colonists. Mr. Percy then delivered up the colony's first patent, and the papers of the colony, and Sir Thomas Gates entered upon his new office. He looked about him. Jamestown was indeed in a ruined condition. The gates were off their hinges, many of the palisades were gone, and dead men's cottages had been torn down for firewood by weak and indolent survivors. Gates could see no hope for the colony which had been planted at so much expense of money and life. His stock of provisions would last but a few weeks, and the Indians were determined in their hostility. Powhatan was at last sure of being rid of his troublesome neighbors. His policy was to starve the English out at least until the taking of Jamestown should be an easy matter. There was but one thing to be done.

The provisions would barely last to get the colony to Newfoundland, where there were chances of meeting with English fishing vessels. Two weeks after the arrival of the Bermuda colonists, four pinnaces, the *Discovery* and the *Virginia*, the *Deliverance* and the *Patience*, lay in the James River ready to sail for Newfoundland. Each man was assigned to his vessel, and the colonists were leaving Jamestown. They hated the poor dismantled village which most of them had hallowed neither by bravery nor self-denial. Some of the more reckless were determined to set fire to the houses, and celebrate the occasion with a conflagration. To prevent this Sir Thomas Gates was the last one to leave Jamestown. As they sailed away, "none dropped a tear, for none had enjoyed one day of happiness." That day they dropped down the stream to Hog Island. As they neared the mouth of James River on the following morning, they met the long boat of Lord Delaware's approaching fleet, sent out to intercept them. Lord Delaware had started from London on the first of April with one hundred and fifty colonists, most of whom were working men. One of the vessels, the *Hercules*, they had lost sight of in a storm—the other two ships sighted the headlands of Chesapeake Bay on the fifth of June. They anchored for the night off Cape Henry, and the men went ashore to refresh themselves, fish, and set up a cross, that the *Hercules* might know of their arrival if she ever reached Chesapeake Bay. While they fished, some Indians came down to them, held intercourse on friendly terms, and were given a share of the fish by Lord Delaware. On returning to the ships, the navigators descried a sail. Lord Delaware gave chase to the strange vessel. To their great joy they found her to be the *Hercules*. The fleet anchored off Point Comfort, where the captain of the fort at this point, Colonel Davis, told them a tale, "mixed both with joy and sorrow"—joy because of the news that the passengers of the *Sea Adventure (Sea Venture)* had not been lost, as had long been believed, sorrow because of the misfortunes of the colony.—Learning that the pinnaces were even now in the river waiting the turn of the tide to sail for Newfoundland, while they had yet provision left Lord Delaware sent out his long boat to turn them back.—The colonists again landed at their deserted town, and on Sunday morning, the tenth of June, Lord Delaware disembarked.

A sermon was preached in the church by Mr. Buck, and Sir Thomas Dale delivered up his papers. Lord Delaware then rose and delivered a short speech, "laying some blames on them," as he afterwards said in a letter to England, "for many vanities and their idleness, earnestly wishing that I might no more find it so, lest I should be compelled to draw the sword of justice to cut off such delinquents, which I had much rather draw in their defense to protect from enemies," and concluding by "heartening them with the knowledge of what store of provisions I had brought for them." The settlement in Virginia had indeed come near to extinction. Had Lord Delaware been a day or two later, the colonists would have been gone past recall. On the other hand, had they delayed their return for a little longer, the Indians would have sacked and destroyed the fort of Jamestown, which was the only thing that could keep them in abeyance, and indeed the colonists had nearly destroyed this themselves. Lord Delaware set all things to work to retrieve the fortunes of England's little colony. He must soon have discovered the nature of the men that he had to govern, for he wrote back home that "an hundred or two of debauched (dissolute)" men "dropped forth year after year—ill-provided for before they came, and worse governed after they are here," men "whom no examples daily before their eyes, either of goodness or punishment, can deter from their habitual impieties or terrify from a shameful death," were not the men to be the "workers in this so glorious a building."

☐☐☐☐☐☐☐☐☐☐☐

Though Lord Delaware had a year's provisions, he did not let the colony depend on these. Captain Argall was sent to fish for cod and halibut, and in the month of August he dropped anchor in "a very great bay," which he called the Delaware. Sir George Somers was sent back to the Bermudas to secure some wild hogs with which to restock the colony. "The good old gentleman, out of his love and zeal," went "most cheerfully and resolutely." He encountered contrary winds, and was forced to the more northern coast of Virginia, but he persevered, and reached the Bermudas at last in safety. Here Sir George Somers labored hard to accomplish his purpose, but he was destined never to leave the islands which bear his name. Finding himself about to die, he exhorted his men to be constant to the Virginia Plantation.

Lacking the courage of their leader, his men, however, embalmed his body and set sail with it for England in their bark of thirty tons burden. Three of their number, [Christopher] Carter, [Edward] Waters, and [Edward] Chard, had volunteered to remain on the island, their comrades promising to return for them. Here they lived, lords of an island abounding in food. When the ship was fairly out of sight, they worked diligently, planting corn and seeds and building themselves a house. They thus lived happily together until good luck befell them. In searching in the crevices of the rocks one day they came upon a very large block of ambergris—a substance secreted in the intestines of whales, of bright gray color, and very valuable as a perfume. Having now become rich, these three men immediately became unhappy. They grew proud, ambitious, and contemptuous. Though, in the words of the old narrative, they were "but three forlorn men, more than three thousand miles from their own country, and but small hope ever to see it again," they now "fell out for superiority." They had words over the merest trifles, and they sometimes went from words to blows. One day, when they were fighting, the dog of one of the men bit his master in disgust, "as if," says the story, "the dumb beast would reprove them of their folly." Matters went from bad to worse, until Chard and Waters, the two prouder spirits of the three, resolved on a duel. Carter became frightened, he preferred even quarrelsome neighbors to solitude, so he hid the duelists weapons. For two long years these unhappy men lived on their island, until their clothes were almost entirely worn from their backs. All this time they kept up a triple war. At last, however ever, "they began to recover their wits." They "concluded a tripartite peace," and made up their minds to build a boat and "make a desperate attempt for Virginia." They had no sooner made this resolution than they descried a sail on the horizon. The vessel stood in for shore, and the three exiles were overjoyed, though "they neither knew what she was or what she would." They ran with "all possible speed" to meet her.

"According to their heart's desire, she proved an Englishman." Those who had returned with Sir George Somers's body attempted to awaken an interest in the Summer Islands, but their stories were considered "travelers's tales." It at last came into the mind of some of the Virginia Company that this might be a good land for a new plantation. A company was formed for the planting of the Bermudas, a patent was granted it, and this vessel which the three lonely men had descried was the first ship sent out to make a trial. The captain found that the three men had been industrious. There was an acre of corn ready to be harvested, with quantities of pumpkins and beans, and a plentiful store of salt pork and cured bacon. The three islanders never became rich from their block of ambergris. The governor of the new colony got an inkling of it. The result was that the colony was thrown almost into a civil war over this treasure.

The governor using it as a loadstone to draw fresh supplies to his colony sent back to the Company only a third at a time of the treasure. Many pieces of it were stolen, and the original finders got no benefit whatever, while it served to produce dissension both in the colony and in England. It often happens that riches prove only something to quarrel about.

Under Lord Delaware's governorship some progress was made in the colony. Hours for labor were from six to ten o'clock in the morning, and from two to four in the afternoon. Two forts were built, and named Henry and Charles for the king's sons. The church was rebuilt, twenty-four feet in breadth and sixty in length, with a chancel (space around altar) of cedar, cedar pews, a black walnut communion table, and handsome wide windows, with shutters to close them in bad weather. The church was kept trimmed with sweet wild flowers. Prayers were held here twice a day, two sermons were preached on Sunday and one on Monday. When Lord Delaware attended church on Sunday, he was accompanied by the officers of the church with high-sounding names, and followed by fifty attendants armed with halberds (weapon) and wearing his lordship's handsome scarlet livery.

In church Lord Delaware's seat was a chair covered with green velvet, and a red velvet kneeling cushion was before him. Such courtly pomp belonged to the age, but it was ridiculous enough in poor little Jamestown. During Lord Delaware's administration, Captain Argall was sent to the Potomac to get corn from the natives, and Captain Percy was dispatched against the Pashiphey Indians to punish them for some misdemeanors. The English very cruelly burnt their cabins, and slew some women and children. Sir Thomas Gates was sent back to England to procure a new supply for the colony. During Lord Delaware's stay in America he was attacked by four or five different diseases. At last to save his life he was obliged to return home. His return threw "a damp of coldness" in England upon the enterprise, so that the adventurers wished to withdraw their payments. Lord Delaware was much distressed by this result. He made a public explanation of the cause of his desertion of the colony, how he had been welcomed to Jamestown with ague, and how this was followed successively by dysentery, cramps, gout, and scurvy.

Such were the malarial influences with which the colonists had to contend. Fortunately, Sir Thomas Dale had already been dispatched with three vessels loaded with men and cattle. He arrived in Virginia in May, 1611, and took the government out of George Percy's hands. In August, Sir Thomas Gates also arrived in Virginia with a fleet of six vessels, three hundred men, a hundred cattle, two hundred hogs, and a good supply of provisions. He brought from England his wife and daughters, but Lady Gates died on the voyage. When Dale had arrived in the spring the colony had already relapsed into old habits. The colonists were found busily occupied playing bowls in the streets of Jamestown. A more permanent reform was begun under the successive administrations of Dale and Gates. During this summer the wisest measure yet tried was adopted—a measure so simple that it seems strange that it was so long missed. Every man was given a little tract of land from which to raise his own support, and the colonists were no longer dependent on a public store and no longer worked for the interests of others. The limits of the colony were fast extended. A new town was built above the falls in the James River, and named Henrico in honor of the heir-apparent to the throne of England, who was a great favorite. Here the Reverend Alexander Whitaker, "the apostle of Virginia," established himself, "bearing the name of God" to the natives. Morning and evening the colonists prayed, "Lord, bless England, our sweet native country." The colony was now governed with a terribly severe code of laws taken from the martial laws of the old countries. Everything was done according to rule. It seems incredible what trivial offenses were punished with death.

For the second time that a man committed the offense of profanity a bodkin (needle) was thrust through his tongue and for the third time the penalty was death. The first time a man stayed away from church he forfeited a week's allowance, the second time he was whipped, and the third offense was punished with death. Desertion of the colony, theft, willfully pulling up a flower, gathering of grapes, or plucking ears of corn belonging to others, the killing of domestic animals, were all punished with the same rigor. He who treated a minister with disrespect was publicly whipped three times and forced to ask forgiveness of the congregation three Sundays in succession. For one offense a man lost his ears and was branded on his hand, for another he was compelled to lay "head and heels together" all night.

If a man refused to give a clergyman a statement of his faith or declined to take his advice on religious matters, he was whipped daily until he repented. Jamestown must now have seen a strict and circumspect body of colonists within her streets. Grants of land were extended. After a time the London Council began giving individuals patents to large tracts. In time plantations came to be scattered along the shores of the James River and its tributaries. The increased use of tobacco made this plant a valuable article of export. The little colony was really beginning to reach forth into something like prosperity.

All this time Powhatan was hostile to the colonists. In one way and another he had possessed himself of many English arms, and had detained a number of Englishmen as prisoners. Pocahontas happened to be among the Potomacs on the river of that name. One account says that she had gone thither—feasting among her friends, but [Ralph] Hamor says that she had been sent to the Potomacs to trade with them. Perhaps also Powhatan distrusted her friendship for the whites. Whatever may have been the cause, Pocahontas was certainly making a stay on the Potomac River. Captain [Samuel] Argall had gone to trade with the Indians on the Potomac. Some friendly Indians informed him that Pocahontas was in the region. A plan for bringing Powhatan to terms immediately suggested itself to the unscrupulous captain. He sent for one of the Indian chiefs, and told him that if he did not give Pocahontas into his hands they would no longer be "brothers nor friends." The Potomac Indians were at first unwilling to do this, fearing that it might involve them in a war with Powhatan. Captain Argall assured them that he would take their part in such a war, and they consented to his plan.

The following story is told of the manner in which Pocahontas was betrayed. The Indian girl manifested no desire to go aboard Captain Argall's vessels, having many a time been on English vessels in her friendly intercourse with the whites. Captain Argall offered an old Indian named Japazaws their resistible bribe of a copper kettle if he would betray Pocahontas into his power. Japazaws undertook to do this with the assistance of his wife, whose "sex," remarks the old writer, "have ever been most powerful in beguiling enticements." The old woman became immediately possessed with an intense desire to visit the English ship, which she said had been there three or four times and she had never been aboard it. She begged her husband to allow her to go aboard, but Japazaws sternly refused, saying she could not go unless she had some woman to accompany her. He at last threatened to beat her for her persistence. The tender heart of Pocahontas was moved with pity, she offered to accompany the woman on board the English vessel.

Japazaws and his wife with the chief's daughter were taken on to the ship, where they were well-entertained and invited to supper. The old man and his wife were so well-pleased with the success of their stratagem that during the whole meal they kept treading on Captain Argall's toes. After supper the captain sent Pocahontas to the gun room while he pretended to have a private conversation with Japazaws. He presently recalled her, and told her that she must remain with him, and that she should not again see Powhatan until she had served to bring about a peace between her father and the English. Immediately Japazaws and his wife set up "a howl and cry," and Pocahontas began to be "exceeding pensive and discontented." The old people were rowed to shore, happy in the possession of their copper kettle and some trinkets. Captain Argall sent an Indian messenger to Powhatan, informing him that "his delight and darling, his daughter Pocahontas," was a prisoner, and informing him that "if he would send home the Englishmen whom he had detained in slavery, with such arms and tools as the Indians had gotten and stolen, and also a great quantity of corn, that then he should have his daughter restored (returned), otherwise not."

Powhatan was "very much grieved," having a strong affection both for his daughter and for the English weapons which he possessed. It was a hard alternative. He sent, however, a message desiring the English to use (treat) Pocahontas well, and promising to perform the conditions for her rescue.

☐☐☐☐☐☐☐☐☐☐

It was a long time before anything more was heard from Powhatan. After three months he sent to the governor by way of ransom seven Englishmen, overjoyed to be free from slavery and the constant fear of a cruel death, three muskets, a broadaxe, a whipsaw, and a canoe full of corn. These were accompanied with a message to the effect that he would further satisfy injuries give the English a large quantity of corn, and be forever their friend when his daughter was delivered up. The English received these things "in part payment," and returned such an answer as this to Powhatan, "Your daughter shall be well-used, but we cannot believe the rest of our arms are either lost or stolen from you, and therefore till you send them we will keep your daughter." The wily old chief was much-grieved at this message, and it was again a long time before anything was heard from him. At last Sir Thomas Dale, taking with him Pocahontas and a hundred and fifty men, embarked in the colony's vessels for a visit to Powhatan. The party sailed up the York River. Powhatan was not to be seen. The English told the Indians that they had come to deliver up the daughter of Powhatan and to receive the promised return of men and arms. These overtures were received with scornful threats and bravadoes, and open hostility. Skirmishing ensued, in which some of the Indian houses were burned and property spoiled. The Indians asked why this had been done.

The English answered by asking why they had shot at them. The Indians excused themselves, laying the blame on some straggling savages. They protested they intended no harm, but were the white man's friends. The English rejoined that they did not come to hurt them, but came as friends. A peace "was patched up" and messengers were sent to Powhatan. The Indians told the English that their imprisoned men "were run off" for fear the English would hang them, but that Powhatan's men "were run after to bring them back." They promised to return them with the stolen swords and muskets on the following day. The English perceived that this story was told only to gain time. Meantime two brothers of Pocahontas came aboard the ship to visit her. They had heard that she was not well, and were overjoyed to find her in good health and contented. While they were visiting with their sister, Mr. John Rolfe and Mr. Sparks were sent to negotiate with Powhatan. They were received kindly and hospitably entertained, but they were not admitted to the presence of the offended chief. His brother Opechancanough saw them and promised to do the best he could with Powhatan, saying that "all might be well." With such slight satisfaction the English were obliged to return to Jamestown, for it was now April and time to sow corn. Pocahontas had been about a year a prisoner at Jamestown. There can be no doubt that she was treated with the greatest friendliness by the colonists. Her feelings had always been warm for the white strangers. Now that she was an innocent and interesting young prisoner among them, what more natural than that she should be honored and petted? Pocahontas was now a woman, being about eighteen to nineteen years of age.

To judge from her portrait she could not have possessed the beauty with which tradition has invested her, but she had at least a pleasant and interesting face, and there must have been some charm in her large black eyes and straight black hair. There was one colonist at least who took a great interest in the young prisoner. Mr. John Rolfe is styled in the different records "an honest gentleman of good behavior," "an honest and discreet English gentleman," "a gentleman of approved behavior and honest carriage." His wife, whose little daughter was born at the Summer Islands and christened Bermuda, must have fallen victim to the malarial influences which did such deadly work among newly-arrived colonists in Jamestown. The subject of the conversion of Pocahontas had weighed heavily upon the mind of Mr. Rolfe. He accordingly attempted to convert her to

Christianity, and in doing so fell in love with her. Pocahontas became a Christian, and what more natural than that the constant friend of the white men should love an Englishman? Long before the trip up the York River Mr. Rolfe had loved the Indian maiden. He wrote a long letter to Sir Thomas Dale asking his advice. Sir Thomas readily consented to the marriage.

Pocahontas, on her part, told her brother of her attachment to Mr. Rolfe. He informed Powhatan, who seems to have been well-pleased with the proposition, for within ten days an old uncle of Pocahontas and two of her brothers arrived at Jamestown. Powhatan had sent them as deputies to witness the marriage of his daughter, and to do his part toward the confirmation of it. Pocahontas was first baptized. It was deemed necessary to give her a Christian name at her baptism.

She was christened Rebecca, and as a king's daughter she was known after this as the Lady Rebecca, and sometimes as the Lady Pocahontas. In April, 1614, the odd bridal procession moved up the little church with its wide-open windows and its cedar pews. The bridegroom was a young Englishman, the bride an Indian chief's daughter, accompanied by two red-skinned warriors, her brothers, and given away by an old uncle.

Perhaps more than one of the colony's ministers officiated. Before the altar with its canoe-like font Pocahontas repeated in imperfect English her marriage vows, and donned her wedding wing. The wedding is briefly mentioned by the old recorders only as something bearing upon the welfare of the colony. It was the first union between the people who were to possess the land and the natives. The colonists doubtless regarded it as a most auspicious event, binding as it did the most powerful chief in Virginia to their interests. Pocahontas's wedding day must have been a festive day in this balmiest of the months of the Virginia climate. From this day friendly intercourse and trade were again established with Powhatan and his people. To the day of his death the old chief never violated the peace which was thus brought about. In still another way the marriage of Pocahontas benefited the colony. The nearest neighbors of the

English were the Chickahominys, a powerful tribe of Indians who were just now free from the yoke of Powhatan, whom they regarded as a tyrant. They had taken advantage of the recent differences between this chief and the colonists to hold themselves exceedingly independent of both. But now that Powhatan and the English were united, the Chickahominys began to fear for their own liberty. They sent a deputation to Sir Thomas Dale desiring peace. Dale visited them, entered their council, and concluded a treaty stipulating that the Chickahominy Indians should call themselves Tassantessus, or Englishmen, as a sign of friendship, furnish three hundred men in case of a Spanish attack on the colony, bring a tribute of corn at harvest time, for which they should receive payment in hatchets, and, lastly, that each of the eight of their chief men who were to see to the performance of this treaty should have a red coat and a copper chain with the picture of King James hung upon it, and "be accounted his noble men." The treaty was confirmed with a great shout, followed by an Indian oration—directed first at the old men, then at the young, and lastly at the women and children.

□□□□□□□□□□□

Early in 1614 Sir Thomas Gates had returned to England and left the government of the colony to Sir Thomas Dale. An old soldier of the Netherlands, Dale was harsh in the enforcement of law, but his strict rule, tempered by a hard-earned wisdom on the part of the Virginia Company, was beneficial, and under his government the little commonwealth gained a sure foothold in America. Commercial jealousy was bitter and relentless in those days. A little French colony of Jesuit missionaries had been planted on the coast of Maine, within the limits of the charter granted by King James. The English now made frequent fishing voyages far north along the coast. Captain [Samuel] Argall set out on a voyage, however, according to one authority, for the express purpose of destroying the Jesuit colony. The Indians at Pemaquid, supposing the captain would be pleased to meet brother white men, informed him that there was a settlement of

Frenchmen at Mount Desert. The faces of Argall and his men instantly depicted an excitement which the Indians took for delight, and they offered a pilot to the harbor of the little colony. The French were scattered about in the woods when they saw an English vessel decked with red, and with the sound of trumpet and drums, bearing down upon their own ship securely anchored in harbor, her sails converted into awnings, and but ten men aboard her. Without a preliminary word Argall opened fire.

[Gilbert] Du Thet on board the French vessel made one wild shot from the ship's guns, but was mortally wounded with a musket ball. The helpless vessel surrendered. Landing and searching the colony's tents, Argall discovered the desk of the commander, [Rene Le Coq de] La Saussaye, opened it, pocketed his royal commission and relocked the desk. Captain Argall demanded his papers when La Saussaye returned from the woods, and when they were found missing, declared that he had neither title nor right to the land on which he was settled.

Argall permitted his men to plunder the colony. The Jesuits remonstrated with him. "Well, it is a pity you have lost your papers," remarked Argall. La Saussaye and a dozen men returned to France in a fishing vessel. The others were carried to the Chesapeake, where Argall represented that they had been without a commission. Dale imprisoned them, and they were threatened with hanging. The unscrupulous Argall became frightened at the result of his deception and confessed the truth, whereupon the prisoners were released. Mr. Ralph Hamor, who had been in Virginia for several years, was upon the eve of returning home, and wished to see Powhatan. He was sent with an interpreter on a commission by Sir Thomas Dale. Powhatan sent the governor word by Hamor that he need have no more fears in regard to his intention. He said, "There hath been enough of blood and war. Too many have been slain already on both sides, and, by me, occasion there shall never be more. I, who have power to perform it, have said it. I am now grown old and would gladly end my days in peace and quietness, and although I should have just cause of resentment, yet my country is large enough and I can go from you. And this answer I hope will satisfy my brother." While Hamor was among the Indians he found an Englishman who had been made a prisoner some three years before. He looked so like an Indian both in complexion and dress that he was recognized only by his speech. He begged Hamor to procure his release. When Hamor made this request Powhatan showed much discontent. "You have one of my daughters," said the chief, "and I am content, but you cannot see one of your men with me but you must have him away or break friendship. If you must need, have him, you shall go home without guides, and if any evil befall you, thank yourselves." "I will," said Hamor, "but if I return not well, you may expect a revenge, and your brother Dale might have just cause to suspect you." Powhatan left his guest in a passion. He entertained him, however, at supper with a "cheerful countenance." About midnight he awoke Hamor and said he would send him and the other man home on the morrow. Powhatan, like all Indians, was a consummate beggar. He always had a list of presents which he desired at the hands of the English. He now told Hamor to remind "his brother Dale" to send him ten great pieces of copper, a razor, a froe for riving shingles, a grindstone, and some fishhooks and nets. Lest Hamor should forget any of these things he made him write them down in a memorandum book which the old chief had got into his possession. He probably had seen Englishmen do this when they wished to remember anything. Hamor wrote the list of things, and the old chief took back the book. Hamor asked him for the book, but Powhatan would not give it up, saying that "it did him much good to show it to strangers." Sir Thomas Dale did not live at Jamestown, but at a more recent plantation on the James River called Bermuda Hundred. Mr. Whitaker was the minister at this place, and here lived Rolfe and his wife. Dale, Whitaker, and Rolfe devoted themselves assiduously to the task of instructing Pocahontas. She was taught the English language and especially educated in the Christian religion. Pocahontas, on her part, was eager to learn. Her husband and Sir Thomas Dale were probably planning to take her to England. One can imagine the training that this Indian woman went through to learn the formalities and refinements of civilized life. But Pocahontas's inclination had always been towards the English. She became so well-educated that she had no desire to return to her father, "nor could well endure the society of her own nation." It is said that "the true affection she constantly bare her husband was much," and if we may believe the quaint words of the old history "he, on the other hand, underwent great torment and pain out of his violent passion and tender solicitude for her." In 1615 a great lottery was drawn in England for the benefit of Virginia. This pernicious resource for money was soon after put a stop to. In this same year a Spanish vessel, the constant dread of the colony, "was seen to beat to and fro off Point Comfort." A boat was at last sent ashore for a pilot. The pilot went out to them and the vessel sailed away with him. Arrived at Spain they endeavored to persuade him to betray the company. He refused, and was imprisoned for four years, at the end of which time he was returned to England.

□□□□□□□□□□

    Sir Thomas Dale had been five years in Virginia when in 1616 he settled the affairs of the colony, left [George] Yeardley as deputy governor, and embarked for England. He took with him Mr. [John] Rolfe, Pocahontas, Tomocomo, or Uttamatomakkin, one of Powhatan's chief men, married to his daughter Matachanna, and other Indians of both sexes. Tomocomo, who was considered among the Indians "an understanding fellow," had been charged by Powhatan to count the people in England and give him an exact idea of their strength. It is said that Opechancanough, who was rising into power among the Indians, also charged Tomocomo to observe whether the English had any trees or grain in their country. The Indian boy Namontack, whom Captain [Christopher] Newport had taken over, had seen hardly anything except London, and had reported great numbers of men and houses, but he made no mention of trees or cornfields. Opechancanough had a strong suspicion, from the colonists's constant desire for corn and the shiploads of lumber which left the James River [often], that England was destitute of these commodities. The vessel reached Plymouth on the 12th of June, 1616. On leaving the vessel Tomocomo was prepared with a long stick and a knife ready to make a notch for every man he saw. He kept this up till "his arithmetic failed him." In traveling by coach from Plymouth up to London, Tomocomo discovered that England did not lack in trees and grain fields. We can imagine the excitement that followed these travelers everywhere. They were all wonders, but especially was the "Princess" Pocahontas. The popular interest in her must have exceeded the usual desire to catch a sight of the King of England and his family. It was even debated, doubtless at the suggestion of the ever-jealous royal dunce, King James, whether Rolfe had not committed high treason in marrying the daughter of a foreign prince without permission of his sovereign. Pocahontas was now mother to a little son, Thomas Rolfe, whom she "loved most dearly."

Immediately on her arrival the Virginia Company took measures for the maintenance of her and her child. Persons of "great rank and quality" took much notice of Pocahontas. She did not like the smoke of London, and was removed to Brentford.

In this year Sir Walter Raleigh had been liberated after thirteen years imprisonment, and went around London renewing acquaintance with familiar objects and noting the changes that had been made. It is very probable that Sir Walter [Raleigh], "the father of Virginia," took pains to see Pocahontas. Captain Smith was at this time between two voyages and his stay in London was limited. He met Tomocomo, and they renewed old acquaintance. "Captain Smith," said the Indian, "Powhatan did bid me find you out, to show me your God—and the king and queen and prince you so much had told us of." "Concerning God," says Smith, "I told him the best I could, the king I heard he had seen, and the rest he should see when he would." Tomocomo, however, denied having seen King James [in person] till Smith satisfied him that he had by the circumstances. Tomocomo immediately looked very melancholy and said, "You gave Powhatan a white dog, which Powhatan fed as himself, but your king gave me nothing, and I am better than your white dog." There was much curiosity "to hear and see the behavior" of Tomocomo, he being a real savage and untutored Indian. [Samuel] Purchas says of him, "With this savage I have often conversed at my good friend, Master Doctor Gulstone [Theodore Goulston], where he was a frequent guest, and where I have seen him sing and dance his diabolical measures." Captain Smith, as he says, desiring to return the courtesy of Pocahontas, had written the following letter to the queen immediately upon hearing of the arrival of Pocahontas.

To the most high and virtuous Princess, Queen Anne of Great Britain. MOST ADMIRED QUEEN—*The love I bear my God, my king, and country hath so oft emboldened me in the worst of extreme dangers, that now honesty doth constrain me to presume thus far beyond myself to present your majesty this short discourse. If ingratitude be a deadly poison to all honest virtues, I must be guilty of that crime if I should omit any means to be thankful. So it is that some ten years ago, being in Virginia, and taken prisoner by the power of Powhatan, their chief king, I received from this great savage exceeding great courtesy, especially from his son Nantequas, the most manliest, comeliest, boldest spirit I ever saw in a savage, and his sister Pocahontas, the king's (Powhatan) most dear and well-beloved daughter, being but a child of twelve or thirteen years of age, whose compassionate, pitiful heart, of desperate estate, gave me much cause to respect her. I being the first Christian this proud king and his grim attendants ever saw, and thus enthralled in their barbarous power, I cannot say that I felt the least occasion of want that was in the power of those mortal foes to prevent, notwithstanding all their threats. After some six weeks fatting among these savage courtiers, at the minute of my execution she hazarded the beating out of her own brains to save mine, and not only that, but so prevailed with her father that I was safely conducted to Jamestown, where I found about eight and thirty miserable, poor, and sick creatures to keep possession of all those large territories of Virginia. Such was the weakness of this poor commonwealth as, had the savages not fed us, we directly had starved. And this relief, most gracious queen, was commonly* brought us by this lady, Pocahontas. Notwithstanding all these passages when inconstant fortune turned our peace to war, this tender virgin would still not spare to dare to visit us, and by her our jars have oft been appeased and our wants still supplied. Were it the policy of her father thus to employ her, or the ordinance of God thus to make her his instrument, or her extraordinary affection to our nation, I know not. But of this I am sure, when her father, with the utmost of his policy and power sought to surprise me, the dark night could not affright her from coming through the irksome woods, and with watered eyes gave me intelligence, with her best advice to escape his fury, which had he known he had surely slain her. Jamestown, with her wild train, she as freely frequented as her father's habitation, and, during the time of two or three years, she, next under God, was still the instrument to preserve this colony from death, famine, and utter confusion, which if in those times had once been dissolved, Virginia might have lain as it was at our first arrival to this day. Since then this business having been turned and varied by many accidents from that I left it at. It is most certain after a long and troublesome war after my departure betwixt her father and our colony, all which time she was not heard of, about two years after she herself was taken prisoner. Being so detained near two years longer, the colony by that means was relieved, peace concluded, and at last, rejecting her barbarous condition, she was married to an English gentleman, with whom at present she is in England, the first Christian ever of that nation, the first Virginian ever spoke English, or had a child in marriage by an Englishman, a matter surely, if my meaning be truly considered and well understood, worthy a prince's understanding. Thus, most gracious lady, I have related to your majesty what at your best leisure our approved histories will account you at large, and done in the time of your majesty's life. And, however, this might be presented to you from a more worthy pen, it cannot come from a more honest heart, as yet I never begged anything of the State or any, and it is my want of ability and her exceeding desert, your birth, means, and authority, her birth, virtue, want, and simplicity, doth make me thus bold humbly to beseech your majesty to take this knowledge of her though it be from one so unworthy to be the reporter as myself, her husband's estate not being able to make her fit to attend your majesty. The most and least I can do is to tell you this, because none hath so oft tried it as myself, and the rather being of so great a spirit, however her stature. If she should not be well-received, seeing this kingdom may rightly have a kingdom by her means, her present love to us and Christianity might turn to such scorn and fury as to divert all this good to the worst of evil, where, finding so great a queen should do her some honor more than she can imagine, for being so kind to your servants and subjects, would so ravish her with content, as endear her dearest blood to effect that your majesty and all the king's honest subjects most earnestly desire.

And so I humbly kiss your gracious hands.

❑❑❑❑❑❑❑❑❑❑❑

Captain Smith went to Brentford with several others to see Pocahontas. She saluted (acknowledged) him modestly, and without a word turned around and "obscured her face as not seeming well-contented." Smith, with her husband [John Rolfe] and the other gentlemen, left her "in that humor" for several hours. The captain was disappointed, and repented having written the queen that she could speak English. But when the gentlemen returned Pocahontas began to talk, and said that she remembered Captain Smith well, "and the courtesies she had done." "You did promise Powhatan," said Pocahontas, "what was yours should be his, and he the like to you. You called him father, being in his land a stranger and by the same reason so must I do to you." Captain Smith tried to excuse himself from this honor.

Knowing the jealousy of the court—he, "durst not allow that title because she was a king's daughter." "Were you not afraid," said Pocahontas, with a look of determination, "were you not afraid to come into my father's country, and caused fear in him and all his people but me, and fear you here I should call you father? I tell you then I will and you shall call me child, and so I will be forever and ever your countryman. They did tell us always you were dead, and I knew no other till I came to Plymouth, yet

Powhatan did command Uttamatomakkin to seek you and know the truth, because your countrymen will lie much." This deception played, it seems, upon the Indians, and to which Rolfe must have been a party, is very strange. It has been conjectured by romancers (historians) that Pocahontas had really loved Smith, but there seems to be no reason to think anything more than that she felt a warm affection for him as a friend of her childhood. Pocahontas, it is said, had been so well-instructed that she "was become very formal and civil after our English manner." During his brief stay in London Captain Smith made frequent visits to Pocahontas, accompanied by courtiers and other friends who wished to see the Indian lady. The gentlemen, said Smith, "generally concluded they did think God had a great hand in her conversion," and said that they had "seen many English ladies worse favored, proportioned, and behaviored." Pocahontas was presented at court, accompanied by Lady Delaware, both to the king [King James] and queen [Queen Anne]. Ben Jonson's *Christmas Masque* was played at court on the 6th of January, 1617. Pocahontas and Tomocomo were present. The following notice of it is found in a letter of the day, "On twelfth night there was a mask, when the new-made Earl (Buckingham) and the Earl of Montgomery danced with the queen. The Virginian woman, Pocahontas, and her father's counselor have been with the king and graciously used, and both she and her assistant were pleased at the mask. She is upon her return, though sore against her will, if the wind would about to send her away." Captain Samuel Argall was about to sail for Virginia as governor of the colony, Rolfe and his wife must return to their home, Tomocomo must go back to tell Powhatan of his observations, but the other Indians were left in England to be educated. While Pocahontas was in England her portrait was drawn and engraved. She is represented in the fashionable costume of the day. Beneath the picture were these words, "Matoaks als Rebecka, daughter to the mighty Prince Powhatan, Emperor of Attanough-Kornouck als Virginia, converted and baptized in the Christian faith, and wife to the worshipful Mr. John Rolfe.—Aged 21.—Anno Domini 1616."

Pocahontas, it is said, was unwilling to leave England. She was destined never to return to Virginia. She died at Gravesend on the eve of her departure for America, being about twenty-two years of age. The few words devoted in Smith's *History* to her death are quite characteristic of the times, "It pleased God at Gravesend to take this young lady to His mercy, where she made not more sorrow for her unexpected death than joy to the beholders to hear and see her make so religious and godly an end." In the parish register at Gravesend is the following blundering entry, which could hardly have referred to any other than Pocahontas, "1616 (old calendar), May 21, Rebecca Wrothe wyff of Thomas Wroth gentleman a Virginia lady borne, here was buried in ye channcell." (Original spelling left intact.) The child of Pocahontas was left in England in the care of Sir Lewis Stukley, and afterwards transferred to the care of his uncle, Mr. Henry Rolfe, a London merchant. He was educated in England and afterwards returned to America. From him descended some of the most respectable families in Virginia. (See page 257 for more info on descendants of Pocahontas through her son, Thomas Rolfe.) There is on record a petition signed by Pocahontas's son, Thomas Rolfe, and addressed to the authorities of the colony in 1641, praying to be allowed to go to the Indian country to visit his mother's sister, known among the white people as Cleopatra.

☐☐☐☐☐☐☐☐☐☐

In spite of all his troubles at Jamestown, Smith, as he says, "liked Virginia well." The remainder of his life was devoted to the furtherance of colonization in the New World. No jealousy kept him from an enthusiastic interest in the welfare of the Virginia colony. He was quick to rejoice over its growing prosperity. Henceforth we see him in the meetings of the Virginia Company, exciting merchants through a desire for gain to adventure voyages, exploring the coast of North Virginia, writing books and pamphlets to draw attention to the American colonies, and traveling over England selling these works. After the failure of the colony of the Plymouth Company in Maine, and the dreary picture of the New England coast given by the colonists, Captain Smith was the first to again attract attention to this part of the New World. He set sail in March, 1614, with two vessels fitted out at the expense of some London merchants, for the purpose of catching whales, or discovering gold mines, and if these failed, of returning with a cargo of fish and furs. Precious metal was not to be found, and whale fishing was pronounced (stated) a "costly conclusion," for they "saw many and spent much time in chasing them, but could not kill any." The best part of the fishing season was now gone, but the sailors spent the remainder of the summer catching and curing codfish. Meantime Captain Smith in a small boat with eight men explored the coast from Penobscot to Cape Cod. He bought large quantities of furs from the Indians along the coast, paying them in trifles. From his observations Smith made a map. He returned to England with a cargo, of furs, leaving Captain Thomas Hunt in command of the second vessel to return by way of Spain, where he was to dispose of the fish. This man, after the departure of Captain Smith, decoyed twenty-four savages (of which one of them was Squanto) on board his vessel and sailed to Spain with them, selling them for slaves in the port of Malaga. This infamous deed, avers (alleges) Captain Smith, was perpetrated for the purpose of making the Indians so hostile as to prevent the establishment of a colony, and thus leave the profitable trade to such adventurers as himself. Smith reached England after having been gone some six months. (See page 257 for more on this story involving the capture of Squanto.)

    He presented his map to Prince Charles, afterwards Charles II, and requested him to change the barbarous names by which its different capes, bays, and rivers were known. The young prince named Cape Ann, which Smith had called Cape Tragabigzanda, after the Turkish lady who had loved him, changed Gosnold's name of Cape Cod to Cape James, changed Massachusetts River to Charles River, and made various other alterations, some of which remain to this day while others are forgotten. Smith gave a lively description of the country. The Plymouth Company, as owners of "the dead patent to this unregarded country," engaged Captain Smith to undertake a voyage in their service.—Soon after the old Virginia Company made him an offer to take the command of a fleet of four vessels.—He was, however, bound in honor to the Plymouth Company and refused. Meantime a vessel which had sailed to the coast of New England in search of gold returned to report an entire failure, and the Plymouth Company's ardor was dampened. Smith had promised to return to Plymouth about Christmas. When he reached this place in the early part of January, 1615, with two hundred pounds in his pocket, ready and eager to again set sail, his hopes were disappointed, and it was too late for him to accept the offer of the other colony. Captain Smith was destined never again to set foot in the New World, though he lived many years after this. But he was always at work for the furtherance of his project. To him New England owes its name. He says that this part of America was formerly known as Norumbega, Virginia, Nuskoncus, and Pemaquida. He expresses particular contempt for the name "Canada" in his orthography, as applied to New England. In his writings Smith dilates upon the fine fishing along the coast of this country. He says that fish are "to be had in abundance, observing but their seasons, but if a man will go at Christmas to gather cherries in Kent, though there be plenty in summer he may be deceived, so have these plenty here each their season." After his experience Smith thought he could plant a colony of three hundred men on this coast, and supply them provisions by trade with the savages. "If they should be untowards, as it is most certain they will," says Smith, "thirty or forty good men will be sufficient to bring them all in subjection." With a sturdy pen Smith presented the advantages of colonization to the men of his day. He despises a tame staying at home, and characterizes the manner of living of many men of his day in descriptions which would not be inapplicable today.

"Then who would live at home idly," exclaims Smith, "or think in himself any worth to live, only to eat, drink, and sleep, and so die, or by consuming that carelessly his friends got worthily, or by using that miserably that maintained virtue honestly, or for being descended nobly and pine with the vain vaunt of great kindred in penury, or to maintain a silly show of bravery, toil out thy heart, soul, and time basely, by shifts, tricks, cards, and dice, or by relating news of other men's actions, shark here and there for a dinner or supper, deceive thy friends by fair promises, and dissimulation in borrowing where thou never meanest (meant) to pay, offend the laws, surfeit with excess, burthen thy country, abuse thyself, despair in want and then cozen thy kindred, yeah, even thy own brother, and wish thy parents death (I will not say damnation) to have their estates."

Opposed to this Smith gives a picture of the delights of a life in the New World. "What pleasure can be more," he says, "than being tired with any occasion ashore in planting vines, fruits, or herbs, in contriving their own grounds to the pleasure of their own minds, their field, orchards, buildings, ships, and other works, to recreate themselves before their own doors in their own boats upon the sea." He describes the pleasures of fishing in a passage which has a flavor like that of Isaac Walton.

"What sport," says Smith, "doth yield a more pleasing content and less hurt and charge than angling with a hook and crossing the sweet air from isle to isle, over the silent streams of a calm sea, wherein the most curious may find profit, pleasure, and content?" Looking at another side of fishing he says, "Is it not pretty sport to pull up twopence, sixpence, and twelvepence as fast as you can haul and veer a line?" Smith says that though a man may work thus only part of his time he will make more than he can spend, "unless he be exceedingly excessive." "And lest any should think the toil might be insupportable," says the persuasive captain, "though these things may be had by labor and diligence, I assure myself there are who delight extremely in vain pleasure that take much more pains in England to enjoy it than I should do here to gain wealth sufficient. And yet I think they should not have half such sweet content, for our pleasure here is still gains, in England charges and loss, here nature and liberty affords us that freely which in England we want or it costeth us dearly." Captain Smith said that he had not been "so ill-bred" as not to have "tasted of plenty and pleasure as well as want and misery" that neither necessity nor discontent (dissatisfaction) forced him to "these endeavors, nor am I ignorant," said he, "what small thanks I shall have for my pains—yet I hope my reasons with my deeds will so prevail with some that I shall not want employment in these affairs (situations), to make the most blind see his own senselessness and incredulity, hoping that gain will make them effect that which religion, charity, and the common good cannot." He wanted to make a colony "of all sorts of worthy, honest, industrious (diligent) spirits—not to persuade them to go only," said he, "but go with them, not leave them there, but live with them there. I will not say but by ill providing and undue managing such courses may be taken as may make us miserable enough, but if I may have the execution of what I have projected, if they want to eat let them eat or never digest me—and if I abuse you with my tongue, take my head for satisfaction."

But anxious as Smith was to colonize New England he was not destined to be father to that as well as to Virginia.

☐☐☐☐☐☐☐☐☐☐☐

Notwithstanding the failure of the Plymouth Company to fulfill their engagement with Captain Smith, he still labored hard to accomplish his object. After "a labyrinth of trouble" Smith was furnished with two vessels by some friends, assisted by Sir Ferdinando Gorges. Smith had planned to plant a colony with but sixteen men. He had indeed wished for a much larger number with which to begin his settlement, "but," says Smith, "rich men for the most part are grown to that dotage through their pride in their wealth, as though there were no accident could end it or their lives." He must therefore content himself with a colony of sixteen, and he believed that, through his friendship with some of the Indians of the New England coast and his experience at Jamestown, he might still succeed. He set sail in March, 1615.

He had gone but a hundred and twenty leagues when he was separated from his other vessel, and lost his masts in a storm. Smith was forced to return under a jury mast to Plymouth, while the other vessel continued her course and returned in August with a profitable cargo. Captain Smith was not, however, to be deterred by accidents. He immediately set sail again in a bark of sixty tons burden, accompanied by his sixteen colonists. This time they were chased by pirates. Their pursuers had thirty-six guns and Captain Smith's vessel but four. His crew begged him to surrender, but this he refused to do until he could do so on fair conditions. He vowed that he would sink rather than be ill-used by the pirates. The pirate's men were astonished that a bark of sixty tons with but four guns should higgle about the terms of surrender. When it became known that Smith was the captain of the vessel it was found that many of the pirates had been soldiers under him, probably in the Turkish wars. They had run away from Tunis with this vessel. They were now destitute of provision and "in combustion amongst themselves." They offered their command to Captain Smith, but he declined the leadership of these mutinous adventurers. His unfortunate bark having escaped this danger again fell in with pirates. This time the enemy consisted of two French vessels. Captain Smith had much ado to force his men to fight. He at last told them that he would blow up his ship rather than yield while he had powder left. So, to use his own expression, the ships "went together by the ears," and the bark at last escaped her pursuers in spite of their shot.

Near Flores (Portugal) Captain Smith's vessel was met by four French privateers, who said they had a commission from their king to take Portuguese, Spaniards, and pirates. They called upon Captain Smith to come aboard them and show his papers. This he did after many fair promises on their part. He was no sooner aboard the French vessel, however, than he was detained, his own ship rifled, manned with French sailors, and his men divided among the different vessels in the fleet. Within five or six days other ships joined them, and the fleet numbered eight or nine sail. They at last surrendered the English vessel to her sailors and returned much of her provision. The crew desired to return immediately to England, but Captain Smith resolved to keep on for his destination. Before he parted with the French fleet the admiral again sent for Smith. While he was on board the admiral's ship a sail was spied and she went in chase. Meantime the mutinous part of Smith's crew set sail for England in the night, leaving him on the French vessel in his "cap, bretches, and waistcoat," as the narrative says, his arms having been left aboard his own vessel, where the sailors divided them among themselves. Captain Smith led a life of excitement aboard the French ship. The admiral's vessel was separated from the others of the fleet in a storm. While she lay off the Azores watching for prizes, Smith occupied himself in writing a narrative of his last voyages. They were soon afterward chased by an English pirate with twelve guns and thirty men, nearly starved. During this fight Captain Smith was imprisoned in the gun room. When the two vessels came to a parley the English endeavored to procure relief from the French, who as usual made fair promises in order to get them in their power. When they found the English pirates were ready to defend themselves to the last, they resolved to barter provision with them. While they were thus occupied they received some shot from a small vessel. The next fight was with a small English fishing smack. During this engagement Captain Smith was confined in the cabin. From this station he could see the captain robbed of all his valuables and half his cargo of fish. His poor clothes were auctioned at the mainmast, and the proceeds did not amount to sevenpence apiece to the pillagers. The next capture was a Scotch ship. Fortunately for her she was not yet loaded, and the French did not get much from her.

They next descried four vessels and "stood after" them. These vessels furled their sails and awaited the approach of the French vessel, "but" say Captain Smith with evident exultation, "our French spirits were content only to perceive they were English red crosses." A short time after this the French ship chased four Spanish vessels coming from the West Indies.

When Spaniards were to be fought Captain Smith was released and ordered to assist, and with an Englishman's hatred of Spain he no doubt fought the Spaniards with some relish. For four or five hours the English fought the Spanish ships, "tearing their sides," says Smith, "with many a shot betwixt wind and weather, yet not daring to board them, we lost them, for which all the sailors ever after hated the captain as a professed coward." A poor little Brazilian vessel was next chased. She was captured after a short fight, with fourteen or fifteen, "the better half," of her crew wounded. She was plundered of seventy chests of sugar, a hundred hides, and seventy thousand silver coins. The plunderers soon after met a Dutch ship. They entrapped the captain aboard under the pretence of showing his commission and then captured his vessel. She was manned with French sailors, who took occasion in the night to run off with the vessel. In a day or two more they met a West Indian man-of-war. For one whole forenoon they fought her. They captured her, and she proved the richest prize of all. From her they took a large quantity of hides, cochineal, coffers of silver, money and coffers containing the King of Spain's treasure, with pillage from many rich passengers. The pirates seemed now content. They had often promised to set Captain Smith ashore on some island or send him home in the next ship they met. They had also promised him a large share in their plunder. On their return voyage for France, Smith was put into the little vessel loaded with sugar. This was separated from the admiral in a storm. She was once hailed by two West India men. When they were answered with the sign of France the vessels went on their way with a parting broadside. Arrived at France, Smith was detained a prisoner in the harbor of Rochelle. He was now accused of being the English captain who had destroyed the French colony at Mount Desert, and was threatened with imprisonment or "a worse mischief." He therefore took the first occasion to escape. A severe storm came on which drove all on board under hatches. The night was very dark—Smith watched for his opportunity and left the vessel in a little boat. He had but a "half pike" for a paddle, the wind was strong, the waves high, and Captain Smith drifted out to sea. For twelve hours he worked away in his little boat, baling out water on a night when the coast was strewn with wrecks. He at last reached a marshy island, nearly drowned and suffering from cold and hunger. He was found here by some hunters. The admiral's ship, meantime, had been wrecked the captain and half his company with much of the plunder lost. Smith pawned the little boat for means to reach Rochelle. Here he lodged a complaint with the judge of the Admiralty, supported by some of the sailors as witnesses. We do not learn that he got anything more than "good words and fair promises," with some paper certifying to the truth of his story, which he presented to the British ambassador at Bordeaux. He received great kindness on all hands, and especially from "the good Lady Chanoyes," who "bountifully assisted" him. Captain Smith returned to England to find that he had been "buried" (slandered) by his mutinous sailors. He took measures to punish the ringleaders.

□□□□□□□□□□□

John Rolfe, who was fond of novel experiments in agriculture as in marriage, is said to have been the pioneer tobacco planter of Virginia. The raising of tobacco paid the planters so well that for many years there was a constant temptation to neglect the planting of sufficient corn for food. In consequence of scarcity in the colony during the year 1616, the Chickahominy Indians were called upon to furnish a tribute of grain according to their treaty. They refused, however, and Yeardley with one hundred of his best shot marched into their country. Here he was received with contempt. The Indians said he was only [Thomas] Dale's man—they had paid Dale their tribute, but would not pay him. A skirmish ensued, in which twelve Indians were killed and as many made prisoners. These were ransomed with corn, and the Indians were glad to rid themselves of the Englishmen by loading their boats. Powhatan was growing old, and began to fear his brother Opechancanough. This Indian was as ambitious and influential as Powhatan, while he was younger, and very popular with Indians and whites. Since Opitchapan was both old and decrepit, Powhatan was the only obstacle between him and chief dominion among the Indians. This wily old chief had never loved the English any too well.

He had on every occasion refused to enter or approach the white settlements. He would not even go to Jamestown to attend the wedding of his daughter. Powhatan now dreaded lest his ambitious brother should betray him into the hands of the English. He therefore retired to a distance from Jamestown, devoting himself to warding off this danger. The old chief expressed great sorrow when he heard of the death of Pocahontas. He was, however, pleased that her son [Thomas Rolfe] was living, and both he and Opechancanough said they would like to see him. When Tomocomo returned Powhatan called upon him for the number of people in England.

"Count," said Tomocomo, "the stars in the sky—the leaves on the trees—and the sand upon the seashore, for such is the number of the people in England." Captain [Samuel] Argall was now governor of the colony and John Rolfe was his secretary.

Argall found Jamestown on his arrival from England neglected, and the streets planted with tobacco. Poor little town! It was never destined to be great.—Sir Thomas Dale had before this preferred to live at Bermuda Hundred.—Virginians were fast becoming a widely scattered community of planters, its situation was unhealthy, and much of its site has since been washed away by the river. There still remain some graves and a church tower built of brick brought all the way from England. In the year 1618 Powhatan died. Opitchapan nominally succeeded him, but Opechancanough was far too ambitious and popular to remain in a subordinate position. The power fell really into his hands. When the English came to Virginia, Powhatan had long since established his reputation as a great warrior, and could well afford to rest on his honors, but it was not so with Opechancanough. Had the English known as much of Indian character as we do today, they would have feared the younger chief, who had yet a career to make, a reputation as a brave to gain. But Opechancanough renewed the treaty of Powhatan, the English proceeded to scatter their settlements wherever good land for the cultivation of tobacco was to be found, and Indians went in and out the planters's houses on peaceful and friendly terms. Argall's government was unscrupulous. He was the first public officer in this new country to make money out of the public store. He seems to have been cruel as well as unprincipled.

Bitter complaints were sent by the colonists to the Company in England. Meantime Lord Delaware, who had spent much money and time in the service of the Company, again embarked with two hundred emigrants to take into his own hand the government of the colony. Unfortunately, he died on the voyage.—Some of the members of the Company soon after sent Argall a very severe letter, accusing him of many wrongs against the Company and colonists.—This was accompanied by a letter to Lord Delaware, with many accusations against Argall. Owing to the death of Lord Delaware both of these letters fell into Argall's hands. In October, 1618, when the news of Lord Delaware's death reached England, Captain Yeardley was appointed governor, and before his departure was knighted and treated with a discourse from King James upon the duty of carrying religion to the Indians. Before he reached Virginia, however, Argall was gone, and had turned into the hands of friends his wrongfully acquired property, quite after the approved manner of public thieves in our time. Sir George Yeardley's government covered the most prosperous years that the colony had yet known. The first representative legislature held within the limits of the United States convened at Jamestown in 1619. The Company had granted the colony an annual assembly of the governor and council with two representatives from each plantation. This assembly met in the chancel of the Jamestown church, and among other things made the following laws. First, against drunkenness, that any man found drunk was to be reproved privately by the minister, if the offense were committed a second time he was to be reproved publicly, the third time he must "lie in bolts" for twelve hours and pay a fine, and if he still persisted he was to suffer such severe punishment as the governor and council should decide upon.

"Against excessive apparel," an offense one would think hardly likely to creep into so young a colony, it was enacted that every man should be assessed "in the church for all public contributions, if he be unmarried, according to his own apparel, if he be married, according to his own and his wife's, or either of their apparel." It was found that many of the colonists being single men did not settle permanently in the colony, but endeavored to make money at tobacco raising, intending to return ultimately to England. The Company resolved to provide wives for the colonists in order to bind them permanently to Virginia. "One widow and eleven maids" were sent over in 1621. The Company in England wished it to be understood that these women had been chosen with great care and came with good recommendations. They were to be "lodged and provided for of diet till they be married." If this did not quickly take place, however, they were to be "put to several householders that have wives till they can be provided of husbands." Moreover, a price was set upon wives. Each man must pay a hundred and twenty pounds of "best leaf tobacco" to defray the expense of his wife's importation, and that there might be no dead loss to the Company if one of the girls should die, the expense of her passage must be divided among the husbands of the others.

Pains must also be taken lest there should be any cheating in the quality of the tobacco. Shortly after thirty-eight more "maids and young women" were exported by the London Company, with the hope that they would be "received with the same Christian piety and charity" as the others, from which we may infer that these did not have to wait long for husbands. In the choice of the last, also, the Company had taken "extraordinary care and diligence." They had "good testimony of their honest life and carriage." This testimony, with the name of each girl, was enclosed for the benefit of the husband. They were labeled, so to speak. The price of wives was raised on this lot to one hundred and fifty pounds of tobacco, with an addition if any of the girls should die. "Their own deserts," say the directions to Virginia authorities, "together with your favor and care, will, we hope, marry them all to honest and sufficient men whose means will reach to present repayment, but if any of them shall unwarily or fondly bestow herself (for the liberty of marriage we dare not infringe) upon such as shall not be able to give present satisfaction, we desire at least as soon as ability shall be, they be compelled to pay the true quantity of tobacco proportioned, and that this debt may have precedence of all others to be recovered." The "maids" were welcomed in Virginia. We can imagine a planter going to Jamestown to get him a "wife" in exchange for a lot of choice tobacco. This sending out of "wives" was one of the wisest measures adopted, for when there were wives in the cabin, and children born in the land, the white [English] men felt that Virginia was indeed their home.

□□□□□□□□□□

In 1621, when Sir Francis Wyatt became governor, the peace with Opechancanough was ratified, and that chief seemed to the English to show decided evidences of a religious inclination. The colony of Virginia had grown and increased, spreading its arms wherever fertile land was to be found. Eighty peaceful plantations lay widely scattered and almost entirely unprotected. Totally unsuspected, the religiously inclined Opechancanough laid his plans for an extermination of the whites. Two days before the massacre the savages guided a white man safely through the woods. Up to the very hour appointed for the work to begin Indians lounged tranquilly about the plantations according to their habit. Within the space of an hour or two more than three hundred men, women, and children fell at the hands of the savages, who burned their houses, butchered their cattle, and mangled their dead bodies. One Indian servant out of affection for his master had revealed the plot on the eve of its accomplishment. By his means Jamestown and the adjacent settlements were warned in the early morning, and thus a much more dreadful destruction was avoided. Great was the consternation in England when the news arrived. The Company no more advised a tender and kindly treatment of the savages. The colonists now hated the Indians with a bitter animosity. They wreaked vengeance on them, they hunted them—they kept great mastiffs and bloodhounds to set upon them. They averred that the dogs took the "naked tanned" savages for "no other than wild beasts," while the Indians themselves feared them "worse than their old devil which they worship, supposing them to be a new and worse kind of devils than their own." Captain Smith was fired with a desire to fight these savages and protect the colony in which he felt so warm an interest. He offered his services to the Company to lead a band of one hundred and thirty men to Virginia, promising to make "a flying camp," with which he would so torment the Indians as either to bring them into subjection or force them to leave the country. He also planned to make such explorations as would bring the two maps of Virginia and New England together. Many favored his project, but others of the Company considered that the expense would be too great, and so were inclined to let the planters take care of themselves.

Smith says he was given to understand that he would be allowed to undertake such an expedition at his own expense and might have the plunder as a reward. But he says, truly, that the plunder to be procured from Indian villages would not amount to twenty pounds in twenty years. The massacre was a great drawback to the Virginia colony. The planters drew together upon some few plantations for safety, and it was some time before the Virginians gained a feeling of security and Virginia's prosperity returned to her. Opechancanough was a savage of the savages, crafty, cruel, and proud. Twenty years later he instituted another massacre of the ever-encroaching settlers. He was supposed to be nearly a hundred years old, and very feeble.

But his fierce ambition had by no means subsided with oncoming age. He led his men, and the deadly work was the most destructive where he was in person. But no resistance to white settlement could avail for the Indians of Virginia.

Opechancanough was taken prisoner. The once straight and active warrior was bent and emaciated. He was so weak that he was carried on a litter from place to place. The muscles of his eyelids were paralyzed so that he could not raise them. He was carried to Jamestown and well-used, but was naturally an object of curiosity. Hearing one day the sound of many footsteps the old chief commanded his attendants to raise his eyelids. He saw himself surrounded by a crowd of people curious to see the famous Opechancanough. He sent for Sir William Berkeley, the governor. "Had it been my fortune," said the proud old man, "to have taken Sir William Berkeley prisoner, I would not have meanly exposed him as a show to my people." Soon after this the old chief was shamefully (righteously) shot in the back by his keeper (bodyguard), no doubt in revenge for his massacre of some family of women and children. [Justice was served.]

❑❑❑❑❑❑❑❑❑❑

Captain Smith's travels and adventures seem to have come to an end while he was yet young. He lived to see successful colonies thriving in the two lands of his affection, Virginia and New England. Had these perished he would no doubt have buckled on his armor again and planted anew. During the later years of his life he published many books, and a general history of Virginia appeared under his supervision, but chiefly written by others, and edited by the Reverend Doctor [William] Symonds. Captain John Smith died in 1631, in the fifty-second year of his age. He was buried in St. Sepulchre's Church, in London, where the following [recorded] inscription was set up to his memory.

"*Here lies one conquered that hath conquered kings, subdued large territories and done things which to the world impossible would seem, but that the truth is held in more esteem. Shall I report his former services done in honor of God and Christendom? How that he did divide from pagans three their heads and lives, types of his chivalry, for which great service in that climate done, brave Sigismundus, King of Hungarion, did give him a coat of arms to wear, those conquered heads got by his sword and spear, or shall I tell of his adventures since done in Virginia, that large continent, how that he subdued kings unto his yoke, and made those heathens fly as wind doth smoke. And made their land, being of so large a station, a habitation for our Christian nation, where God is glorified, their wants supplied, which else for necessaries might have died? But what avails his conquest? Now he* lies interred in earth, a prey for worms and flies. Oh may his soul in sweet Elysium sleep until the Keeper, that all souls doth keep, return to judgment and that after thence with angels he may have his recompense." Of Smith's explorations, [William] Robertson says in his famous *History of America*, "After sailing three thousand miles in a paltry vessel, ill-fitted for such an extensive navigation, during which the hardships to which he was exposed, as well as the patience with which he endured and the fortitude with which he surmounted them, equal whatever is related of the most famous Spanish discoverers in their most daring enterprises, he returned to Jamestown, he brought with him an account of that large portion of the American continent now [in 1774] comprehended in the two provinces of Virginia and Maryland, so full and exact that after the progress of information and research for a century and a half his map exhibits no inaccurate view of both countries, and is the original upon which all subsequent delineations and descriptions have been formed." Of the private character of our great captain we may judge by what one of Smith's former soldiers says of him, "I never knew a warrior yet but thee, from wine, tobacco—debts—dice—oaths so free." Captain Smith was in his own day and until our time honored as the hero of Virginia. But there is a pedantic pride which loves to show its knowledge by unhorsing the heroes of history. In our own time the writings of Wingfield, Newport, and others, recently brought to light—have been used to discredit the narratives of Smith. Men have even assailed him with bitterness, and a recent writer intimates that he was a "gascon and a beggar," though the same author thinks that Virginia ought to erect a monument to his fame! Men were not so careful of historical accuracy in the days of James I as they are today.

History in our sense of the word was hardly known in English literature. The public expected travelers to please them with well-varnished stories. That Smith may have allowed his imagination too much play in setting down romantic facts from memory is not improbable. It was the bad fashion of travelers in the sixteenth and seventeenth centuries [to embellish]. But the statements of [Christopher] Newport, [Edward] Wingfield, and [John] Ratcliffe, all enemies to Captain John Smith, and who yet say more to confirm than to contradict him, are certainly not entitled to half the weight of Smith's writings. For, on any theory, Wingfield was grossly incompetent—Newport was as helpless as a porpoise when he set foot on land, not efficient in exploring and foolish in negotiating, while Captain Ratcliffe was an adventurer sailing under the false flag of an assumed name. There are two fields in which we are able to test Captain Smith's veracity. His map of the region about the Chesapeake remains today a wonderfully accurate chart, when we consider that he lacked the use of modern instruments for survey. His descriptions of the country are always correct, and his accounts of the manners and customs of the Indians are in the main true to the life, as we know the slow-changing Algonquin tribes of today. Now, if we remember the solid qualities of Smith—if we remember the fact that at the beginning of the settlement at Jamestown he was excluded from the council and condemned by the other leaders, and that he was afterwards the one man who could manage the settlers and the savages, the man who, by the sheer force of necessity, was brought to the front and made president—we shall see how little ground there is for these aspersions of his character. Add to this that he was, after his return, a member of the London Council of the Company, and that the Virginia Company and the Plymouth Company competed for his services, and we can understand how little he deserves to be condemned on the testimony of the incompetent, whom he pushed to the wall for the sake of saving the colony. Make what reductions we may in his own narrative or in the testimony of his friends, accept for truth all that is said by his enemies, and on any possible theory of events John Smith remains, of all that quarrelsome company, the one man whose disinterestedness, courage, address, perseverance, and weight of character fitted him to save colonists from the result of their own folly (stupidity) and from the craft (danger) of the savages (Native Americans). Is such a hardy leader of forlorn hopes, such an explorer of new rivers, such a terror to crafty savages, likely to be found in the person of "a gascon (braggart) and a beggar?" Not Virginia alone, but the nation ought to erect a monument to the first explorer, the first defender, and the first historian of the country (America).

◻◻◻◻◻◻◻◻◻◻

SMITH'S DELIVERANCE BY POCAHONTAS

This story of Captain Smith's deliverance was not mentioned in his [memoir] *True Relation*, published in England in 1608, nor in the historical notices printed with his *Map of Virginia* at Oxford, 1612. It first appears while Pocahontas was in England in 1616 or 1617, in a letter addressed by Smith to the queen in behalf of the "Lady Rebecca" or Pocahontas. Nor does any account of his romantic deliverance appear in [Edward] Wingfield's very brief narrative. The circumstantial account first appears in the *General History of Virginia*, published in 1624. This book was gathered out of the writings of many writers, and was edited by Dr. [William] Symonds, though it was issued in Smith's name. In consequence of its not appearing in the earlier accounts, the incident has of late years been very generally given up by historians as a romantic tale invented by the gallant captain after the daughter of Powhatan became famous as the first convert to Christianity, and the first Indian woman married to an Englishman. We have thought it better to give the narrative in the text as it is given in Smith's *General History*, and to reserve a statement of its doubtfulness for this note. Nor do we consider it quite clear that the pleasing story must be given up. There are yet so many unsolved questions about Jamestown and about Pocahontas that we may have to return to the old belief in the veracity of Smith. In the *True Relation*, published in 1608, he praises Pocahontas as "a child of ten years old, which, not only for feature, countenance, and proportion much exceeded any of the rest of his [Powhatan's] people, but for wit and spirit the only nonpareil of his country." If we suppose that this child had delivered Smith, but that for some motive unknown to us he or his editor suppressed the account, this praise seems natural. If not, why should he thus praise this Indian girl? He mentions farther on that she was sent as a messenger to intercede for certain savages that had been detained. Why should Powhatan send so young a child to accompany a messenger on a difficult mission? Why entrust his daughter to the whites? If she had delivered Smith all this would be natural enough. It is all very difficult on any other supposition. Again Pocahontas was always afterwards a friend and benefactor to the whites, helping and warning them. She was especially devoted to Smith, and when she was married to Rolfe she had been made to believe that Captain Smith was dead. When she met Smith in England she was much moved. All of these things are of the same piece with Smith's story of her interference in his behalf. The *True Relation* [memoir] was published somewhat mysteriously. Some copies bear the name of Thomas Watson, with a preface explaining that it was a printer's blunder, others the name of John Smith, others read "By a Gentleman of Said Colony." This variation is clearly made in the same form of the title page. The initials "I. H." are signed to the preface. Who is I. H.? Why this halting about the name of the author? It is confessed that the editor came upon his copy at second or third hand, that is, we suppose that it had been copied in MS. He also confesses to omitting what he thought "fit to be private." All account of the adventurous voyage is left out either by the author or the editor. Some sentences are incomprehensible even to so careful an editor as Mr. Charles Deane, who reprinted the tract in 1866, and the name of Captain Smith does not appear in it throughout. Can anyone doubt that the *True Relation* was carefully revised, not to say corrupted, in the interest of the Company and of the colony? And if so, what more natural than that the hostility of so powerful a chief as Powhatan would be concealed? For the great need of the colony was a fresh supply of colonists. Nothing would have so much tended to check emigration to Virginia as a belief that the most powerful neighboring prince was at enmity with the settlement. (The same reason may have procured the omission of the fight at

Kecoughtan-Hampton, as related in this book, though indeed that story has a marvelous sound as told in the *General History of Virginia, New England and the Summer Isles*.) While, therefore, much doubt is thrown upon the incident of Smith's deliverance by Pocahontas on account of its omission from the earlier accounts [by Smith], there are some reasons for believing it to be true.

THE SURVIVORS OF THE ROANOKE COLONY

William Strachey, who makes the statement about the slaughter of the survivors of the colony by Powhatan, in his *History of Travaile into Virginia Britannia*, has the following curious sentence, "At Peccarecamek and Ochanahoen, by the relation of Machumps [an Indian], the people have houses built with stone walls, so taught them by those English who escaped the slaughter at Roanoke, at what time this our colony under conduct of Captain Newport landed within the Chesapeake Bay, where the people had up tame turkeys and take apes in the mountains, and where at Ritanoe, the werowance (werowance) Eyanoco preserved seven of the English alive—four men, two boys, and one young maid (who escaped and fled up the river Chanoke)—to beat his copper, of which he had certain mines at Ritanoe." That is to say, if we disentangle it rightly, that Eyanoco, chief at Ritanoe, preserved the lives of seven of the English settlers, to beat his copper and build his houses, and that these colonists were yet alive when Captain Newport landed at Jamestown. From another very obscure passage we infer that Machumps or some other Indian had told Strachey that Powhatan, instigated by his priests, had sent into the country where these captives were, and put them to death after the settlement of Jamestown, where the survivors of Roanoke had "twenty odd years peaceably lived intermixed with those savages." This massacre may have been to prevent communication with Jamestown by rival chiefs through the captives. If, indeed, Strachey were not imposed on by the facile invention of an Indian storyteller making a tale to suit the demands of his auditors, as others had invented gold mines and an easy route to the Pacific to gratify the whites. Strachey evidently believes his story, for he refers to it again and again, proposing at one time to make it a ground for alliance with neighboring chiefs against Powhatan. Lawson's *History* (1718) is quoted in the *Transactions of the American Antiquarian Society*, as citing a tradition among the Hatteras Indians "that several of their ancestors were white people, and could talk from a book, the truth of which is confirmed by gray eyes being among these Indians and no other." But this proves little about the Roanoke colony. If Strachey had finished his book we should perhaps have known more, for he promised a fuller account in a future chapter. But he was, we fear, a somewhat eager collector of stories, though there is nothing inherently improbable in his account of the fate of the whites. But what shall we do with the apes which the Indians caught in the mountains of North Carolina?

PREVIOUS MARRIAGE OF POCAHONTAS

William Strachey referred to in Note 2, uses these words in an account of Powhatan's family, "and besides young Pocahontas, a daughter of his, using sometime to our fort in times past, now married to a private captain called Kocoum some two years since." As Indian marriages were often fast and loose affairs, and as Powhatan sold his daughters in marriage, and gave away his wives when he tired of them, it might well be that Pocahontas was living with a husband when Argall captured her. The English, with the religious prejudices of the time, would not think much of the sanctity of a pagan marriage, and would not halt at anything that stood in the way of the conversion of Pocahontas to Christianity. But it is worthwhile to remember that Strachey probably wrote his book, according to the best judges, more than two years after his return to England, and that he could only know of the marriage to a private captain or petty chief, two years previous to his writing, by report of others, and that he may very well have mistaken a report of the marriage of any other of Powhatan's daughters for that of Pocahontas. If she had been previously married, we should probably not have wanted for others to certify that fact, and there would then have been no need of the suggestions of various writers mentioned in the text as to the causes of her residence on the Potomac. Or might he not have written as late as the early part of 1616, before Rolfe's arrival in England? And this "private captain," may he not be John Rolfe, transformed by some confusion of memory or mistake of a copyist into Kocoum? We nowhere [can] find the word *captain* applied to an Indian. Strachey's book was first printed from the manuscript in the British Museum in 1849.

Nathan Hale

Nathan Hale

Preface

Many a man dies at what appears to onlookers the very zenith of fame—the very summit of success. But as time moves on, its relentless finger first dims—then absolutely effaces, his personal records, so that, even to the generation immediately following him, his former fame becomes incredible. The marvel is not when a man's standing is in time lowered, but rather when some invisible power—call it what you will—through slow, revolving years, lifts him ever higher, until his fame becomes a national crown of glory and bids fair—like that of the dead at Thermopylae, or the victors at Marathon, or of individuals like Washington and Lincoln—to last as long as time shall last. If sometimes true of mature men, this has seldom been true of very young men. Indeed, so short is this list that but two names are recalled as of abiding interest, one, that of Arthur Henry Hallam, enshrined in the imperishable lines of *In Memoriam*, the voicing of [Alfred] Tennyson's love and sorrow, while to Colonial America and the year of our national independence, and to Yale, his alma mater, belong the splendid story of a youth who courageously gave up a life that he had willingly risked for his country, accepting an ignominious death with more than Spartan firmness, at the age of twenty-one years, three months, and sixteen days. Both of these names, perhaps especially that of Nathan Hale, seem destined to go on increasing in radiant influence and strong inspiration century after century. Such souls, however, are not accidents, but are the perfected fruit of generations of character and growth. Their development may sometimes appear due to opportunity, and the strength of the soul that is in them, lacking that opportunity, might have lain hidden. It is an inspiring fact that, as we study the early days of our country, we find so many men and women bearing naturally, in their everyday life, these splendid traits of character. Wealth did not then abound—character did. The patriot of today may be pardoned if, as he contrasts the past and the present, he remembers with a sigh the simple, early life of the American people, and the splendid ability of the sons and daughters who went forth from those unpretentious homes to meet responsibilities, to conquer difficulties, and to lay broad the foundations for the noblest republic the world has yet known.

The story we present of Nathan Hale is that of a boy reared in one of those rural homes, presided over by upright parents whose children were trained to master life, to meet death fearlessly, and all unconsciously to win ever-growing reverence.

The story of this boy, of his home, and of the future to which his training led him, is well-worth our closest and earnest consideration. It is impossible to claim originality in any important detail in the sketch of a life so brief as Nathan Hale's. Especially is this true when that life has been so carefully studied and so ably presented by such men as the Honorable Isaac W. Stuart, Mr. Benson J. Lossing, Professor Henry P. Johnston, George Dudley Seymour, Esquire, and the Reverend Anson Phelps Stokes, Secretary of Yale University—all men who have come under the spell of that brave boy, and who have portrayed him as they believed him to have been. This little book differs from their writing, to which it is greatly indebted, principally in the fact that it pictures him as seen through a woman's eyes, lifted above all mortal loss, transfigured as have been all who have made the Great Surrender for "right because it is right," and who have gone forward, victorious through seeming defeat.

It is today a recognized fact that no life worthy of our reverence, or even a life calculated to awaken our fear, is the result of accident. Whatever may be the character, its basis has been the result of long-developing causes. This, the life of Nathan Hale well illustrates. He was born at a time and under influences that were sure to develop the best qualities in him. He was an immediate descendant of the best of the Puritans on both sides of the sea. His great-grandfather, John Hale, was the son of Robert Hale, who came to America in 1632. John Hale graduated from Harvard in 1657 and was the first pastor settled in Beverly, Massachusetts, remaining there until he died, an aged man. An ardent patriot, this John Hale, in 1676, gave about one-twelfth of his salary, some seventy pounds, for defense in King Philip's War. When need arose in the French War, he went to Canada as a volunteer, for a threefold purpose—so that he might accompany a number of his own parishioners, act as chaplain for one of the regiments, and fight when his aid was needed. Living during the witchcraft trials, he was one of the first to be convinced of the mistaken course pursued. We are not certain as to his approval or disapproval of the progress of the excitement in regard to witchcraft until it became intensely personal to his own family. His wife was, fortunately as the results proved, accused by some misguided person of being a witch. The well-known nobility of her life, and her lovely character, at once convinced all who knew the circumstances that some terrible mistake had been made by her accuser. And if a mistake had been made in her case, why not in others? At once the deadly power of the delusion was broken and, happily, the tide turned back forever. There was no question after this of the Reverend Mr. Hale's viewpoint as to witchcraft. In the very darkest depths of the witchcraft delusion, some illustrations of splendid courage and noble unselfishness were exhibited. Gruesome as it is, we cannot forbear quoting the example of one Giles Corey, condemned to die as a witch, who knew that if he did not confess he had bewitched people, his estate, which he wished his wife and family to inherit, would be forfeited, and that he would be pressed to death instead of being hanged. Being hanged is a comparatively brief experience, while the other way is prolonged and agonizing. But, for the sake of his family, brave old Giles Corey calmly faced this terrible, lingering death. He must have won from some, if not from all, the feeling that a stout-hearted and generous man had proved his love for his own as no mere words could have done. John Hale appears to have been a worthy ancestor of the youth Nathan Hale, who, a hundred years later, so freely made a sacrifice of his life. John Hale's son, Samuel, was Nathan's grandfather—he made his home in Portsmouth, New Hampshire. One of Samuel Hale's sons, bearing his own name, Samuel, was a Harvard man.

Another son, Richard, Nathan's father, born February 28, 1717, looking about to find the best farming lands for the support of a future family, moved to Connecticut, and became a farmer in South Coventry, thirty miles east of Hartford. Distinguished from the beginning for his success in whatever he undertook in business affairs, and also as a man of singularly upright character, Deacon Richard Hale won the warmest regard of all who knew him. His advice and help were sought, both in political and religious affairs, to the full limit of the time at his command.

His farm was among the best in that section. The house that he first occupied—probably one already on the place—was as comfortable and convenient as the usual homes of the earlier colonists. Later a larger house was built, big enough to accommodate a family of a dozen or more, and many guests as well. The house in which Nathan lived as a boy is still standing, and has fortunately come down to us with almost no mutilation. Though the forms and the voices of those who dwelt in them have long since vanished, there still linger about these vacant rooms the most tender and inspiring memories of the lives once developing there, now gone forward, nothing wasted or lost, as we will believe, of anything permanent they strove for or cared for in their dear, earthly home. To this home Richard Hale, married May 2, 1746, at the age of twenty-nine, brought his young bride, Elizabeth Strong. If Richard Hale's pedigree was a good one, his wife, Elizabeth Strong, came from a family even more finely endowed. The first of her ancestors who came to America was Elder John Strong. He was one of the founders of Dorchester, now a part of Boston, later he helped to found Northampton, Massachusetts. Mrs. Hale's grandfather, Joseph Strong, represented Coventry for sixty-five sessions in the General Assembly of Connecticut, and when he was ninety years of age he presided over the town meeting, suggesting by that deed a man of some vigor, for town meetings were no play days in those early years. His descendants, active in whatever their hands found to do—in the ministry, the law, business, or politics, were long prominent in New England and New York, and doubtless many are today still helping to mold their country's future. The son of this Justice Joseph Strong was also named Joseph, and called Captain Joseph Strong. In 1724 he married his second cousin, Elizabeth Strong. He, too, was a noted man among the colonists. She, later, became the "grandmother" to whom Nathan so warmly alludes in one of his last letters to his brother. Captain Joseph Strong and his wife were the parents of Elizabeth Strong who, in her nineteenth year, married Richard Hale. To Elizabeth Strong Hale we can give but a passing notice.

There is not, it is believed, one word that she wrote now in existence, nor any record left, of that gracious womanhood, save a name on an obscure gravestone. But what brave-hearted mother would not count it well-worthwhile to leave, for the coming years, the impress she left upon her many children, one of them alone destined to carry to coming generations of Americans the assurance that such a son could only have been borne by one of the noblest of mothers. Dying at the age of forty—April 21, 1767—after a married life of twenty-one years, she had performed all the duties then expected from the mistress of a farmer's household in a section where the principal help that could be secured in any time of need came from the voluntary kindnesses of neighbors, for, like one large family, they felt it necessary to "lend a hand" whenever any one of their number was in need. Mrs. Hale had been the mother of twelve children when she died. Two of her children, named David and Jonathan, were twins. One of the twins, Jonathan, died when only a week old. David lived to be graduated from Yale and to become a minister at Lisbon, Connecticut. A little daughter, Susanna, lived but a month, but ten of Mrs. Hale's twelve children grew to maturity. Nathan, the sixth child, born June 6, 1755, was the first of the ten to die, leaving to his surviving brothers and sisters a memory that in later years must have been an unfailing inspiration. He was delicate at first, but owing to his mother's care he later became as robust in body as he was in mind. For an older brother, Enoch, the plan was formed of sending him to college to prepare for the ministry, a custom then prevalent among many of the large and prosperous families in New England. Nathan was at first destined for a business life, but because of the urgent desire of his mother, heartily seconded by that of his grandmother Strong, he was allowed to enter college with his brother Enoch in 1769, when he was fourteen years old, this was two years after the death of his mother. Four of Mrs. Hale's immediate relatives were graduates of Yale—a fine illustration of the value those progressive pioneers attached to education. As a boy Nathan was to his mother what he later became to all who knew him, and the bond between such a mother and such a son must have been very tender and strong.

It is a comfort to those who know what such mothers desire for their children, to remember the gladness and hope with which this mother, overworked and dying long before her time, looked forward to the days coming to her children. For Nathan, through her influence, was to become one of Yale's noblest sons. As Nathan's mother died nine years before he did, we understand the full meaning of the line in Judge [Francis Miles] Finch's poem, *The Sad of Earth, the Glad of Heaven*, written many years later in honoring Nathan's splendid sacrifice. The poem to which the line belongs, read more than sixty years ago on the one hundredth anniversary of the Linonian Society, an organization of Yale College of which Nathan Hale had been an early and an active member, had much influence in rousing first Yale men, and then other patriotic Americans, to recognize Nathan Hale as one of America's bravest martyrs. Mrs. Hale died in 1767. About two years later Deacon Hale married again, bringing to his home this time a widow, Mrs. Abigail Adams, of Canterbury, who must have been well-fitted to take her place as the new head of the family. No ignoble mother could rear such children as she had reared, and Deacon Hale's second choice of a wife proved a wise and happy one. Providence appears to have smiled upon him when he opened his doors and invited Mrs. Adams and her children to share his home, and even the affection of some of his sons.

It is said that two of Deacon Hale's sons fell in love with her youngest daughter, Alice Adams, who, at Deacon Hale's desire, came to live permanently in the family in 1770 or 1771, while his second son, John, married her eldest daughter, Sarah Adams, on December 19, 1770. The lives of both these women, Sarah and Alice Adams, are sufficient witnesses to the high character of the new mother added to the Hale household. To several of his biographers it has seemed quite probable that Nathan Hale wrote one of his last two letters to this mother. We grant that it may have been addressed to her, while intended for the reading of another. In regard to the marriage of John Hale and Sarah Adams it may be as well to state here that, after a married life of thirty-one years, John Hale died suddenly in December, 1802, his health probably undermined by his service in the Revolutionary War, where he held the rank of major. His widow, desiring to carry out what she believed would have been his wishes, "bequeathed £1000 to trustees as a fund, the income of which was to be used for the support of young men preparing for missionary service"—probably among the Indians, as this was before the support of foreign missions was undertaken in America—"and in part for founding and supporting the Hale Library in Coventry, to be used by the ministers of Coventry and the neighboring towns." Included in the bequest for founding the still existing so-called "Hale Donation" was a portrait of the donor's husband, Major John Hale—well-painted, for the period, and now of great interest. Mrs. John Hale died a few months after her husband. It is easy to believe that, though born of different parents, the Hale and Adams families were congenial mentally and morally, and that Deacon Richard Hale was a wise and fortunate man in his choice of a second mother for his children.

According to his mother's and grandmother's wishes, it was early decided that Nathan should be prepared to enter college. After the fashion of those times, he and two of his brothers began their preparatory studies under the direction of the Reverend Joseph Huntington, Doctor of Divinity, then pastor of the church in Nathan's native town. He is said to have been a man noted for his intellectual power, for his patriotism, and for his courteous manners. It may be well to say here that, in those early days, the New England ministers usually settled in one pastorate for life, and they were not only teachers in spiritual things, but were noted for their courteous and dignified manners, so that even before he entered college Nathan Hale must have had ample opportunities for the cultivation of the easy manners and courteous deportment which are said by all who knew him to have been so marked in him. Nathan Hale, as a boy, had one more asset that must have helped to insure his future success, and that did, as we believe, help him to die nobly. He was not overindulged—he had always the spur of effort to urge him forward. It was told of him, many years after his death, by the woman he had loved and who had known him well all his later years, Mrs. Alice Adams Lawrence, that whatever he did, even as a boy, he did with all his heart, as if it engrossed his whole mind. Whether it was work, or study, or play, he gave all his energies to the doing of it. Such a disposition, together with his fine home training, must have helped to insure his success in Yale.

In September, 1769, accompanied by Enoch, an older brother, Nathan Hale entered the freshman class at Yale. His personal traits easily won the hearts of his classmates, while his quick understanding, his high scholarship, and his loyalty to the college standards made him as popular among tutors and professors as among his classmates. It is pleasant to know that, from the time we first learn of him until we see him standing beside the fatal tree, he appears to have won all hearts worth winning. But Nathan Hale had yet another gift that would surely endear him to college students of today as much as it doubtless did to his own classmates. He was a powerful athlete. So great was his skill in this line that, to successive generations of Yale men, the "broad jump" made by Nathan Hale remained unequaled. It is said to have taken place on what is now called "The Green" in New Haven, not far from the Old State House, and for many years the spot was marked to designate the length of the jump. Even during the years when his courageous death appeared to be well-nigh forgotten, "Hale's jump" was vividly remembered. But he not only "jumped," he excelled in all games then popular in college, besides being a capital shot with his rifle, as well as a fine swimmer. Hale could, it is said, lay one hand on the top of a six-foot fence and easily vault over it, and, though this astonishing feat is reported as occurring while he was a teacher, he used to delight his companions by showing them how to stand in a hogshead with his hands on his hips, leap over the first hogshead, land in a second, leap from that into a third, and from that out on to the ground—all this before he was twenty.

Imagine the delight of the "other fellows" standing around to watch Hale go through his various stunts in athletics! It almost makes one feel as if one had been a student and shared in the cheering when Hale did these things, so easy to himself, so difficult to the onlookers. Then fancy the talk at the supper tables, when the candles burned brightly and the eatables tasted twice as good because "old Hale" had won laurels for "old Yale" that afternoon by some "splendid" deed, as the boys called it. Whatever he did, we may be sure that it was done well and with all his might, and that nobody equaled him.—This much for the athletic life of Hale in his student days.—It was only natural to such a man that whatever he was—friend, student, teacher, or soldier—he should carry zest and earnestness to all his work, even as he carried his manliness, his courtesy, and his unquenchable spirit. Let us now turn to the record of his years of successful work at Yale. It has been said that whatever he did, he did with all his might, and his brain work was as notable in its results as were the strength and agility of his body. In those early days the college bell rang for prayers, as the beginning of the day's work, at half past four in summer and an hour later in winter, and there are men still living who remember, in later years and at later hours, the wild rushes half-dressed students used to make, adjusting what they could of their hastily donned clothing on their race to morning chapel. Hale, however, as well as his companions a hundred and forty years ago, were accustomed to early rising, and able to fill every hour of their long days with work or play. The course of study then was much shorter than it is now, but if lacking in quantity it certainly made up in some of its qualities.

We doubt if freshmen today would outshine their fellows of that very early time if their declamations on Fridays were required to be in Latin, Greek, or Hebrew, "no English being allowed save by special permission." Science as we now know it had not entered into the college course, but the little then known, and the other studies considered essential, comparatively limited as they must have been, were taught so thoroughly that the men who carried away a college diploma carried a sure guarantee that they had been carefully taught whatever was then considered essential to a college education. Although it is true that science was then in comparative infancy, it is also true that it was deeply absorbing to young Hale. Some of his most valued books were scientific, and, aside from the studies he was obliged to pursue, he eagerly absorbed educational theories and the best literary works then available. As a college student, he stood high, as a thinker and as one interested in the finest pursuits of his period, he ranked equally high. Before he was nineteen he had won the permanent friendship and ardent admiration of a man who was then his tutor, Timothy Dwight, later the renowned president of Yale College, and to the end of his long life a loyal servant of his dear friend, Nathan Hale. Another warm friend, a classmate, destined to be notable in future years, was James Hillhouse, later United States senator, the first man to leave the stamp of beauty on his native city, New Haven, in the wonderful elms of his planting. In addition to these two noted men, many of Hale's warmest friendships were formed at college among the leading men of his own and of other classes. At least two or three of these were his companions in arms, to whom we may refer later.

Of his scholarship, one sure test remains. At graduation, of the thirty-six men in his class, he ranked among the first thirteen. In one other important line Nathan Hale made a notable mark in college, namely, in his intense interest in Linonia. This society had been founded in 1753 "to promote in addition to the regular course of academic study, literary stimulus and rhetorical improvement to the undergraduates," and to create friendly relations among its members. The organization lived a long and honorable life, and did a most helpful work among its members. Nathan Hale was the first in his class to become its Chancellor, later styled President. He was for some time also its scribe, and many of his entries in the Linonian reports are still "clear throughout and well-preserved" as is his signature at the end, after the passing of more than a hundred years. During his college course his name occurs in the reports of almost every meeting of the society. At one time he delivered "a very interesting narration" at another, "an eloquent extemporaneous address." On various occasions he is said to have taken part in some of the plays that were frequently acted (staged), and to have proposed questions for discussion. Besides taking part in the society and college exercises (classes), he enjoyed frequent correspondence with a number of his classmates on themes of taste and criticism and of grammar and philology. As incoming

Chancellor at the end of the college year of 1772, Hale responded in behalf of Linonia to the parting address from one of the graduating class. Hale's farewell address to the Linonians of the class of 1772 is preserved to Yale College on the society records.

In reading it one must remember that the speech was made by a boy of seventeen. The dignity of the address, the assured ease with which he speaks, the sense of the Yale bond, as strong then as it ever has been, all show the only boyish thing about the speaker, namely, his sense of the superiority of Linonia, then nearly twenty years old, to the struggling new society of "The Brothers," less than eight years old. All this brings before us very vividly a boy in years, but a man in thoughts and aspirations, ardent and scholarly, and full of a noble ambition that looked forward, as do all ambitious students in their college days, to years of generous life. A few paragraphs quoted from various parts of the quaintly courteous speech will illustrate alike the youth and the maturity of the speaker. He said, "The high opinion we ought to maintain of the ability of these worthy gentlemen" [the retiring members of the Society] "as well as the regard they express for Linonia and her sons—tends very much to increase our desire for their longer continuance. Under whatsoever character we consider them, we have the greatest reason to regret their departure. As our patrons, we have shared their utmost care and vigilance in supporting Linonia's cause, and protecting her from the malice of her insulting foes. As our benefactors, we have partaken of their liberality, not only in their rich and valuable donations to our library, but, what is still more, their amiable company and conversation." [This is a fine portrait of Hale painted (described) by himself, says a friend of Hale today.] "But as our friends, what inexpressible happiness have we experienced in their disinterested love and cordial affection! We have lived together not as fellow students and members of the same college, but as brothers and children of the same family, not as superiors and inferiors, but rather as equals and companions. The only thing which hath given them the preeminence is their superior knowledge in those arts and sciences which are here cultivated, and their greater skill and prudence in the management of such important affairs as those which concern the good order and regularity of this Society. Under the prudent conduct of these our once worthy patrons, but now parting friends, things have been so wisely regulated, as that while we have been entertained with all the pleasures of familiar conversation, we have been no less profited by our improvements in useful knowledge and literature." Hale's direct address to the parting members is as follows, "Kind and generous Sirs, it is with the greatest reluctance that we are now all obliged to bid adieu to you, our dearest friends. Fain (gladly) would we ask you longer to tarry—but it is otherwise determined, and we must comply. Accept then our sincerest thanks, as some poor return for your disinterested zeal in Linonia's cause, and your unwearied pains to suppress her opposers.—Be assured that we shall be spirited in Linonia's cause and with steadiness and resolution strive to make her shine with unparalleled luster.—Be assured that your memory will always be very dear to us, that though hundreds of miles should interfere, you will always be attended with our best wishes. May Providence protect you in all your ways, and may you have prosperity in all your undertakings! May you live long and happily and at last die satisfied with the pleasures of this world, and go hence to that world where joys shall never cease, and pleasures never end! Dear Gentlemen, farewell!" Not only in speeches but also in deeds Hale proved his love for Linonia.

    He is said to have contributed some of his own books to the library of the Society, and to have cooperated with Timothy Dwight and James Hillhouse in promoting its growth. In time the library owned more than thirteen thousand volumes. These three Linonians were always considered its real founders, and were so honored at the Society's centennial anniversary on July 27, 1853. Timothy Dwight, the first of that name to be president of Yale College, was, like Nathan Hale, a descendant of Elder Strong who founded Northampton, Massachusetts. Dwight graduated in 1769, the year Hale entered college. He then became a tutor and was a personal friend of Hale's. He was a teacher of extraordinary power and was made president of Yale in 1795. He was one of the most remarkable men of his time, molding the moral and religious, as well as intellectual, character of the college so that his influence extended not only over the whole state but, to a great degree, over the whole United States. He was a fine illustration of the great abilities that centered in so many of the leading families of the colonists. Such connections as this man add even a higher luster to the genealogy of Elizabeth Strong Hale, and lessen our wonder that a son of hers, while hardly more than a boy, could face the duty and calmly accept the responsibility that he felt rested upon him. As may easily be inferred, the Hale boys, Enoch and Nathan, were not forgotten by their home friends while making honorable records in college, and forming pleasant friendships outside the college walls—then the happy lot of all the best men in college—among the cultured families of what was then a small New England city.

An instance of the friendships Nathan made in New Haven is shown by the words of Aeneas Munson, MD, formerly of that city. When an aged man he spoke in the warmest terms of Hale's fine qualities as he observed them when he was a boy in his father's house, and he treasured a letter to his father from Hale in 1774 which will be given farther on. Of home letters, happily a few from their father in Coventry to his two sons in college are still preserved, these prove, as no words of any stranger could, his constant and practical interest in all that concerned them.

They show us how an upright father tried to influence his boys's religious characters while distant from them, and at the same time they show the economies which even well-to-do fathers then had to exercise in providing for their sons while at college. The first letter also shows that Nathan must have entered college when fourteen years and three months old, having been born in June, 1755, and entering college in September, 1769. We here give the first letter, with all its quaint old spelling, and after it two others written during successive years. We may smile at their old-time expressions, but we must own to a sincere admiration for the kind and thoughtful father, so interested in his boys, and so solicitous concerning their health "after the measles." [Coventry, December 26th, AD 1769] DEAR CHILDREN, I received your letter of the 7th instant and am glad to hear that you are well-suited with living in college and would let you know that we are all well through the Divine Goodness, as I hope these lines will find you. I hope you will carefully mind your studies that your time be not lost and that you will mind all the orders of college with care. I intend to send you some money the first opportunity perhaps by Mr. Sherman when he returns home from of the [circuit court] he is now on. If you can hire horses at New Haven to come home without too much trouble and cost I don't know but it is best and should be glad to know how you can hire them and send me word. If I don't hear from you I shall depend upon sending horses to you by the 6th of May—if I should have known opportunity to send you any money till May and should then come to New Haven and clear all of it would it not do? If not you will let me know it. Your friends are all well at Coventry—your mother sends her regards to you—from your kind and loving father, Richard Hale. [Coventry, December 17th, 1770] DEAR CHILDREN, I have nothing special to write but would by all means desire you to mind your studies and carefully attend to the orders of college. Attend not only prayers in the chapel but secret prayer carefully. Shun all vice especially card playing. Read your Bibles a chapter night and morning. I cannot now send you much money but hope when Senior Strong comes to Coventry to be able to send by him what you want. From your loving father, Richard Hale. [Coventry August 13th, 1771] LOVING CHILDREN—by a line would let you know that I with my family through the Divine Goodness are well as I hope these lines will find you. I have heard that you are better of the measles. The cloth for your coat is not done. But will be done next week I hope at furthest. I know of no opportunity we shall have to send it to New Haven and have laid in with Mr. Strong for his horse which his son will ride down to New Haven for one of you to ride home if you can get leave and have your clothes made at home. I suppose that one measure will do for both of you. I am told that it is not good to study hard after the measles—hope you will use prudence *(cautiousness) in that affair (situation). If you do not one of you come home I don't see but that you must do without any new clothes till after commencement. I send you eight pounds (dollars) in cash by Mr. Strong—hope it will do for the present. Your loving father, Richard Hale.* Some students of today in college with elder brothers might protest vigorously at the idea of new suits provided for two boys of different sizes being fitted for the larger, though the younger might find some consolation in the fact that he would have plenty of room in which to grow! At all events, good Deacon Hale's kindly letters give us a very friendly feeling toward him, revealing as they do his love for his boys. The letters also suggest indirectly the happy homecoming of these college boys, riding thither on horseback over many miles, buoyed up by high spirits, college news, and the prospect of vacation. In their home, as time went by, they found the two new members of the family, their stepmother's daughters, Nathan to find in Alice Adams, the youngest, some of the happiest inspirations of his manly young life. It is pleasant to linger a moment and try to realize the pride Deacon Hale must have felt in his boys, and their delight in being once more home with him and with all the family circle. We can fancy them as they sat around that generous board—none the less generous, we are sure, because of the homecoming of the "Yale boys." Deacon Hale was a man of remarkable energy—"a driver," in other words. As a rule, in the busiest season of the year he would finish his meal before the family was half through theirs, rise, return thanks, and be off to the field, leaving the others to resume their seats around the table. Alice Adams used to say of him, "I never saw a man work so hard for both worlds as Deacon Hale." One amusing incident was long in circulation and laughed over by many who did not know the energetic haymaker by name. As it really happened to Deacon Hale, it is worth telling as an example of the energy that has characterized his descendants. One haying season Deacon Hale hired a tall, brawny countryman, of uncommon strength, to help him house his crop. While in the field he took upon himself the task of "packing" the load, the hired man's duty being to pitch

it onto the cart. The man began his work too slowly to suit Deacon Hale, who soon called out, "More hay!"

This call he repeated three or four times, as cock after cock (pile) of hay was still somewhat lazily pitched up to him. Finally his tardy helper, becoming sensible that his easy way of working was being rebuked, set himself to work with a will equal to the Deacon's, and at last pitched the hay up so rapidly that his employer was unable to "pack" it properly upon the cart.

Very soon, therefore, to the dismay of both men, the whole load slipped off in one great mass on to the ground, carrying the Deacon along with it! "What do you want now, Deacon?" shouted the "Hercules" by his side with a satisfied grin.—"More hay!" instantly replied the discomfited Deacon, nimbly scrambling back to his place on the cart.—Despite this little accident at the beginning of the afternoon, it is safe to state that a generous storage of hay took place before sunset. But happy as were these college days and homecomings, and rich as were the harvests gleaned in them, the four years in college halls sped swiftly, and in 1773 Enoch Hale and Nathan turned their faces toward the future, the one to a long life and faithful Christian service, the other toward the briefest of mortal days, but to a service whose memory will not end till his college walls shall have crumbled, and the names of all its heroic sons faded from the earth.—For even though stones may crumble, influence lives on.—It has already been said that at graduation Nathan Hale stood among the first thirteen in a class of thirty-six. On Commencement Day, September 3, 1773, he took part in a forensic debate on the question, "Whether the education of daughters be not, without any just reason, more neglected than that of sons." In *Memories of a Hundred Years* Dr. Edward Everett Hale says, "As early as 1772 there appears at Yale College the first question ever debated by the Linonian Society. 'Is it right to enslave the Africans?' I think, by the way, that this record, bad spelling and all, is made by my great-uncle, Nathan Hale." These debates show how seriously, even in the colonial period, men were thinking of the urgent problems of later days. In the debate first mentioned, the others taking part in it were Benjamin Tallmadge, Ezra Sampson, and William Robinson. Some account of Major Tallmadge's after life is given in later pages. Sampson was, for a time, a clergyman, and then became an editor, first in Hudson, New York, and then of the *Courant (Hartford Courant)*, at Hartford, Connecticut. William Robinson was a direct descendant of Pastor John Robinson of Leyden. He studied for the ministry and was ordained in 1780 at Southington, Connecticut.

In the winter of that year—which was one of the coldest and most severe on record—he walked the whole distance from Windsor to Southington, about thirty miles, on snowshoes, to be installed as pastor, an office he held for forty-one years.

☐☐☐☐☐☐☐☐☐☐

College days behind them, Nathan, now eighteen years old, and Enoch pressed on toward their future. Here, to some extent, we part with Enoch, catching only occasional glimpses of him in a few straggling letters to his brother. It is probable that, as he intended to enter the ministry, he soon began his theological studies. In 1775 he was licensed to preach. Nathan, however, turned toward teaching as the next step in his career. In the meantime Nathan's love for Alice Adams had not prospered. An older brother, John, had married Alice Adams's elder sister Sarah, and the mother and sister of Alice thought that she should not wait four or five years for Nathan. Perhaps they decided that two intermarriages in one family were quite enough, anyway, they induced Alice to accept the offer of a prosperous merchant of Coventry, Mr. Elijah Ripley, and a short time before Nathan's graduation her marriage had apparently terminated their personal relations. Nathan Hale was at this time an unusually good-looking young man, [possibly] almost six feet in height, well-proportioned, with broad chest, athletic, as we have seen, and with a handsome, intelligent face, blue eyes, light brown hair of a rich color, and a winning smile. These, added to a musical voice and gracious manners, gave him a personal charm that attracted all who saw him. As a teacher he combined unusual tact and manly dignity, making his discipline in school as effective as it was reasonable. He also proved to be as skillful in imparting knowledge as he had been in acquiring it, and his success as a teacher was assured from the outset. His first school was in East Haddam, Connecticut. There was then much wealth and business activity in the town, although, to a man fresh from college and the city, it appeared to be a very quiet place, as one or two of his early letters indicate. Yet there too he did with all his might what his hands found to do, and soon proved that not only his work, but his social qualities, were endearing him to new friends, some of whom remembered him with pleasure during their own long lives, one of them saying of Nathan Hale in her own old age, "Everybody loved him, he was so sprightly, intelligent, and kind," and, she added withal, "and so handsome!" He had many correspondents among classmates and friends. Sometimes he was stimulated to put his thoughts into rhyme by some poetical epistle he received. One such was from Benjamin Tallmadge, then in Wethersfield. Tallmadge had apologized for his muse and Hale, in pure boyish fun, with a fine disregard of whether he was invoking the muse or mounting Pegasus, replied as follows, "But here, I think you're wrong, to blame your generous muse and call her lame, for when arrived no mark was found of weakness, lameness, sprain or wound." Then, invoking her himself, he describes her as if she were indeed the winged steed, "With me in charge (a grievous load) along the way she lately trode, in all, she gave no fear or pain, unless, at times, to hold the rein."

At last, on his supposed arrival at Wethersfield, he invites Tallmadge's judgment on the appearance of the equine muse, thus, "Now judge, unless entirely sound if she could bear me such a round. It's certain then your muse is healed, or else, came sound from Wethersfield." Before the end of the first term (October, 1773, to mid-March, 1774) in East Haddam, however, his work had aroused attention elsewhere, and in May, 1774, he took charge of a school in New London, called the "Union School"—a larger school and a more lucrative position than that at East Haddam. In it Latin, English, arithmetic, and writing were taught. The salary was seventy pounds a year with a prospect of an increase, and he was allowed to teach private classes as well. It will not surprise those acquainted with human nature that, as we will allow him to tell in a letter to a relative, he soon had a class of some twenty young ladies between the unusual hours of five and seven in the morning! It does not take a very vivid imagination to picture the vivacity of these twenty young ladies, the becomingness of their simple but pretty gowns, and the zest with which each studied, nor, on the other hand, the ill-concealed, bantering interest of the big brothers of the same—asking perhaps, now and then, with mock gravity, if mother thought "Patty" would be so prompt every morning at five o'clock if old Parson Browning were the teacher! But whatever might have been the dominant interest of the young ladies, "Master Hale" was quite as practical in his teaching in the early hours of the day as with the boys in the later classes. An uncle of his, Samuel Hale, was for many years at the head of the best private school in New Hampshire, numbering among his pupils some of the leaders in Revolutionary times.

To him, September 24, 1774, Nathan wrote a letter from which we give the following extracts, "*My own employment is at present the same that you have spent your days in. I have a school of thirty-two boys, about half Latin, the rest English. The salary allowed me is 70 £ per annum. In addition to this I have kept, during the summer, a morning school, between the hours of five and seven, of about 20 young ladies for which I have received 6 [shillings] a scholar, by the quarter. Many of the people are gentleman of sense and merit. They are desirous that I would continue and settle in the school, and propose a considerable increase in wages. I am much at a loss whether to accept their proposals. Your advice in this matter, coming from an uncle and from a man who has spent his life in the business, would, I think, be the best I could possibly receive. A few lines on this subject and also to acquaint me with the welfare of your family—will be much to the satisfaction of your most dutiful nephew, Nathan Hale.*" A letter to Enoch Hale, containing allusions to the excited feeling in the colony at this time, runs as follows. [New London, September 8th

1774] DEAR BROTHER, I have a word to write and a moment to write it in. I received yours of yesterday this morning. Agreeable to your desire I will endeavor to get the cloth and carry it on Saturday. I have no news. No liberty pole is erected or erecting here, but the people seem much more spirited than they did before the alarm. Parson [Samuel] Peters of Hebron, [Connecticut] I hear has had a second visit paid him by the sons of liberty in Windham [New York]. His treatment, and the concessions he made I have not as yet heard. I have not heard from home since I came from there. Your loving brother, Nathan Hale. A letter from Hale to his friend the senior Dr. Aeneas Munson of New Haven has been mentioned. It runs as follows. [New London, November 30, 1774] SIR, I am very happily situated here. I love my employment, find many friends among strangers, have time for scientific study and seem to fill the place assigned me with satisfaction. I have a school of more than thirty boys (students) to instruct, about half of them in Latin, and my salary is satisfactory. During the summer I had a morning class of young ladies—about a score—from five to seven o'clock, so you see my time is pretty fully occupied profitably, I hope to my pupils and to their teacher. Please accept for yourself and Mrs. Munson [Susanna Howell] the grateful thanks of one who will always remember the kindness he ever experienced whenever he visited your abode. Your friend, Nathan Hale. On one occasion, as Hale left his house after paying a visit, Dr. Munson observed, "That man is a diamond of the first water, calculated to excel in any station he assumes. He is a gentleman and a scholar, and last, though not least of his qualifications, a Christian." The son of Dr. Munson (who bore his father's name), when an aged man, said, "I was greatly impressed with Hale's scientific knowledge, evinced during his conversation with my father. I am sure he was equal to [John] Andre in solid acquirements, and his taste for art and talents as an artist were quite remarkable. His personal appearance was as notable. He was almost six feet in height, perfectly proportioned, and in figure and deportment he was the most-manly man I have ever met. His chest was broad, his muscles were firm, his face wore a most benign expression, his complexion was roseate, his eyes were light blue and beamed with intelligence, his hair was soft and light brown in color, and his speech was rather low, sweet, and musical. His personal beauty and grace of manner were most charming. Why, all the girls in New Haven fell in love with him," continued Dr. Munson, "and wept tears of real sorrow when they heard of his sad fate. In dress he was always neat, he was quick to lend a helping hand to a being in distress, brute or human, was overflowing with good humor, and was the idol of all his acquaintances." Young masters of schools, public or private, unmarried and attractive, usually rank next in popularity to other professional men—ministers, lawyers, or doctors, as the case may be—and a boy of nineteen, the object of as much attention as Nathan Hale must have received, might well be pardoned if his head had been slightly turned, in thus becoming the admired teacher of a large class of young ladies. One special mark of stability of character appears to have characterized this young man in a greater degree than is always the case at the present day. Detached as he was, as he supposed irrevocably, from the woman he loved, he appears to have carried himself with almost middle-aged dignity, and, what is not a little to his credit, even his intimate friends among his classmates could not, by the most delicate cross-questioning, draw from him anything suggesting more than a pleasant interest in any of the young ladies with whom he was thrown in contact. A letter that will be given in its proper place shows his courteous and cordial interest in the little city he left when he entered the army, yet it is rather a noteworthy fact that one of his classmates, writing to him during his camp life, had to suggest that, as the young ladies he had taught were always inquiring when he had heard from "Master," it would doubtless give them pleasure if he could find time to write some one of them a note with friendly messages to others, to show that he still remembered them. Many young men would hardly have needed such a suggestion. But Nathan Hale, so far as we can learn, while given to warm friendships among his classmates, and to the cultivation, while in New Haven, Haddam, and New London, of the society of the best families, appears, from the beginning, to have taken life seriously. Disappointed in the love of the one woman for whom he cared, he had turned with sincere absorption to the work to which he felt himself called before entering on the theological course it is thought that his father had planned for him. There is further evidence of Hale's notable gifts as a teacher. Colonel Samuel Green, who had been a pupil of Hale in New London, said of him, in old-time phrase, "Hale was a man peculiarly engaging in his manners—these were mild and genteel. The scholars, old and young, were attached to him. They loved him for his tact and amiability. He was wholly without severity and had a wonderful control over boys. He was sprightly, ardent, and steady bore a fine moral character and was respected highly by all his acquaintances. The school in which he taught was owned by the first gentlemen in New London, all of whom were exceedingly gratified by Hale's skill and assiduity." A lady of New London, who was for some time an inmate of the same family with Hale, adds her testimony, "His capacity as a teacher was highly appreciated both by parents and pupils. His simple and unostentatious manner of imparting right views and feelings to less cultivated understandings was unsurpassed by any other person I have ever known." He was, as we see, a successful teacher, and, as we learn elsewhere, had serious thoughts of remaining a teacher. Unexpectedly, however, events verified the truth of the old adage, "Man proposes God disposes." A great historical drama was to be enacted before the eyes of the wondering world, and events were ripening that were to form a great epoch in history. America was being led first to protest against the unjust exactions laid upon its people, and then to resist the oppressions that were being forced upon it.

Gradually the idea prevailed that a taxation which might have been acceptable, if coupled with representation in Parliament, was absolutely intolerable without representation, and the Stamp Act in 1765 struck the first note of intense opposition. Thenceforward the political clouds grew darker and the warning incidents multiplied. And yet, as a people, Americans were walking as if their personal plans lay easily in their own control. Scores of young men were fitting themselves for ordinary callings, Nathan Hale among them. His father's plans combining with his own appeared to be that he was to teach for a while, and then follow his brother Enoch into the ministry. As it proved, his days as a teacher were numbered. He was never to enter a pulpit, though he was to utter one sentence that, graven upon bronze or granite, will last while America lasts. He was to teach, by his last, unpremeditated words, and by an example more potent than any other in American history, what all generations of Americans must venerate—the sublimity of a complete sacrifice. Smoldering discontent on the part of the Americans, waxing stronger and stronger for a decade, and the aggressive course of action on the part of the British authorities, finally culminated in a sudden outbreak, as matches applied to gunpowder, and on the 19th of April, 1775, the first blood of the American Revolution was shed. Settlement after settlement, big and little, learned the facts as rapidly as couriers on horseback could carry them, and the thirteen colonies arrayed themselves against one of the most powerful monarchies of the world. The story is too well-known to need recalling here, save as it draws Nathan Hale toward his doom. Within a few days after the fatal 19th of April, four thousand Connecticut volunteers were on their way to Boston to help Massachusetts in its earliest struggle with the English.

    Un-uniformed, undisciplined, straight from whatever had been their ordinary vocation, with whatever they owned in the way of arms and ammunition, they went hurrying toward Boston. Israel Putnam, renowned veteran of the "Old French War," was plowing in his fields at Pomfret, Connecticut, when he heard the stirring news. Leaving his plow in the furrow, he hastened to his house, left a few orders for the management of his farm and the comfort of his family, and marched at the head of a body of volunteers toward the camp near Boston. We are told that, in some households, families sat up all night, the fathers melting their pewter plates into bullets for ammunition to be used by their sons, and the mothers and sisters fashioning for them, with all possible speed, the clothing they could not go without. On the arrival of the news from Boston, the people in New London at once held a meeting. Honorable Richard Law, District Judge of Connecticut and Chief Justice of the Superior Court, was chairman. Hale was one of the speakers. At that meeting a company was selected from the already existing militia and ordered to start for Boston the next morning. This company Nathan Hale, with his keen sense of duty, could not then join. But, for a few succeeding weeks, in addition to his regular work in school, he did all in his power to keep alive the interest of the young men in the town concerning their duties as Americans.

With his enthusiastic nature, and broad comprehension of what might soon confront the country, it is probable that his seriousness and his activity were never greater than during the few weeks intervening between his speech at the political meeting and his departure from New London to enter the military service of his country. Of course his becoming a soldier would greatly interfere with the plans that his father had made for him, and he at once wrote home on the subject, stating that "a sense of duty urged him to sacrifice everything for his country" but he added that as soon as the war was ended he would comply with his father's wishes in regard to a profession. The father was quite as patriotic as the son. He immediately assented to his son's desires. In those days, however, correspondence could not be conducted so swiftly as at present, and some time must have elapsed before this matter was positively settled between the two. As the war went on, and doubtless none the less wholeheartedly after the news of Nathan's death had been received, Mr. Hale did all he could for the comfort of passing soldiers. It is said of him that many a time he sat at the door of his hospitable home and watched for passing soldiers that he might take them in and feed them, and, if necessary, lodge and clothe them. He often forbade his household "to use the wool raised upon his farm for home purposes, that it might be woven into blankets for the army." Anxious as had been young Hale to join the army, he appears to have deferred making any decided plans until he had received the necessary permission from his father. Having received it, he at once took steps for securing his dismissal from his school and his admission into the army. During the weeks of waiting it had become known that he was anxious to enlist, and a military appointment was waiting his acceptance. To secure his dismissal, on July 7 he addressed the following letter to the proprietors of his school—a letter that for a young man of twenty is as dignified as it is patriotic. *GENTLEMEN, having received information that a place is allotted me in the army, and being inclined, as I hope for good reasons, to accept it, I am constrained to ask as a favor that which scarce anything else would have induced me to, which is, to be excused from keeping your school any longer. For the purpose of conversing upon this and of procuring another master, some of your number thinks it best there should be a general meeting of the proprietors. The time talked of for holding it is six o'clock this afternoon, at the schoolhouse. The year for which I engaged will expire within a fortnight, so that my quitting a few days sooner, I hope, will subject you to no great inconvenience. School keeping (teaching) is a business of which I was always fond, but since my residence in this town, everything has conspired to render it more agreeable. I have thought much of never quitting it but with life, but at present there seems an opportunity for more extended public service. The kindness expressed to me by the people of the place, but especially the proprietors of the school, will always be very gratefully remembered by, gentlemen, with respect, your humble servant, Nathan Hale.*

☐☐☐☐☐☐☐☐☐☐☐

The place "allotted" to him was that of lieutenant in the third company of the 7th Connecticut regiment, commanded by Colonel Charles Webb. No doubt exists that Lieutenant Nathan Hale was the same Nathan Hale who had won distinction in all his college work, in his subsequent teaching, and in all the events thus far associated with his early manhood, with this difference, he was now lifted to a line of service that in his opinion seemed the highest possible for him to follow, and no one who studies his subsequent course can question that in this following he found the loftiest consecration thus far possible to him. Perhaps unconsciously he was to verify the poet's assertion, "So nigh is grandeur to our dust, so near is God to man, when duty whispers low, thou must, the youth replies, I can." With no trace of merely personal ambition, but with that splendid power of absorption in duty as in work, Nathan Hale followed in the steps of those devoted American patriots whose blood, so freely shed at Lexington, was calling upon their countrymen to shed theirs as freely, should duty demand it. Dead almost one hundred and forty years, we still are thrilled by proofs of the splendid manhood henceforth to be so prominent in every remaining day of Hale's brief life. A few letters to friends, a fairly comprehensive diary for a few months, his camp book, and the recollections of a few of the officers and of his body servant, give a moderately complete picture of Nathan Hale for a few brief weeks, during which time he had been doing all in his power to perfect himself and the men under him in the duties of soldiers. By the middle of September the Connecticut troops, having received orders from General Washington to proceed to the camp near Boston, the 7th Regiment, containing Lieutenant Hale's company, went to the spot appointed, remaining there during the winter, and leaving for New York, again by Washington's orders, in the spring.

Of these intervening months, so momentous to the little army whose many members were impatient for the close of the war, Nathan Hale himself gives us vivid pictures, of the work he was trying to do, of the men he was meeting, of the religious life he was in no sense forgetting, and of his own deepening patriotism. Letters written to him show the attitude of friends at home, and their interest both in the affairs of the country and in him personally. The following letter [below] from Gilbert Saltonstall, a young Harvard graduate and warm friend of Hale while in New London, shows how fully the men at home, as well as those in the army, entered into the anxieties of the times.

[New London, October 9th, 1775] DEAR SIR, by yours of the 5th I see you're stationed in the mouth of danger—I look upon *your situation more perilous than any other in the camp—should have thought the new recruits would have been posted at some of the outworks, and those that have been inured (accustomed) to service advanced to defend the most exposed places—but all things are concerted, and ordered with wisdom no doubt—the affair (spying) of Dr. Church is truly amazing—from the acquaintance I have of his public character I should as soon have suspected Mr. Hancock or Adams as him.* [Of this Dr. Church (Surgeon General of the United States Army during the American Revolution, John Fiske writes] "In October, 1775, the American camp was thrown into great consternation by the discovery that Dr. Benjamin Church, one of the most conspicuous of the Boston leaders, had engaged in a secret correspondence with the enemy. Dr. Church was thrown into jail, but as the evidence of treasonable intent was not absolutely complete, he was set free in the following spring, and allowed to visit the West Indies for his health. The ship in which he sailed was never heard from again." [He is listed as dead in 1778.] Then follow accounts of an affair (spying by Dr. Church) on Long Island Sound, and extracts from a paper two days old just brought from New York, describing army matters in the North. "I have extracted all the material news—should have sent the paper but it's the only one in town and everyone is gaping for news, your sincere friend, Gilbert Saltonstall." Another, also from Saltonstall, reads in part as follows.

[November 27th 1775] ESTEEMED FRIEND, *Doctor Church is in close custody in Norwich Gaol (jail), the windows boarded up, and he denied the use of pen, ink, and paper, to have no converse with any person but in presence of the Gaoler (jailer), and then to converse in no language but English. What a fall. Your and etc, Gilbert Saltonstall.* A letter already referred to as showing Hale's interest in New London and its people, also his feeling as to camp life, is here given. "Betsey" was one of his pupils in his early morning classes. Note the little touch of good-natured fun in the last paragraph. [To Betsey Christophers at New London—Camp Winter Hill—October 19th 1775] DEAR BETSEY, *I hope you will excuse my freedom in writing to you, as I cannot have the pleasure* of seeing and conversing with you. What is now a letter would be a visit were I in New London but this being out of my power, suffer me to make up the defect in the best manner I can. I write not to give you any news or any pleasure in reading (though I would heartily do it if in my power) but from the desire I have of conversing with you in some form or other. I once wanted to come here to see something extraordinary—my curiosity is satisfied. I have now no more desire for seeing things here, than for seeing what is in New London, no, nor half so much neither. Not that I am discontented—so far from it, that in the present situation of things I would not except a furlough were it offered me. I would only observe that we often flatter ourselves with great happiness could we see such and such things, but when we actually come to the sight of them our solid satisfaction is really no more than when we only had them in expectation. All the news I had I wrote to John Hallam—if it be worth your hearing he will be able to tell you when he delivers this. It will therefore not (be) worthwhile for me to repeat. I am a little at a loss how you carry at New London—Jared Starr I hear is gone. The number of Gentlemen is now so few that I fear how you will go through the winter but I hope for the best. I remain with esteem your sincere friend, and humble servant, Nathan Hale.

The next letter refers to the time when, on account of their personal privations (extreme poverty), the Connecticut troops were thinking seriously of withdrawing from the struggle (military life and army service) and returning to their homes.

[New London, December 4th 1775] DEAR SIR, the behavior of our Connecticut troops makes me heartsick—that they who have stood foremost in the praises and good wishes of their countrymen, as having distinguished themselves for their zeal and public spirit, should now shamefully desert the cause, and at a critical moment too, is really unaccountable—amazing. Those that do return will meet with real contempt, with deserved reproach. It gives great satisfaction that the officers universally agree to tarry—that is the report, is it true or not?—May that God who has signally appeared for us since the commencement of our troubles, interpose, that no fatal or bad consequence may attend a dastardly desertion of his cause. I want much to have a more minute account of the situation of the camp than I have been able to obtain. I rely wholly on you for information, your Gilbert Saltonstall. To explain some of Saltonstall's references to the feelings of some of the Connecticut troops, we quote from Captain Hale's diary of October 23, "10 o'clock went to Cambridge with field commission officers to General Putman to let him know the state of the regiment and that it was through ill usage upon the score of provisions that they would not extend their term of service to the 1st of January 1776."

Other letters to Hale from New London friends, among them one from an officer absent on furlough, speak freely of the anxieties of those watching the progress of the reenlistments, and the home reception that would be given to any leaving the army. Another letter from Saltonstall reads as follows.

[New London, December 18th 1775] DEAR SIR, I wholly agree with you in ye agreeables of a camp life, and should have tried it in some capacity or other before now, could my father carry on his business without me. I proposed going with Dudley (possibly Dudley Saltonstall), who is appointed to commission a twenty gunship in the Continental Navy, but my father is not willing, and I can't persuade myself to leave him in the eve of life against his consent. Yesterday week the town was in the greatest confusion imaginable, women wringing their hands along street, children crying, carts loaded 'till nothing more would stick on, posting out of town, empty ones driving in, one person running this way, another that, some dull, some vexed, more pleased, some flinging up an entrenchment, some at the Fort preparing ye guns for action, drums beating, fife's playing, in short as great a hubbub as at the confusion of tongues, all of this occasioned by the appearance of a ship and two sloops off the harbor, supposed to be part of Wallace's Fleet. When they were found to be friends, vessels from Newport with passengers ye consternation abated. [A postscript runs as follows.] The young girls, B. Coit, S. and P. Belden [Hale's pupils] have frequently desired their compliments to Master, but I've never thought of mentioning it till now. You must write something in your next by way of P. S. that I may show it them. Favored by copies of these letters by Saltonstall, one must regret all the more that so few of Hale's own letters have been discovered, ten being the limit. Within a comparatively short period, however, some sixty more records—mostly letters written to Hale—have come to light, preserved, as it is now seen, by the same "orderly care" that marked his interest in all the correspondence of his friends.

In them are expressed, in letter after letter, the affectionate interest and warm admiration of the writers. It is now said that Hale kept these letters with him down to the date of his tragic mission. We can easily imagine the glow of satisfaction that must have filled his brotherly soul in the few spare moments he could devote to these letters.

Brief extracts are made from his diary, fortunately preserved for evidence as to his work and growing interest in the duties he had entered upon. The diary was found in the camp book brought to his family by Asher Wright, Hale's attendant in camp before he left New York. In the diary, under date of November 19, 1775, this entry is made, "*Robert Latimer, the Major's son went to Roxbury today on his way home. The Major who went there today and returned this evening but accounts that the HMS Asia, man-of-war, stationed at New York was taken by a schooner armed with spears and etc. This account not credited.*" A month after the return from camp mentioned above, Robert Latimer wrote to Captain Hale, his former teacher, the following interesting and diverting letter. [December 20th 1775] *DEAR SIR, as I think myself under the greatest obligations to you for your care and kindness to me, I should think myself very ungrateful if I neglected any opportunity of expressing my gratitude to you for the same. And I rely on that goodness, I have so often experienced to overlook the deficiencies in my letter, which I am sensible will be many as maturity of judgment is wanting, and though I have been so happy as to be favored with your instructions, you can't sir, expect a finished letter from one who has as yet practiced but very little this way, especially with persons of your nice discernment. Sir, I have had the pleasure of hearing by the soldiers, which is come home, that you are in health, though likely to be deserted by all the* men you carried down with you, which I am very sorry for, as I think no man of any spirit would desert a cause in which, we are all so deeply interested. I am sure was my mammy willing I think I should prefer being with you, to all the pleasures which the company of my relations can afford me. I am sir with respect, your sincere friend and very humble servant, Robert Latimer. [P. S.] My mammy and Aunt Lamb, presents compliments. My mammy would have wrote, but being very busy, thought my writing would be sufficient—my respects to Captain Hull. (Addressed to Captain Hale) Here is a second letter from the same ardent friend (Robert Latimer) of Captain Hale. His admiration for his former teacher is evident in every line. [New London March 5th 1776] DEAR SIR, as my letter meet with such kind reception from you, I still continue writing and hope that the desire I have of improving, added to the pleasure, I take in hearing often from so good a friend, will sufficiently excuse me for writing so often—I received your kind letter sir, per the post and can't deny but your approbation, of my writing, gives me the greatest pleasure, and should be afraid of its raising my pride, did I not consider that your intention in praising my poor performance, must be with a design, of raising in me an ambition, to endeavor to deserve your praise—and I hope that instructions conveyed in such an agreeable manner, will not, be thrown away upon me—you write sir that you have got another fifer, and a very good one too, as I hear, which I am very glad to hear, though I sincerely wish I was in his place—have not any news. So will conclude—I am servant with respect your friend and student, Robert Latimer. [P. S.] My mammy and aunt present compliments and etc. Only one thought dims the pleasure with which we read these two letters—the consciousness of the depth of distress that must have filled that loyal boy's heart to overflowing when he learned of the tragic death of his hero friend. Two notable records from Captain Hale's diary are these. "November 6.—*It is of the utmost importance that an officer should be anxious to know his duty, but of greater that he should carefully perform what he does know. The present irregular state of the army is owing to capital neglect in both of these.* November 7.—*Studied ye best method of forming a regiment for a* review, of arraying the companies, also of marching round ye reviewing officer. A man ought never to lose a moment's time. If he put off a thing from one minute to the next, his reluctance is but increased." Later in November, when the men in his company were unwilling to reenlist, this notable entry was made, signed with his full name. "28 Tuesday.—*Promised the men if they would tarry another month, they should have my wages for that time.* Nathan Hale." These brief quotations, proving as they do Hale's intense devotion to duty, and his practical efforts to hold his men to their duty, show how clearly he understood the tremendous responsibility resting upon the commander-in-chief as given in Washington's own words in letters to friends and to Congress, soon to be quoted, and that, known or unknown to Washington, there were men among his officers fully aware of the condition of the army, and as anxious to serve it as was their magnificent leader. We here quote from Washington's letters, the first one was written to a friend. "*I know the unhappy predicament in which I stand, I know that much is expected of me, I know that without men, without arms, without ammunition, without anything fit for the accommodation of a soldier, little is to be done, and what is mortifying, I know that I cannot stand justified to the world without exposing my own weakness, and injuring the cause, by declaring my wants which I am determined not to do farther than unavoidable necessity brings every man acquainted with them. My situation is so irksome to me at times, that if I did not consult the public good more than my own tranquility, I should long ere this have put everything on the cast of a die. So far from my having an army of twenty thousand men, well-armed, I have been here with less than half that number, including sick, furloughed, and on command, and those neither armed nor clothed as they should be. In short, my situation has been such, that I have been obliged to conceal it from my own officers.*" The second letter was written to Congress, "*To make men well-acquainted with the duties of a soldier, requires time. To bring them under proper discipline and subordination, not only requires time, but is a work of great difficulty, and in this army where there is so little distinction between officers and soldiers requires an uncommon degree of attention. To expect, then, the same service from raw and undisciplined recruits, as from veteran soldiers, is to expect what never did, and perhaps never will happen.*" On the 23rd of December, 1775, Hale began his first and only trip to Connecticut for the sake of securing additional enlistments. If on this one visit home he became engaged—as some have believed—to the woman he had so long loved, now a widow of about nineteen, Alice Adams Ripley, we may infer that love brightened his embassy even though patriotism inspired it. No record remains of the glorified hours he may have spent in Coventry. We have good reason to believe that, if he survived the war, he expected to marry the woman he had so faithfully loved. After a few brief days in his home, he left it, never to return, speeding on his way to serve his country's needs. If this new zest entered his life at this time, we can easily imagine as he fared on, striving to arouse his countrymen to their duty as patriots, that the happiest hours of his life were urging him forward to the most perfect service he could render in the present, and to unlimited hopes and ambitions for the future he might well expect was awaiting him. Crowned by human love, and with unlimited opportunities to serve his country, who can tell by what "vision splendid" he was "on his way attended?" Who can help rejoicing that such days, brief as they were, and uplifting as they must have been, were given to this man, now past twenty? Details concerning that trip are scanty. We know for a certainty that, starting from camp December 23, 1775, he returned to it the last week in January, 1776, having been in New London and other places seeking recruits, and going back with the recruits he himself had secured, joined by others coming from the various towns in Connecticut, and all heading toward the camp around Boston. He received his commission as captain in the new army in January, being still in Colonel Webb's regiment, which now became the nineteenth of the Continental Army. For a few weeks he followed the routine of his earlier months there, doing all that was possible to assist his brother officers in perfecting the discipline of the raw troops, deepening their patriotism, and proving himself a soldier, as devoid of fear as he was rich in all manly qualities. Not a word of regret can be found in his diary.

Acknowledging in a letter to a former pupil, Miss Betsey Christophers of New London, that the novelty and glamour of camp life had worn off, he asserts, with intense ardor, that nothing would tempt him to "accept a furlough" or shrink in any manner from any of his duties as a soldier. And so the weeks passed on. During the winter heavy cannon from Fort Ticonderoga had been brought through the snows over the Green Mountains. The cannon were placed on Dorchester Heights which commanded the British camp, thus compelling the British general to choose between attacking the American army and evacuating the city. In a letter written in April, 1776, to his half-brother, John Augustine, Washington wrote thus regarding this time, "The enemy—apprehending great annoyance from our new works, resolved upon a retreat, and accordingly, on the 17th (March) embarked in as much hurry, precipitation and confusion as ever troops did—leaving the King's property in Boston to the amount, as is supposed, of thirty or forty thousand pounds in provisions and stores." Washington's victory in this maneuver, his first great success, tremendously cheered the hearts of all patriotic Americans. Congress gave him a vote of thanks, also a gold medal—"the first in the history of independent America"—in commemoration of the event. Here again we catch a glimpse of the delight that must have thrilled the hearts of all his officers, not least among them that of Nathan Hale. But Washington, proving himself in these earlier events, as he was to, year after year, through successive discouragements (lack of confidence) "the first in war" turned toward New York as his next base.

In the letter just quoted, Washington wrote further, "Whether they [the enemy] are now bound, I know not, but as New York and Hudson's River are the most important objects they can have in view—therefore as soon as they embarked, I detached a brigade of six regiments to that government and when they sailed another brigade composed of the same number, and tomorrow another brigade of five regiments will march. In a day or two more, I shall follow myself, and be in New York ready to receive all but the first." Uncertain as to his power to hold New York, Washington promptly took the next step that appeared open to him, carrying in his heart a heavy weight of care, and realizing, as perhaps no other man did, that only divine assistance could give him final success.—He was bent upon a desperate mission, but to it, with sublime patience, he gave every energy of his masterly mind, and the entire consecration of all that he possessed.—Well, was it for him that the power which controls nations was quietly working with him. Well, also, that in his army were men ready for any enterprise of danger, for any sacrifice that duty might demand. Washington proceeded to New York, to ultimate victory, to final and permanent fame. Nathan Hale went also, simply as a captain of a Connecticut company—he not to victory, not to immediate fame, but to something higher in one sense than either victory or fame and to a service well-worth a man's doing. Nathan Hale belonged to the first brigade dispatched to New York—that of General Heath.

After rapid marching, considering the state of the roads, "Hale found himself" (March 26th) "for the third time" among his New London friends. The next day they "embarked in high spirits on fifteen transports and sailed for New York."

On March 30th the troops "disembarked at Turtle Bay, a convenient landing place" near what is now East 45th Street. Not far from that spot, within six months, Nathan Hale was to win a victory that time can never dim, even if, for a time, it appeared to have covered his memory with a pall. But in that landing day no shadows were apparent—only hope, and the zest inevitable in a soldier's life. A minor honor was soon to come to Nathan Hale.

Late in 1775 Enoch Hale was licensed to preach. In the summer of 1776 he attended Commencement at New Haven, from July 23 to 26. He makes note in his diary of friends and classmates whom he saw, also that he obtained the degree of Master of Arts for Nathan and himself. Of the latter his record states, "Write to brother to tell him I have got him his degree." One or two more letters of Hale are extant from which only partial extracts have been made. One that was written on the 3rd of June, 1776, we give with more fullness, omitting only some unimportant clauses. This letter has especial value as an illustration of the fact that most of us now and then have received letters that seemed casual in themselves, but have, to our surprise and often to our deep sadness, proved to be farewell letters. It is not probable that, in the hurried days that followed, further messages were sent to his grandmother, to his former pastor and beloved teacher, Mr. [Joseph] Huntington, and to his sister Rose [Elizabeth Hale Rose] and her family. In the late autumn of 1776, after they had learned his fate, and in the years that followed, one can easily imagine how precious seemed these appreciative words, embalming as it were the abiding affection of the man who wrote them. Hale's reference to "the Doctor" also recalls the fact that, from the immediate family of Deacon Richard Hale, five men—three sons, one stepson, and [also] one son-in-law (surgeon Samuel Rose)—entered the Revolutionary Army, one son dying in 1776, one son in 1784, his health having been ruined while in the service, and one son in 1802, his life perhaps shortened by his exposures [to war]. Whatever else may have been lacking in that one family, patriotism certainly was not deficient—the patriotism that does not count the cost to one's self, but the gain to one's country. The following is the letter referred to, written to his brother Enoch. [New York, June 3rd 1776] *DEAR BROTHER, Your favor of the 9th of May and another written at Norwich I have received—the first mentioned one the 19th of May ultimo (previous). You complain of my neglecting you—it is not, I acknowledge, wholly without reason—at the same time I am conscious to have written to you more than once or twice within this half year. Perhaps my letters have miscarried. Continuance or removal here depends wholly upon the operations of the war. It gives pleasure to every friend of his country to observe the health which prevails in our army. Dr. Eli (Surgeon of our Regiment) told me a few days since, there was not a man in our*

Regiment but might upon occasion go out with his firelock. Much the same is said of other Regiments. The army is improving in discipline, and it is hoped will soon be able to meet the enemy at any kind of play. My company which at first was small is now increased to eighty and there is a sergeant recruiting who, I hope, has got the other ten which completes the company. We are hardly able to judge as to the numbers the British army for the summer is to consist of—undoubtedly sufficient to cause us too much bloodshed. I had written you a complete letter in answer to your last, but missed the opportunity of sending it. This will find you in Coventry—if so remember me to all my friends—particularly belonging to the family. Forget not frequently to visit and strongly to represent my duty to our good Grandmother Strong. Has she not repeatedly favored us with her tender, most important advice? The natural tie is sufficient, but increased by so much goodness, our gratitude cannot be too sensible. I always with respect remember Mr. Huntington and shall write to him if time admits. Pay Mr. Wright a visit for me. Tell him Asher is well—he has for some time lived with me as a waiter. Asher this moment told me that our brother Joseph Adams was here yesterday to see me, when I happened to be out of the way. He is in Colonel Parson's Regiment. I intend to see him today and if possible by exchanging get him into my company. Yours affectionately, Nathan Hale. [P. S.] Sister Rose talked of making me some linen cloth similar to brown Holland (linen) for summer wear. If she has made it, desire her to keep it for me. My love to her, the Doctor [Samuel Rose], and little Joseph.

As Washington had supposed probable, the English decided upon the occupation of New York. In July and August the largest army ever collected in one body upon the American continent prior to 1861, an English (British) army numbering nearly thirty-two thousand men, with a formidable fleet and large munitions of war, gathered at Staten Island. Washington, in the meantime, was occupying a portion of Brooklyn and a portion of the city of New York, fortifying each place and preparing to defend it to the extent of his ability with his small army, never so well-fed—nor so thoroughly disciplined as that of the British.

Human wisdom would have assumed that the British army would soon succeed in restoring English control, but the best-laid plans miscarry, and a power interposes that helps the weaker and hinders the stronger army. The English did their best to be ready for the coming conflict, and we know that Washington spared no pains in preparing for the worst that might come. On August 20, Nathan Hale wrote the following letter to his brother Enoch—the last letter that he ever wrote, so far as we know, to reach its destination. It shows that his heart was absorbed in the duties of the conflict he was sharing, and it also shows how wholly he was leaving the ultimate issue to a higher power. [New York, August 20, 1776] *DEAR BROTHER, I have only time for a hasty letter. Our situation this fortnight or more has been such as scarce to admit of writing. We have daily expected an action—by which means, if anyone was going and we had letters written, orders were so strict for our tarrying in camp that we could rarely get leave to go and deliver them. For about 6 or 8 days the enemy have been expected hourly, whenever the wind and tide in the least favored. We keep a particular lookout for them this morning. The place and manner of our attack time must determine. The event we leave to Heaven. Thanks to God! We have had time for completing our works and receiving our reinforcements. The militia of Connecticut ordered this way, are mostly arrived. Colonel Ward's Regiment has got in. Troops from the southward are daily coming. We hope under God to give account of the enemy whenever they choose to make the last appeal. Last Friday night, two of our fire vessels (a sloop and schooner) made an attempt upon the shipping up the river. The night was too dark, the wind too slack for the attempt. The schooner which was intended for one of the ships had got by before she discovered them, but as Providence would have it, she run athwart, a bomb catch, which she quickly burned. The sloop by the light of the former discovered the HMS Phoenix—but rather too late—however she made shift to grapple her, but the wind not proving sufficient to bring her close alongside, or drive the flames immediately on board, the Phoenix after much difficulty got her clear by cutting her own rigging. Sergeant Fosdick, who* commanded the above sloop, and four of his hands were of my company, the remaining two were of this Regiment. The General has been pleased to reward their bravery with forty dollars each except the last man that quitted the fire sloop who had fifty. Those on board the schooner received the same. I must write to some of my other brothers lest you should not be at home. Remain, your friend and etc., brother Nathan Hale. Aside from this letter, the following brief quotations from his diary are all that remain to us in the handwriting of Nathan Hale. Till he lays down his pen for the last time we see him absorbed in the cares and duties of the life about him, fearlessly facing whatever remains to him of life and service. "August 21st. *Heavy storm at night.—Much and heavy Thunder.—Captain Van Wyke, and a Lieutenant and Ensign of Colonial McDougall's Regiment killed by a shock.—Likewise one man in town, belonging to a Militia Regiment of Connecticut.—The storm continued for two or three hours, for the greatest part of which time [there] was a perpetual lightning, and the sharpest I ever knew. 22nd. Thursday. The enemy landed some troops down at the Narrows on Long Island. 23rd. Friday. Enemy landed more troops. News that they had marched up and taken Station near Flatbush, their [advance guards] being on this side near the woods—that some of our riflemen attacked and drove them back from their post, burnt 2 stacks of hay, and it was thought killed some of them—this about 12 o'clock at night. Our troops attacked them at their station near [Flatbush], routed and drove them back 1½ miles.*" One of the facts most perplexing to General Washington was what appeared to be Sir William Howe's delay in making an attack. Indeed, to an outsider unfamiliar with military tactics, Howe's conduct resembles the cruel pleasure a cat sometimes takes in tormenting a mouse that it knows cannot escape. The uncertainty as to what the next British move might be caused much anxiety. Remembering that Howe's force had arrived the last of June, one sees how leisurely must have been his preparations for attack, and how assured his hope of victory.

The expected attack occurred on August 27. The Americans were defeated and driven within their works, their losses being great, especially in prisoners. The Nineteenth Regiment was held in reserve, but Captain [William] Hull wrote that they were near enough to witness the carnage among their fellow soldiers. The night after the battle the enemy encamped within a few hundred yards of the defeated Americans. On the 29th, Washington decided upon a retreat to New York, and it was affected that night. If the English had suspected that the Americans were withdrawing their forces from Brooklyn, it is easy to imagine the carnage that would have ensued. So great was Washington's anxiety at this time that he is said not to have slept during forty-eight hours, and rarely to have dismounted from his horse. One account of the [notable] retreat is as follows.

"A disadvantageous wind and rain at first prevented the troops from embarking, and it was feared that the retreat could not be affected that night. But about eleven o'clock a favorable breeze sprung up, the tide turned in the right direction, and about two o'clock in the morning, a thick fog arose, which hung over Long Island, while on the New York side it was clear. During the night, the whole American army, nine thousand in number, Washington embarking last of all, with all the artillery, such heavy ordnance as was of any value, ammunition, provision, cattle, horses, carts, and everything of importance, passed safely over. All this was affected without the knowledge of the British, although the enemy was so nigh that they were heard at work with their pickaxes and shovels. In half an hour after the lines were finally abandoned, the fog cleared off and the enemy were seen taking possession of the American works. One boat on the river—within reach of the enemy's fire was obliged to return, she had only three men in her, who had loitered behind to plunder." That opportune appearance of the fog must have seemed, to more than one devout heart, as helpful as some of the remarkable interpositions of Providence described in the old Biblical stories. Hale's company, with its many seamen, rendered effective service in this passage from Long Island. Every student of history, and especially of military history, can recall certain decisive hours in momentous battles when some utterly unforeseen event has entirely changed the

face of affairs, and given the victory into unexpected hands, thus, a mistake in the understanding of a phrase used by his captors made [John] Andre a prisoner, and saved the capture of West Point by the English, while Waterloo, Gettysburg, and many another decisive battles has hinged on seeming chance—chance truly, if there is no power working for righteousness among the affairs of nations. The position of the American army, however, now appeared more perilous than ever. Two war vessels had moved up the East River and were followed by others. Active movements among the British troops were reported by all the scouts, but the enemy's designs could not be penetrated.

□□□□□□□□□□

Writing of these events afterward, Captain [William] Hull said, "It was evident that the superior force of the British would soon give them possession of New York. The Commander-in-Chief, therefore, took a position at Fort Washington at the other end of the island. To ascertain the further object of the enemy was now a subject of anxious inquiry with General Washington." In a letter to General Heath at this crisis Washington wrote as follows, "As everything in a manner depends upon obtaining intelligence of the enemy's motions, I do most earnestly entreat you and General Clinton to exert yourselves to accomplish this most desirable end. Leave no stone unturned, nor do not stick at expense, to bring this to pass, as I never was more uneasy than on account of my want of knowledge on this score." [Henry Phelps] Johnston, in his valuable life of Nathan Hale [Nathan Hale 1776], says, "If he [Washington] had been anxious to fathom Howe's plans before the latter began the campaign from Staten Island, he was infinitely more so now. It was not enough to keep a ceaseless watch across the East River. Like every other commander in history, all through the contest he came to depend much on intelligence gained through the 'secret service.' " [Isaac William] Stuart, the earliest reliable biographer of Hale, in writing of spies says, "The exigency of the American army which we have just described, would not permit the employment, in the service proposed, of any ordinary soldier, unpracticed in military observation and without skill as a draughtsman—least of all of the common mercenary, to whom, allured by the hope of a large reward, such tasks are usually assigned. Accurate estimates of the numbers of the enemy, of their distribution, of the form and position of their various encampments, of their marchings and counter marchings, of the concentration at one point or another, of the instruments of war, but more than all of their plan of attack, as derived from the open report or the unguarded whispers in camp of officers or men—estimates of all these things, requiring a quick eye, a cool head, a practical pencil, military science, general intelligence, and pliable address, were to be made. The common soldier would not answer the purpose, and the mercenary might yield to the higher seductions of the enemy, and betray his employers." During the war with the French and Indians, American officers had learned the need of trained men who could keep the commanders informed both of the movements and of the plans of the opposing forces.

Washington had learned this unforgettable lesson in Braddock's campaign, and, as full commander and wholly responsible not only for the immediate safety but for the future success of his little army, he realized the necessity of obtaining the most accurate information possible. A corps collected from the best men in the army was organized, and its command was given to Lieutenant Colonel Thomas Knowlton. He had gained experience as a ranger in the French and Indian War, and was noted for his coolness, skill, and bravery at Bunker Hill. One hundred and fifty men and twenty officers were considered sufficient for the work assigned to this special corps, known as Knowlton's Rangers. They were divided into four companies. Two of the captains of these men were chosen from Knowlton's own regiment, the other two—one of them Nathan Hale—were from other companies. There can be little doubt that Nathan Hale was proud of his enrollment in this brave corps. After Hale's services were ended, one brief record remained of "moneys due to the Company of Rangers commanded late by Captain Hale." After the 1st of September, about which time this company of Rangers was organized, it was constantly on duty wherever its services were required, and one can easily imagine Nathan Hale's enthusiasm in his enlarged duties. Knowlton spoke to some of his officers of the wishes of the commanding general for someone to enter upon this special secret service—wishes that so appealed to Hale that he at once seriously considered offering himself for the hazardous undertaking. Captain Hull, two years his senior in age, and one year in advance of him in Yale, a close friend while in college and during their subsequent days, shall describe the personal interview between himself and Captain Hale in regard to this matter. It is said that many remonstrated with Hale at his decision, but Hull's statement shows the arguments of a practical man against which Hale had to contend. In his memoirs Captain Hull writes thus of his last interview with Captain Hale, "*After his interview with Colonel Knowlton, he repaired to my quarters and informed me of what had passed. He remarked 'I think I owe to my country the accomplishment of an object so important and so much desired by the commander of her armies—and I know of no other mode of obtaining the information than by assuming a disguise and passing into the enemy's camp.' He asked my candid opinion. I replied that it was an act which involved serious consequences, and the propriety of it was doubtful, and though he viewed the business of a spy as a duty, yet he could not officially be required to perform it, that such a service was not claimed of the meanest soldier, though many might be willing, for a pecuniary compensation, to engage in it, and as for himself, the employment was not in keeping with his character. His nature was too frank and open for deceit and disguise, and he was incapable of acting a part equally foreign to his feelings and habits. Admitting that he was successful, who would wish success at such a price? Did his country demand the moral degradation of her sons, to advance her interests? Stratagems are resorted to in war, they are feints and evasions, performed under no disguise, are familiar to commanders, form a part of their plans, and, considered in a military view, lawful and advantageous. The tact with which they are executed exacts admiration from the* enemy. But who respects the character of a spy, assuming the garb of friendship but to betray? The very death assigned him is expressive of the estimation in which he is held. As soldiers, let us do our duty in the field, contend for our legitimate rights, and not stain our honor by the sacrifice of integrity. And when present events, with all their deep and exciting interests, shall have passed away, may the blush of shame never arise, by the remembrance of an unworthy though successful act, in the performance of which we were deceived by the belief that it was sanctioned by its object. I ended by saying that, should he undertake the enterprise, his short, bright career would close with an ignominious death. He replied, 'I am fully sensible of the consequences of discovery and capture in such a situation. But for a year I have been attached to the army, and have not rendered any material service, while receiving a compensation for which I make no return. Yet,' he continued, 'I am not influenced by the expectation of promotion or pecuniary reward. I wish to be useful, and every kind of service necessary for the public good, becomes honorable by being necessary. If the exigencies of my country demand a peculiar service, its claims to perform that service are imperative!' He spoke with warmth and decision. I replied, 'That such are your wishes cannot be doubted. But is this the most effectual mode of carrying them into execution? In the progress of the war there will be ample opportunity to give your talents and your life, should it be so ordered, to the sacred cause to which we are pledged. You can bestow upon your country the richest benefits, and win for yourself the highest honors. Your exertions for her interests will be daily felt, while, by one fatal act, you crush forever the power and opportunity Heaven offers for her glory and your happiness.' I urged him for the love of country, for the love of kindred, to abandon an enterprise which would only end in the sacrifice of the dearest interests of both. He paused—then affectionately taking my hand, he said, 'I will reflect, and do nothing but what duty demands.' He was absent from the army, and I feared he had gone to the British lines to execute his fatal purpose." Just how soon after this conversation Captain Hale left camp on his perilous mission, cannot now be determined. We only know that it must have been early in September, during the first week or ten days. He proceeded with Sergeant Hempstead by the safest route, and reached Norwalk (Connecticut) before finding a place to cross Long Island Sound. Sergeant [Stephen] Hempstead alone has furnished the few details of Captain Hale's final preparations. He had decided to assume civilian's dress, probably that of an educated man seeking employment as tutor among the Americans still living in New York. Hempstead says he was dressed in a brown suit of citizen's clothes, with a round, broad-brimmed hat. On parting he gave Hempstead his private papers and letters, and his silver shoe buckles, to take care of for him. It is, we think, not an undue inference that the letters and private papers he left in Hempstead's care were all to be sent to his family. These doubtless included personal letters to them, for no man such as we know Nathan Hale to have been would have faced a journey from which he might never return without some words of explanation, and possible farewell, to those he loved at home. There is one fact that all who believe in the sanctity of personal confidences and possible farewells will be glad to remember—that not one private word from Nathan Hale to Alice Adams Ripley, or from her to him, has ever been exploited to satisfy the curiosity of those who have no right to share it.

Hempstead left Captain Hale, who, now fully committed to his hazardous quest, set forth on the armed sloop *Schuyler* with Captain [Charles] Pond—one of the captains in the 19th Regiment—in command, across the Sound to Long Island. When he landed Captain Hale said farewell to the last American friend he was to be with, so far as we have any record. Assuming that he reached this point on or near the 15th of September, one or two other facts suggest themselves. It is known that the Declaration of Independence had been carried to the American camp as early as possible after its announcement in July, had been read to the troops assembled for that purpose, and had been received with unbounded enthusiasm. It is probable that both Colonel [Thomas] Knowlton, later in command of the Rangers, and Captain Hale, one of its officers, were present at that reading and joined in the huzzas. Singularly enough, neither one of these two men was a citizen of the United States for three months. Two months later Colonel Knowlton fell in the battle of Harlem Heights, on September 16th, six days before Nathan Hale's execution. Knowlton's last words are said to have been, "I do not care for my life, if we do but win the day." From the moment of his leaving New York, the mind of such a man as Nathan Hale must have had solemn foreshadowings of the possible result, of the tremendous risk he was facing. Men do not grow old by the passing of years so much as by the endurance of great experiences, and in the few brief days that were left to Nathan Hale we know really nothing of his whereabouts, of what risks he ran, of how often he barely escaped recognition as a spy, where he slept, of any possible friends whom he may have encountered, or of any moment when his very life seemed to hang on the accidental glance of an enemy's eye.—Finally dawned the 21st of September.—Hale had fully accomplished his mission. There are conflicting accounts as to what occurred on the last evening of Nathan Hale's life, some going into minute details of occurrences that were assumed to have taken place. One with considerable plausibility says that, as the time had elapsed which he had expected to spend among the British (at the end of which time a boat was to be sent across the Sound for him), Hale, having finished his quest, had entered a tavern kept by a certain Widow Chichester. She was a staunch friend of the Tories, and her house was the constant resort of Tories and British men and officers.

While Hale was sitting in the tavern, apparently at his ease among the men there assembled, someone passed him whose face he thought familiar—a man who glanced at him sharply and then passed from the room. Later it was said to have been his own cousin who betrayed him. Fortunately, there is not a word of truth in the assertion. Although Deacon Hale writes that his son was undoubtedly betrayed by someone, it appears to have been effectually disproved that he was betrayed by a relative—a cousin who, it is stated, had never seen him, and therefore could not have recognized him. A much more probable rumor is that he was recognized by a loyalist woman who might easily have seen him before the American army retreated farther north on the island, and been impressed by his personal appearance and by his prowess in kicking the football over the trees in the Bowery.

This feat Hale is said to have performed. The report goes on to say that a man suddenly entered saying that a boat was approaching, and that Hale, supposing this boat to have been sent for him, at once left the room and went to the shore. If there is any truth in this narrative, it is very possible that here Hale committed his one indiscretion. In his joy at seeing the friends who had been sent for him, he may have uttered words of such joyous welcome that the officer who heard them must have known that this was someone expecting a boat, and presumably a boat from the opposite shore. At all events, it is stated that Hale, seeing his mistake when several marines presented their guns, turned to fly, stopping only when told by the officer to stand or be shot. These events are said to have taken place at Huntington, Long Island, about forty miles from New York.

But more than a century after Hale's death a British Orderly Book was found, containing the statement, dated September 22nd, 1776, that follows, "*A spy from the enemy (by his own full confession) apprehended last night, was this day executed at 11 o'clock in front of the artillery park.*" This, with other knowledge obtained about the position of the ship by whose crew he was said to have been taken, gives reason for believing that the arrest was not made at Huntington by the crew of that ship, but in the city of New York. The order proves also that, once apprehended, he made not the slightest attempt at concealment, or any effort to escape his doom. The information gained by Hale's brother Enoch in New York supports this belief as to his capture. All that we actually know is that he was captured while attempting to make his way back to his friends, and that this must have been the sharpest moment in his experience. Before it, he had hopes of escape, after his capture he knew that his doom was certain, and his splendid soul adapted itself quietly and bravely to the inevitable. That fatal night—the night of the 21st of

September was in many respects the most terrible that New York has ever passed through. A fire had broken out near the docks at two in the morning, and was spreading with fearful rapidity toward the upper part of the city, the blaze carried northward by a strong breeze. It looked at one time as if nothing could stop the conflagration, and that the whole city would be destroyed. For a time the enemy believed that the Americans had deliberately set fire to their own city in order to expel the hated British. Later this was found to be untrue, as the fire proved to have started in a low drinking house where several coarse fellows were carousing. The fire swept on, destroying more than five hundred houses, one fifth of all the buildings then in the city, and was stopped only near Barclay Street by a sudden sharp change in the wind, which blew the fire southward toward the already burning district.

Report says that the provost marshal was given authority by Howe to dispose summarily, without the delay of a trial, of any Americans found rushing about the burning buildings, assuming, of course, that they were intent on the destruction of more buildings, rather than on the natural desire of saving what they could of their own property, and that as a result of this authority, more than one hapless householder was thrown into his own burning home. Up to this point, the early or late evening of the 21st, there is more or less of unsolvable mystery in regard to Hale's movements, but from the memoirs of Captain William Hull, Nathan Hale's college friend and companion in arms, we have what appears to be unimpeachable evidence as to Hale's arrest and being brought to General Howe's headquarters.

Quoted from Captain Hull, the information he received from an English officer through a flag of truce. *"I learned the melancholy particulars from this officer, who was present at Hale's execution and seemed touched by the circumstances attending it. He said that Captain Hale had passed through their army, both of Long Island and [New] York Island. That he had procured sketches of the fortifications, and made memoranda of their number and different positions. When apprehended, he was taken before Sir William Howe, and these papers, found concealed about his person* betrayed his intentions. He at once declared his name, his rank in the American army, and his object in coming within the British lines. Sir William Howe, without the form of a trial, gave orders for his execution the following morning. He was placed in the custody of the provost marshal. Captain Hale asked for a clergyman to attend him. His request was refused. He then asked for a Bible—that too was refused. 'On the morning of his execution,' continued the officer, 'my station was near the fatal spot, and I requested the provost marshal to permit the prisoner to sit in my marquee while he was making the necessary preparations. Captain Hale entered, he was calm, and bore himself with gentle dignity. He asked for writing materials, which I furnished him, he wrote two letters, one to his mother and one to a brother officer. He was shortly summoned to the gallows. But a few persons were around him.' "

He was condemned to die in the early morning of the 22nd, but in the confusion prevailing throughout the city on account of the spreading fire, at one time threatening the whole town, Provost Marshal [William] Cunningham must have been that morning very fully occupied, and it was late in the forenoon before he completed his preparations for Hale's execution.

At eleven o'clock Cunningham was ready, and, as it proved, Nathan Hale was ready also. Quietly standing among the few who had gathered to see him die, and it is said in response to a taunt from Cunningham that if he had any confession to make now was the time to make it, Hale responded, glancing briefly at Cunningham and then calmly at the faces about him, "*I only regret that I have but one life to lose for my country.*" For once in his life Cunningham must have been astounded. With no plea for mercy, no shrinking from the worst that Cunningham could do, this man, still almost a boy in years, had shown himself utterly beyond his power—had lifted himself forever from the doom of a victim to the grand estate of a victor. One sharp, brief struggle and Nathan Hale was free—dead, but victorious! Indefinite as are most of the details, there are some unwritten points that may confidently be assumed. That 22nd of September was a Sabbath day, a day associated in Nathan Hale's mind with religious observances, prayers at the family altar, readings of the Bible, and gatherings of his friends within church walls. Whether or not his family knew the dangerous quest on which he had ventured, he knew that he was not absent from their memories, and that the family were bearing him in their thoughts that Sabbath morning. No other day could have made that assurance so real to him, and this thought was probably one of his strongest earthly consolations and inspirations while he was awaiting the slow but relentless preparations for his death. No wonder that he bore himself "calmly and with dignity," as Captain Montresor said of him. No wonder that he died bravely—seemingly without a tremor of soul. In his last words Nathan Hale, true and faithful in every relation and every act of his brief life, gave to his country more than his life, more than all the hopes he was relinquishing so freely for her sake. In one short, indomitable breath of patriotism, he uttered words that will be forgotten only when American history ceases to be read. William Cunningham, Provost Marshal of the English forces in America, murderer and inhuman jailer, would have laughed to scorn the idea that any being, human or divine, could preserve Nathan Hale's last words for the inspiration of coming generations, yet a kindly British officer, Captain John Montresor, carried them to Hale's friends. Cunningham has left a record of brutality unsurpassed in American history. He is himself said to have boasted that he had caused the death of two thousand American soldiers. We know that any reference to the prison ships in New York Harbor sets Cunningham before us as a cowardly murderer, starving men to death by depriving them of rations which the English supplied for them, and which he sold, pocketing the proceeds. He stands alone on a pedestal of infamy. The letters that Hale had written and left, as he hoped, to be delivered to his friends, Cunningham ruthlessly destroyed, giving as his reason that "the rebels should not know that they had a man in their army who could die with so much firmness." Though Hale's letters were destroyed, the English officer, John Montresor, aide to General Howe—a gentleman in whose presence we may safely assume that

Cunningham, cowardly as all brutal men are, had not dared to maltreat Nathan Hale as he was known to maltreat other prisoners—that very Sunday evening spoke of Hale's death to General [Israel] Putnam and Captain Alexander Hamilton at the American outposts where he had been sent with a flag of truce by General Howe to arrange for an exchange of prisoners. More was learned when a flag of truce was sent two days later to the British lines by General Washington, in answer to the one on September 22. Two friends of Hale, Captain Hull and Lieutenant Colonel Samuel Webb, were among those who went with the flag.

Through these flags of truce—and perhaps others—were obtained all the positive knowledge that Hale's friends were ever able to secure, but the unvarnished story, told by Captain Montresor, gave all that was essential to reveal to his friends his manly attitude when in the presence of General Howe, and his calmness and dignity when he was awaiting execution, while his last unpremeditated (unplanned) but immortal words, in reply to Cunningham's taunt, proved to all his friends that he had died as he had lived—a Christian patriot, and a hero. We may suppose that Nathan Hale himself had not the remotest idea that anything concerning his death would ever be made known to his friends save that, detected as a spy, he had died as the penalty he had known would follow capture. The words spoken by Nathan Hale, as his last earthly thought, seem to prove that the thought, breathed from the depths of his fearless soul, shall live as long as pure patriotism thrills the souls of mortal men [everywhere].

◻◻◻◻◻◻◻◻◻◻◻

From Enoch Hale's diary, parts of which were first published by his famous grandson, Edward Everett Hale, we learn how the news reached the Hale family. Enoch writes as follows. [September 30.—Afternoon—*Ride to Reverend Strong's [his uncle] Salmon Brook [Connecticut]. Hear a rumor that Captain Hale, belonging to the east side of Connecticut River near Colchester, who was educated at College, was sentenced to hang in the enemy's lines at New York, being taken as a spy, or reconnoitering (observing) their camp. Hope it is without foundation. Something troubled at it. Sleep not very well. October 15. Get a pass to ride to New York.—Accounts from my brother Captain are indeed melancholy! That about the second week of September, he went to Stamford, crossed to Long Island (Dr. Waldo writes) and had finished his plans, but before he could get off, was betrayed, taken and hanged without ceremony. Some entertain hopes that all this is not true, but it is a gloomy, dejected hope. Time may determine. Conclude to go to the camp next week.*] He afterwards wrote that Webb, one of Washington's staff, brought word to Washington that Nathan Hale, "being suspected by his movements that he wanted to get out of New York, was taken up and examined by the general [Howe] and some minutes being found upon him, orders were immediately given that he should be hanged. When at the gallows, he spoke and told that he was a Captain in the Continental Army, by name Nathan Hale." To those who have experienced the long weeks of distressing anxiety that often fall to the lot of those whose friends are in battle, or carried prisoners to unknown camps, no words are needed to depict the anxiety among Nathan Hale's family until particulars of his noble death were finally learned. It is a solemn but perhaps a comforting fact that the deepest human distress seems, after a few generations have passed, to have been "writ in water." Bitter as must have been those early sorrowful hours, the only later reminder of the tears that then flowed is given in the statement that one who had loved him could not speak of him fifty years later without tears in her eyes. Of how many wept for him we can form no conception. Indeed, we should have pitied any warmhearted girl or young man who knew him, and had shared his joyous young life, who could have heard of his tragic death without tears almost as bitter as for one intensely loved. Duly Enoch Hale and his family learned all that ever will be known of the last days of their beloved, and now honored, dead. The following letter of Deacon Richard Hale's—good man and uncertain speller that he was—was written to his brother Samuel at Portsmouth, New Hampshire, a few months after Nathan's death had become known.

[Coventry, March 28th 1777] DEAR BROTHER, I received your favor of the 17th of February last and rejoice to hear that you and your family were well—your observation as to the difficulty of the times is very just. So gloomy a day we never saw before but I trust our cause is just and for our consolation in the times of greatest distress we have this to support us that there is a God that judgeth in the earth if we can but take the comfort of it. As to our being far advanced in life if it do but serve to wean us from this present troublesome world and stir us up to prepare for a world of peace and rest it is well. The calls in Providence are loud to prepare to meet our God and O that he would prepare us. You desired me to inform you about my son Nathan. You have doubtless seen the Newburyport paper that gives the account of the conduct of our kinsman Samuel Hale toward him in New York as to our kinsman being here on his way to New York. It is a mistake but as to his conduct toward my son at New York. Mr. Cleveland of Cape Ann first reported it. Near us I suppose when on his way from the Army where he had been Chaplain. Home was probably true. Betrayed he doubtless was by somebody. He was executed about the 22nd of September last by the accounts we have had. A child I set much by, but he is gone. I think the severest trial I ever met with. My 3rd son Joseph is in the army over in the Jerseys and was well the last time we heard from him.—My other son that was in the service belonged to the militia and is now at home.—My son Enoch is gone to take the smallpox by inoculation. Brother Robinson and family are well. We are all through the Divine Goodness well. My wife joins in love to you and Mrs. Hale and your children. Your loving brother, Richard Hale. For a while after Nathan Hale's death, in the crowding events of the Revolution, his personal friends appear to have been his chief mourners. One lady is said to have told Professor Kingsley of New Haven that she had never seen greater anguish than that experienced by Deacon Hale and his family when they heard of Nathan's death. What the news meant to his "good Grandmother Strong" we are not told. For her, so faithful and unselfish in her loving, we can but be glad that if she went home all the earlier for this blow, she must have gone all the more serenely, assured that if the earth was the poorer, heaven was the richer, because the grandson she had loved so truly was there awaiting her. Mrs. Abbot, daughter of Deacon Richard Hale's son, Joseph Hale, lived at her grandfather's from 1784 till her marriage in 1799. Many years ago she wrote to her cousin, "From my earliest recollection I have felt a deep interest in that unfortunate uncle. When his death or the manner of it was spoken of, my grief would come forth in tears. Living in the old homestead I frequently heard allusions to him by the neighbors and persons that worked in the family, much more so than by near relatives. It seemed the anguish they felt did not allow them to make it the subject of conversation. Was it not so with your mother?" Reverend Edward Everett Hale refers in a historical address to the fact that in his own early days the name of Nathan Hale was seldom mentioned in his presence. We of today can but wish that somewhat of the luster from the radiant halo that was to encircle his memory and to grow brighter as the years pass on, might have comforted them. Yet each one of that sorrowing family has long since learned to rejoice that, as nobly as any martyr has ever died for his country, their lad went forth into the eternities.

The poem which follows was published in *Songs and Ballads of the Revolution*, collected by Mr. Frank Moore. It is not known when these verses first appeared, but they are among the earliest tributes to Hale after his death. It is thought possible, by some students of Revolutionary history, that the lines may yet prove valuable in throwing light upon the manner of Hale's capture and death, as they are probably based on accounts current at that time of which records have not yet appeared.

CAPTURE AND DEATH OF NATHAN HALE (By an unknown poet of 1776) *The breezes went steadily through the tall pines, a-saying "Oh! Hush!" a-saying "Oh! Hush!" As stilly stole by a bold legion of horse, for Hale in the bush, for Hale in the bush. 'Keep still!' said the thrush as she nestled her young, in a nest by the road, in a nest by the road, 'for the tyrants are near, and with them appear, what bodes us no good, what bodes us no good.' The brave captain heard it, and thought of his home, in a cot by the brook, in a* cot by the brook. With mother and sister and memories dear, he so gaily forsook, he so gaily forsook. Cooling shades of the night were coming apace, the tattoo had beat, the tattoo had beat. The noble one sprang from his dark lurking place to make his retreat, to make his retreat. He warily trod on the dry rustling leaves, as he passed through the wood, as he passed through the wood, and silently gained his rude launch on the shore, as she played with the flood, as she played with the flood. The guards of the camp, on that dark, dreary night, had a murderous will, had a murderous will. They took him and bore him afar from the shore, to a hut on the hill, to a hut on the hill. No mother was there, nor a friend who could cheer, in that little stone cell, in that little stone cell. But he trusted in love from his father above—in his heart all was well—in his heart all was well. An ominous owl with his solemn bass voice sat moaning hard by, sat moaning hard by. 'The tyrant's proud minions most gladly rejoice, for he must soon die, for he must soon die.' The brave fellow told them, no thing he restrained, the cruel general, the cruel general, his errand from camp, of the ends to be gained, and said that was all, and said that was all. They took him and bound him and bore him away, down the hill's grassy side, down the hill's grassy side. Twas there the base hirelings, in royal array, his cause did deride, his cause did deride. Five minutes were given, short moments, no more, for him to repent, for him to repent, he prayed for his mother, he asked not another, to Heaven he went, to Heaven he went. The faith of a martyr, the tragedy showed, as he trod the last stage, as he trod the last stage. And Britons will shudder at gallant Hale's blood, as his words do presage, as his words do presage. Thou pale king of terrors, thou life's gloomy foe, go frighten the slave, go frighten the slave, tell tyrants to you their allegiance they owe. No fears for the brave, no fears for the brave.

    The body of the martyr spy was never found. For many years there appears to have been some interest, but little knowledge, as to the place of Nathan Hale's execution. During the last one hundred and thirty-eight years, writer after writer has described his life and all the events connected with it as they are believed to have occurred, and, as was inevitable under the circumstances, some things have been written that the critical historian cannot endorse. Until near the end of the nineteenth century no reliable information, even as to the place of his execution, had been gained. The late Mr. William Kelby, librarian of the New York Historical Society, "*an accepted authority on all subjects of this and kindred nature,*" is said to have undertaken to locate the exact spot where it occurred, and met with at least partial success. Writing on the subject [of Nathan Hale] in 1893 he says in substance, "When the British took possession of New York in September, 1776, after the battle of Long Island, General Howe occupied the Beekman House on Fifty-First Street and First Avenue as his headquarters, while the army extended across the island to the north of him. The corps of Royal Artillery occupied part of the high ground between Sixty-Sixth and Seventy-Second Streets, where they parked their guns and formed a camp. Close to the camp were the old "five-mile stone" on the way to Kingsbridge, and a tavern long known as "The Sign of the Dove." The exact location of this tavern is shown from a survey of 1783 as being west of the post road on Third Avenue between Sixty-Sixth and Sixty-Seventh Streets. It belonged, with four acres of land attached, to the city corporation. The extract already shown on page 82 is from an Orderly Book (discovered by Mr. Kelby) kept by an officer of the British Foot Guards. Other entries read as follows. October 6.—*The effects of the late Lieutenant Lovell to be sold at the house near the artillery park.* October 11.—*Majors of Brigade to attend at the Artillery Park near the Dove at five this afternoon.*" The story of Hale's confinement in the Beekman greenhouse at Fifty-First Street and First Avenue on the night of September 21, 1776, is generally accepted. Former stories of the place of execution are disproved by the first extract from the Orderly Book, while the others indicate the location of the artillery park. It therefore appears that Hale was executed upon some part of this common land of the corporation of the city of New York, and it is probable that his body was buried there. The tract is now covered mainly by buildings devoted to educational and philanthropic uses. Possibly the dust of the martyr spy may lie in the grounds of the Normal, or Hunter, College. Other materials, found since Mr. Kelby wrote, confirm his conclusions and make Third Avenue, not far north of Sixty-Sixth Street, the most probable spot of Nathan Hale's death. The noblest educational institutions in New York City could have no more appropriate foundations than those laid above the bodies of patriots who have died, not only for the freedom of the city, but for that of the whole land. For a time, as was inevitable, a pall seemed thrown over the memory of Nathan Hale, and at first only the love of his own family strove to commemorate his life and death. A stone was erected to his memory in the cemetery at South Coventry, near the spot where his father expected to be buried. It still stands there and has been declared to be one of the best examples of the lettering of the times. It bears this inscription, "Durable stone preserve the monumental record. Nathan Hale, Esquire, a Captain in the army of the United States, who was born June 6th, 1755, and received the first honors of Yale College, September 1773, resigned his life a sacrifice to his country's liberty at New York, September 22nd, 1776." One by one were placed near his, his father's stone (his father died at eighty-five), and those of other members of his family. These graves are in a common burial lot near the Congregational Church in South Coventry where the family had worshiped.

In November, 1837, the Hale Monument Association was formed for the purpose of erecting at Coventry—a fitting memorial of the martyr-soldier. Congress was applied to for several years, but was slow in appropriating money to honor the dead—strangely unlike England in honoring her martyrs, as will be seen later. Appeals were made to the State legislature, and Stuart, Hale's earliest biographer and sincere admirer, used his influence as a legislator in securing an appropriation of twelve hundred and fifty dollars. The women of Coventry redoubled their zeal, and by fairs, teas, etc., raised a sufficient sum, added to the grant from the legislature and contributions from some prominent men of the country, to pay for the cenotaph. It is a pyramidal shaft, resting on a base of steps, with a shelving projection one-third of the way up the pedestal. The material is of hewn Quincy granite. It was designed by Henry Austin of New Haven. It is fourteen feet square at the base and forty-five feet high. It was completed under the superintendence of Solomon Willard, architect of Bunker Hill Monument, at a cost of about four thousand dollars. The inscription reads—Captain Nathan Hale—1776—Born at Coventry, June 6, 1755—Died at New York, September 22, 1776—"I only regret that I have but one life to lose for my country." The monument stands on elevated ground. "Its site is particularly fine—on the north it overlooks a beautiful lake, while on the east it looks through a captivating natural vista to greet the sun." With the planning of this monument began the revival of interest in Nathan Hale's short but splendid career [and life] that is still gathering strength and will eventually establish his name among those of the bravest American patriots.

☐☐☐☐☐☐☐☐☐☐☐

When Captain [John] Montresor told Hale's dismayed friends of the terrible doom that had befallen their comrade, it must have seemed as if all the influence Hale might have had in a prolonged life, all that could come to such a man had been sacrificed. We must not blame them if the question involuntarily rose in their hearts, "Why such waste? Why was such an influence so permanently destroyed?" Curiously enough, many years passed with little special notice by the public of Hale's death. But the leaven (influence) of patriotism works, even though slowly and step by step Hale was coming to his own. Little by little the memory of his sacrifice for his country, and the fact that he had left words that should glow with increasing splendor, took possession of those who had ears to hear and hearts to remember. Old Linonia in Yale did not forget the splendid boy, once its Chancellor, who died as he had lived. Linonia's records still bear, in clear and perfect lines, reports his hand had written when he was its most assiduous member. Others might have forgotten him, Linonia had not. On its one-hundredth anniversary, July 27, 1853—Commencement Week—the poet of the occasion was Francis Miles Finch, Yale, 1846, later Judge of the New York Court of Appeals. As poet, Mr. Finch of course recalled many former members of the society. He ended with a poem on Nathan Hale in which he held his listeners spellbound as stanza after stanza, magnetic in proportion to their truthful beauty, fell from his lips. There has been a further service to his country by Judge Finch. His own character has been graven (engraved) into two different poems—the one just referred to, and one that he wrote later. The latter poem had, undoubtedly, a powerful influence in causing our national Decoration Day to be celebrated throughout the United States. The story of this poem is interesting. In a town in Mississippi, certain Southern women went on a spring day, soon after the close of the Civil War, to cover with flowers the graves of their beloved dead. The gracious and tender thought must have come to them that in the graves of aliens buried among them lay those as deeply mourned in Northern homes as were those they themselves had loved.

Certainly no sweeter suggestion could have been more tenderly carried out than that which led these bereaved women to spread flowers over the graves of those who were once their enemies. Mr. Finch was told of this incident, and the lines he wrote show his appreciation of the "generous deed."

The poem, *The Blue and the Gray*, did much to heal the wounds in both North and South. The two poems by Judge Francis Miles Finch are quoted here, the first with the drumbeat pulsing through it, the second in musical, flowing lines that carry in them sorrow, loyalty, and the community of a common bereavement. HALE'S FATE AND FAME *And one there was—his name immortal now—who dies not to the ring of rattling steel, or battle—march of spirit—stirring drum, but, far from comrades and from friendly camp, alone upon the scaffold. To drumbeat and heartbeat a soldier marches by, there is color in his cheek, there is courage in his eye, yet to drumbeat and heartbeat in a moment he must die. By starlight and moonlight he seeks the Briton's camp, he hears the rustling flag, and the armed sentry's tramp. And the starlight and moonlight his silent wanderings lamp. With slow tread* and still tread he scans the tented line, and he counts the battery guns by the gaunt and shadowy pine, and his slow tread and still tread give no warning sign. The dark wave, the plumed wave! It meets his eager glance and it sparkles beneath the stars like the glimmer of a lance. A dark wave—a plumed wave—on an emerald expanse. A sharp clang, a steel clang! And terror in the sound, for the sentry, falcon-eyed, in the camp a spy hath found, with a sharp clang, a steel clang, the patriot is bound. With calm brow, steady brow, he listens to his doom, in his look there is no fear, nor a shadow trace of gloom, but with calm brow and steady brow he robes him for the tomb. In the long night, the still night, he kneels upon the sod, and the brutal guards withhold even the solemn word of God! In the long night, the still night, he walks where Christ hath trod. Beneath the blue morn, the sunny morn, he dies upon the tree, and he mourns that he can lose but one life for Liberty, and in the blue morn, the sunny morn, his spirit wings are free. His last words, his message words, they burn, lest friendly eye should read how proud and calm a patriot could die, with his last words, his dying words, a soldier's battle cry! From fame leaf and angel leaf, from monument and urn, the sad of earth, the glad of heaven, his tragic fate shall learn, and on fame leaf and angel leaf, the name of Hale shall burn. THE BLUE AND THE GRAY By the flow of the inland river, whence the fleets of iron had fled, where the blades of the grave grass quiver, asleep are the ranks of the dead.—Under the sod and the dew, awaiting the judgment day, under the one the Blue, under the other, the Gray.—These in the robes of glory, those in the gloom of defeat, all with the battle blood gory, In the dusk of eternity meet.—Under the sod and the dew, waiting the judgment day, under the laurel, the Blue.—Under the willow, the Gray. From the silence of sorrowful hours the desolate mourners go, lovingly laden with flowers, alike for the friend and the foe.—Under the sod and the dew, waiting the judgment day, under the roses, the Blue, under the lilies, the Gray.—So, with an equal splendor, the morning sun rays fall, with a touch impartially tender, on the blossoms blooming for all. Under the sod and the dew, waiting the judgment day, broidered with gold, the Blue mellowed with gold, the Gray. So when the summer calleth on forest and field of grain, with an equal murmur falleth the cooling drip of the rain. Under the sod and the dew, waiting the judgment day, wet with the rain, the Blue, wet with the rain, the Gray. Sadly, but not with upbraiding, the generous deed was done, in the storm of the years that are fading no braver battle was won.—Under the sod and the dew, waiting the judgment day, under the blossoms, the Blue, under the garlands, the Gray.—No more shall the war cry sever, or the winding rivers be red, they banish our anger forever when they laurel the graves of our dead! Under the sod and the dew, waiting the judgment day, love and tears for the Blue, tears and love for the Gray.—On the one hundred and tenth anniversary of the evacuation of New York by the British—November 25, 1893—a bronze statue of Nathan Hale was presented to the city of New York. It was given by the New York Society of the Sons of the American Revolution, a society founded in 1876 to perpetuate the memory and deeds of the War for American Independence. The presentation was made by the president of the society, Mr. Frederic Samuel Tallmadge, the grandson of Major Tallmadge, Hale's classmate and fellow captain. The statue is of bronze and is by Frederick MacMonnies of Paris. It represents Hale bareheaded, bound about his arms and his ankles, ready for his death. It was placed in City Hall Park where Hale was, for a time, supposed to have been executed. On the pedestal are graven (engraved) his last wonderful words. During the exercises at the unveiling of this statue Dr. Edward Everett Hale said, "The occasion, I suppose, is without a parallel in history. Certainly, I know of no other instance where, more than a century after the death of a boy of twenty-one, his countrymen assembled in such numbers as are here to do honor to his memory and to dedicate the statue which preserves it. He died near this spot, saying, 'I am sorry that I have but one life to give for my country.' And because that boy said those words, and because he died, thousands of other young men have given their lives to his country, have served her as she bade them serve her, even though they died as she bade them die." The day's celebration was concluded by a dinner of the New York Society of the Sons of the American Revolution. Dr. Hale spoke on this occasion also. He said in part, "Let us never forget that this is the monument of a young man—that he is the young man's hero. Let us never forget how the country then trusted young men and how worthy they were of the trust. It was at the very time of which I spoke that [George] Washington first knew [Alexander] Hamilton and asked him to his tent. Hamilton had already won the confidence of [Nathanael] Greene. Hamilton was, I think, in his nineteenth year. [Henry] Knox, who commanded Hamilton's regiment, was, I think, twenty-four. [Charles] Webb, who commanded Hale's regiment, was twenty-two. When, the next year, Washington welcomed [Marquis de] Lafayette, whom Congress appointed major-general, he [Lafayette] was not twenty. And Washington himself, before whom others stood abashed, had only attained the venerable age of forty-four. The country needed her young men. She called for them and she had them. It is one of those young men who, dying at twenty-one, leaves as his only word of regret that he has but one life to give to her." Although it is now known that Hale was not executed near City Hall Park, in some respects there could be no more fitting location for a monument to him than this, perhaps the busiest conflux of human beings that anywhere crowd this great city. Thousands pass this statue, learning from it their first lessons in American history. Hundreds have stopped, seeing this bareheaded, dauntless man, evidently doomed to die, to try to learn whence he came and why he stands there, appealing to the noblest patriotism—patriotism that must touch the heart of any man who knows the love of country. Since this statue was placed, memorials of various kinds to Nathan Hale have been erected in several parts of the country. The schoolhouses in which he taught, although not occupying their original sites, have been restored, and are in possession of patriotic societies. Today, Yale, endowed with buildings costing millions, is learning that stone and mortar, in edifices however beautiful do not enshrine their noblest memories. Through a few friends of Yale, a statue of Nathan Hale by Bela Lyon Pratt has recently been placed near the oldest college building, Connecticut Hall. This building has been restored to the appearance it bore when Nathan Hale dwelt therein. Who shall say that the statue of the bound boy, facing death so manfully, will not prove one of Yale's noblest endowments? Still another beautiful statue of Nathan Hale by William Ordway Partridge may be seen in the city of St. Paul, Minnesota. Happily, Nathan Hale's ability to die for his country is but one side of a Yale shield from which gleam the names of hundreds of her sons, who, doubtless as ready to die for their country as he, had they been in his place, have proved their power to live for God and for their native land. Everywhere, in all quarters of the world, the Nathan Hale spirit of unselfish devotion has inspired the sons of Yale to the noblest service they could render, and every man, young or old, who passes the statue of Nathan Hale will realize that hosts have lived lives inspired by the same splendid spirit. Hale himself went forth from his alma mater filled with the hopes and ambitions that have filled the souls of many men, all unconscious of the fact that the finest heroism and the highest self-sacrifice lay just before him, but conscious that he meant to be ready for the best that life could give him. He was ready, and life for him was the power to die as he died.

☐☐☐☐☐☐☐☐☐☐☐

Descriptions of Nathan Hale by Friends

Joseph Huntington. A somewhat full description of the Reverend, is well-worth placing among the friends of Nathan Hale. It was impossible for such a boy as Nathan to have been under the care of such a man as Dr. Huntington, first as pastor and then as his private teacher in his preparation for college, without having been strongly influenced by him. Indeed, scanning (reading) these old records of a parish of a hundred and fifty years ago, we cannot help feeling a strong personal attraction toward the Reverend Joseph Huntington. Few men more fully prove the claim that many of the early New England pastors were eminently fitted to lead their people heavenward and also in the practical development of their daily lives.

Dr. Huntington lived a life evidently inspired by the finest ideals, and also by shrewd common sense, always so dear to the heart of a New Englander. It is a pleasure to recall the story of this man's useful life, and realize that besides the reverence almost invariably accorded to "the minister" in those days, he must have held the everyday affection and wholesome trust of his people. Year by year he proved himself not only their pastor, but a friend full of all kindly sympathies, never above a hearty laugh when mirth was rampant, or a sympathetic tear for hearts wrung with anguish. He was born in Windham, Connecticut, in 1735. His ancestors came from England about 1640 and the family ultimately settled in Windham. His father, a man of somewhat arbitrary character, had determined that Joseph should be a clothier, and forced him to remain in that business until he was twenty-one. His intellectual ability was thought to be somewhat remarkable and his moral character so good that his pastor advised him to begin a course of study for the ministry.

He completed his preparation for Yale College in an unusually short time, and was graduated there in the year 1762. His call to be settled over the First Church in Coventry was received so soon after his graduation that we are forced to believe that his theological course must have been brief. The parish in Coventry had been greatly reduced in numbers. The meeting house had been allowed to go to decay, and the religious life of the parish was in a corresponding state of depression. His ordination services were held out of doors—whether because the assemblage was too large for the church, or because the building was too dilapidated, does not appear. The first thing Mr. Huntington did after his settlement was to urge upon his people the project of building a new meeting house. They responded so heartily that in a short time they had built the best church in the whole region, having expended for it about five thousand dollars—a large sum in those days. Dr. Huntington does not appear to have been a laborious student. He had few books of his own, largely depending upon borrowing. But he had a remarkable memory and the power of so making his own whatever he read that his scholarship and his originality appear never to have been questioned. The Reverend Daniel Waldo says of him that he was rather above the middle height, slender and graceful in form, and that he seemed to have had an instinctive desire to make everybody around him happy. This, added to his uniform politeness, caused him to be very popular in general society.

The Reverend Mr. Waldo adds that Dr. Huntington was fond of pleasantry and gives this instance. A very dull preacher who had studied theology with him was invited by his people to resign, and they paid him for his services chiefly in copper coin.

On telling Dr. Huntington how he had been paid, he was advised to go back and preach a farewell sermon from the text, "Alexander the coppersmith did me much evil." Many such anecdotes and repartees of Dr. Huntington were current in Coventry for years after his death. This brief summary of Dr. Joseph Huntington's life shows that the men to whom Richard Hale entrusted the preparation of his three sons for entering Yale was not only a Christian, but a gentleman of the finest culture.

He was able not only to impart to Enoch, Nathan, and David Hale the rudiments of scholarship requisite for entering Yale, but to inspire such boys with the keenest appreciation of courtesy, broad mental endowments, and a wholesome zeal for high public service. The correspondence concerning the Union School in New London shows that Dr. Huntington gave Nathan Hale the necessary recommendation for the place. It is on record in Hale's diary that on December 27, 1775, the day after his arrival home from Camp Winter Hill, he visited Dr. Huntington, and in one of his New York letters he wrote, "*I always with respect remember Mr. Huntington and shall write to him if time permits.*" Admitting that Nathan Hale's father and mother were his most important early friends, we believe that Dr. Huntington, as pastor, tutor, and friend during the six years before Hale entered college, may have stood not far behind the parents in deep influence upon his character—that splendid character, destined to be one of the beacon lights of our country's history.

Alice Adams. Studying the lives of the founders of our republic, we are interested in noting the early marriages that so often occurred, and which seem to have been justified by the early mental maturity of the young men and women in the eighteenth century. With early marriage, large families were the rule and not the exception, and eulogize the forefathers of New England as much as one may, no one at all familiar with the lives of the mothers of those generations can question the share that the foremothers had in broadening the lives and inspiring the characters of the husbands and sons in that early period. Nathan Hale showed the power of heredity, and Alice Adams, the woman he is said to have loved, proved well that she too had come of no unworthy stock. It has been given few women to be so worthily loved as was Alice Adams, from the time we catch our first glimpse of her till the last, in her eighty-ninth year.

She was born in June, 1757. Her mother married Deacon Hale when Alice was in her thirteenth year. We do not know when Alice first met Nathan Hale, but we do know that while both were very young they found out that they loved each other, and proceeded to engage themselves without consulting their elders. Nathan had several years of work preparatory to his profession still before him, and, acting as they supposed in the best interests of both the boy and the girl—the mother and elder sister Sarah promptly discouraged the engagement and it was broken. In February, 1773, while Nathan was still at Yale and before she was sixteen, Alice was married to Elijah Ripley, a prosperous merchant at Coventry. Within two years Mr. Ripley died, aged twenty-eight, leaving behind him a little son, also named Elijah, who died in his second year. After Mr. Ripley's death, Mrs. Ripley with her baby boy returned to Deacon Hale's home almost as an adopted daughter, comfortably provided for by the estate of her late husband. A member of the Hale family, she must have seen that whatever was true of Nathan Hale in the days when they were boy and girl together, he, now a Yale graduate and a man among men, first as teacher and then as soldier, was even more worthy of her love than in their early days. It is probable that they corresponded more or less, though happily none of the letters of either are preserved for the curious to delight in. All we know is that in December, 1775, a year after her husband's death, Nathan Hale stopped in Coventry while absent from camp on army business, and the broken engagement has been said to have been then renewed, this time without opposition. Having been married and widowed, and having lost her little son, Alice Adams Ripley was now free to listen to the claims of the first love that had entered her heart. What the few brief months that remained to Nathan Hale must have meant to Alice Ripley, believing in him and caring for him, only the noblest women can comprehend.

In regard to the letters written by Nathan Hale on the morning of his execution, one of these letters is said to have been written to his mother. One or two of his biographers have inferred that this must be an error, and that it was written to his father or to a brother. With the natural delicacy always so conspicuous in him, a letter to his "mother," so called, in reality the mother of one whom we believe to have been his betrothed wife, Alice Adams Ripley, who would show it to Alice and undoubtedly give it to her, was probably what he would have written. The others would know what he had written, but Alice Adams would doubtless possess the letter. Alice Adams was to live many, many years, to become one of the most notable women in the city in which she dwelt, so honored that a copy of her portrait has long hung in the Athenaeum, Hartford's finest shrine for such portraits. It was said of her that for several years after Nathan's death she had no intention of marrying, but, after a widowhood of ten years, events—some say changed circumstances—led her to accept an offer of marriage from William Lawrence, of Hartford, which was thenceforth her home. For many years she was naturally associated with the social life of that city. Whatever letters may have passed between Nathan Hale and Alice Adams Ripley, no trace of them remains today.

For this we can only be grateful that, unlike other unfortunate lovers—Robert Browning and Elizabeth Barrett Browning, for instance—not one word remains of their correspondence. That belonged to him and to her alone. It is fortunate that no mere curiosity hunter can feast his eyes or gossip over the words these two people wrote to each other. To Alice's husband, Nathan's father gave the powder horn she once spoke of as having seen Nathan working upon in his customary intense fashion, "doing that one thing as if there was nothing else to be thought of at that time." It being given to Mr. Lawrence by Nathan's father, to whom it must have been dear, proves that Mr. Lawrence, as well as his wife, was a welcome addition to the Hale family. Mr. Lawrence in turn gave it to his son William, and it is now treasured by the Connecticut Historical Society.

Mrs. Lawrence lived well into the nineteenth century, dying in 1845, in her eighty-ninth year. She was thoroughly appreciated in Hartford (Connecticut), but it is from the pen of a granddaughter, in a note written to the Honorable [Isaac William] Stuart, that the best description of Mrs. Lawrence is given. Speaking of her grandmother she said, "In person she was rather below the middle height, with full, round figure, rather petite. She possessed a mild, amiable countenance in which was reflected that intelligent superiority which distinguished her even in the days of [Timothy] Dwight, [Lemuel] Hopkins, and [Joel] Barlow in Hartford—men who could appreciate her, who delighted in her wit and work, and who, with a coterie of others of that period who are still in remembrance, considered her one of the brightest ornaments of their society. A fair, fresh complexion—bright, intelligent, hazel eyes, and hair of a jetty blackness (un-dyed), will give you some idea of her looks—the crowning glory of which was the forehead that surpassed in beauty any I ever saw, and was the admiration of my mature years. I portray her, with the exception of the hair, as she appeared to me in her eighty-eighth year. I never tired of gazing on her youthful complexion—upon her eyes which retained their youthful luster unimpaired, and enabled her to read without any artificial aid, and upon her hand and arm, which, though shrunken much from age, must in her younger days have been fit study for a sculptor. Her character was everything that was lovely. A lady who had known her many years, writing to me after her death, says, 'Never shall I forget her unceasing kindness to me, and her noble and generous disposition. From my first acquaintance with her, and amid all the varied trials through which she was called to pass, I had ever occasion to admire the calm and Christian spirit she uniformly exhibited. To you I will say it—I never knew so faultless a character—so gentle, so kind. That meek expression, that affectionate eye are as present to my recollection now as though I had seen them but yesterday.' Such is the language of one who had known her long and well and whose testimony would be considered more impartial than that of one who like myself had been the constant recipient of her unceasing kindness and affection." When she died, the story of the early home of the Hales found its completion.—Shall we pity them or congratulate them that in those long ago days so many sorrows came to them? Testing their strength, developing their faith, and fitting them, as their days went by, for life and service beyond.—The following chivalric poem was written by Nathan Hale—perhaps in camp. It expresses his mental as well as emotional appreciation of Alice Adams. It is here given exactly as it appears in the original manuscript, with almost no punctuation marks. It is probable that this is a first rough draft, intended to be improved at some future time. There are marks on the margin of the paper which show that the writer had possible alterations (corrections) in mind.

[To Alicia] *Alicia, born with every striking charm, the eye to ravish or the heart to warm fair in thy form, still fairer in thy mind with beauty, wisdom, sense with sweetness joined great without pride, and lovely without art. Your looks, good nature words, good sense impart, thus formed to charm. Oh deign to hear my song whose best, whose sweetest strains to you belong. Let others toil amidst the lofty air by fancy, led through every cloud above, let empty follies build her castles there, my thoughts are settled on the friend I love. Oh friend, sincere of soul, divinely great, shedest thou for me a wretch, the sorrowed tear, what thanks can I in this unhappy state return to you but gratitude sincere 'tis friendship pure that now demand my lays a theme sincere that aid my feeble song raised by that theme I do not fear to praise since you're the subject where due praise belong. Ah dearest girl in whom the gods have joined the real blessings, which themselves approve can mortals frown at such an heavenly mind when Gods propitious shine on you, they love far from the seat of pleasure now I roam the pleasing landscape, now no more I see, yet absence never shall take my thoughts from home nor time efface my due regards for thee.*

Benjamin Tallmadge. One year older than Nathan Hale, [he] was Hale's classmate and one of his correspondents. Like Hale he became a teacher for a time, and then, entering the army, served with distinction throughout the war. He was entrusted by Washington with important services. In October, 1780, he was stationed with Colonel [John] Jameson at North Castle. He had been out on active service against the enemy and returned on the evening of the day when Major [John] Andre had been brought there and had been started (headed) back to [Benedict] Arnold for explanations. This was four years after the death of Hale. Listening to the account of the capture, and the pass from Arnold, Tallmadge at once surmised the importance of retaining Andre and insisted upon his being brought back. When Andre was once more in American hands, Tallmadge is said to have been the first to suspect, from the prisoner's deportment as he walked to and fro and turned sharply upon his heel to retrace his steps, that he was bred to arms and was an important British officer. Major Tallmadge was charged with his custody, and was almost constantly with him until his execution. Tallmadge writes, "Major Andre became very inquisitive to know my opinion as to the result of his capture. In other words, he wished me to give him candidly my opinion as to the light in which he would be viewed by General Washington and a military tribunal if one should be ordered. This was the most unpleasant question that had been propounded to me, and I endeavored to evade it, unwilling to give him a true answer. When I could no longer evade his importunity and put off a full reply, I remarked to him as follows, 'I had a much loved classmate in Yale College, by the name of Nathan Hale, who entered the army in the year 1775. Immediately after the battle of Long Island, General Washington wanted information respecting the strength, position, and probable movements of the enemy. Captain Hale tendered his services, went over to Brooklyn, and was taken just as he was passing the outposts of the enemy on his return.'—Said I with emphasis—'Do you remember the sequel of this story?' 'Yes,' said Andre, 'he was hanged as a spy. But you surely do not consider his case and mine alike?' I replied, 'Yes, precisely similar, and similar will be your fate.' He endeavored to answer my remarks, but it was manifest he was more troubled in spirit than I had ever seen him before." Major Tallmadge walked with Andre from the Stone House where he had been confined to the place of execution, and parted with him under the gallows, "overwhelmed with grief," he says, "that so gallant an officer and so accomplished a gentleman should come to such an ignominious end." What would have occurred if Andre had not been recalled, but had reached Arnold—whether both could have escaped by boat to the HMS *Vulture* as did Arnold, whether Arnold, leaving Andre to his fate, could have escaped alone under these suspicious circumstances, or whether [Alexander] Hamilton and the others, who were dining with Arnold when the news of Andre's capture reached him, could have managed to hold both until Washington's arrival, cannot now be surmised.

We only know that to Major Tallmadge belongs the credit of the recall and retention of Andre as a prisoner, thereby preventing the loss of West Point. Major Tallmadge remained in the army and was greatly trusted by Washington, rendering important assistance in the secret service. He tool, part in many battles and in time became a colonel. For sixteen years he was in Congress. He died at the age of eighty, leaving sons and grandsons who won honored names in various callings.

William Hull. When Captain William Hull, impelled by a strong natural caution, spoke as forcibly as he could of the disastrous results that might follow Nathan Hale's acceptance of the office of a spy in his country's service, he described not only the result of the failure which seemed almost inevitable, and which would result in a disgraceful death, but also the contempt that would be felt among his fellow officers should he be successful. Hale, as we have seen, deliberately chose these dangers that appeared so appalling, and lost his life in the manner [previously] predicted by Hull. Could Captain Hull, on that September day in 1776, have looked forward to other days in 1812, when, because of his surrender of Detroit, he himself would stand as the most disgraced man in the American army, he would have wondered what disastrous set of causes could have doomed him to lower depths of discredit than he had imagined possible for his friend Hale. This is the story of Captain Hull as told by his grandson, the Reverend James Freeman Clarke, a Unitarian clergyman, and an author of high repute. After remaining in the army throughout the Revolutionary War, where he distinguished himself on repeated occasions, constantly rising in rank, he settled in Massachusetts, practicing law, becoming prominent as a legislator, and finally as one of the Massachusetts judges.

In 1805, as General Hull, he was appointed governor of the territory of Michigan by President Jefferson, and removed thither, stipulating that in case of war he should not be required to serve both as general and governor, as he did not believe the duties of both could be successfully administered by the same person.—The outbreak of the war of 1812, which occurred while Madison was President, found what was then the northern frontier of America, wholly unprepared for hostilities.—The country was new, with dense forests and few roads. There were no adequate means of land defense, and no adequate navy to patrol the lakes. The British, as usual, had all the vessels needed, well-drilled soldiers, and, more terrible than all, more than a thousand Indians, ready to commit any atrocities upon defenseless white settlers. As Hull had insisted, another officer was appointed to command the troops, such as they were, but this officer became ill and Governor Hull was forced to take command. In the meantime, no amount of urgent entreaties could induce the authorities (generals) at Washington to send reinforcements to the assistance of the defenseless settlers.

The American troops were unprepared to maintain their own position, and absolutely unable to conquer and annex Canada, as the government expected them to do. General Hull found himself with some eight hundred men facing more than fifteen hundred British regulars, and threatened in the rear by a thousand Indians. What President Madison or any of his officers would have done, we cannot say. They appear to have thought that it was General Hull's duty to annihilate the British army, effectually dispose of the Indians, and present Canada to the American government. General Hull, however, was a practical soldier. He knew the fate that would await the women and children in his territory, to say nothing of his small army, if he risked a battle and was defeated, as he surely would be, so he did what seemed to him the only possible thing to save the people of Michigan. He surrendered. Canada remained un-annexed, the white settlers of Michigan were not delivered to the tender mercies of the Indians, and General Hull paid the penalty of the independent stand he had taken. He probably foresaw that he must face a terrible ordeal. The whole country appeared to be roused against him, and Hull at once became the best-hated man in America. A court martial was appointed. At first it was hoped that he would be convicted of treason, but the evidence showed that this charge could not be sustained. He was tried for cowardice in face of the enemy, found guilty, and sentenced to be shot. The latter part of the sentence President Madison remitted, in consideration of his past eminent services in the army. So, stamped with indelible disgrace by all who did not know the facts, a ruined and dishonored man, in his sixty-first year General Hull went back to the farm in Newton that had come to him through his wife. Here, surrounded by the most devoted affection, he passed his few remaining years. A ruined and discredited man he truly was—the reputation and the honor due him from his countrymen irrevocably lost and by no fault of his own. Yet his grandson, the Reverend James Freeman Clarke asserts that he was not once heard to say an unkind word about the government that had treated him so cruelly. After his death, in 1825, one of his daughters wrote the story of his life from his own writings, and the Reverend James Freeman Clarke sketched for the world an outline of his grandfather's services in Michigan. This shows that the man who, in his youth, tried to dissuade his friend Nathan Hale from accepting the role of martyr, himself, in his old age, bravely and gently endured a martyrdom compared to which the ostracism he predicted for Hale, even if he succeeded in his mission, was but a passing dream.

Stephen Hempstead. To Stephen Hempstead, a sergeant in Nathan Hale's company in 1776, we are indebted for the most reliable account that is known of Hale's movements after he left New York in the service from which he was not to return. Sergeant Hempstead removed to Missouri after the war, and this account was first published in the *Missouri Republican* in 1827. His own words describing his last days with Hale are these, "*Captain Hale was one of the most accomplished officers, of his grade and age, in the army. He was a native of the town of Coventry, state of Connecticut, and a graduate of Yale College—young, brave, honorable—and at the time of his death a Captain in Colonel Webb's Regiment of Continental Troops. Having never seen a circumstantial account of his untimely and melancholy end, I will give it. I was attached to his company and in his confidence. After the retreat of our army from Long Island, he informed me, he was sent for to headquarters, and was solicited to go over to Long Island to discover the disposition of the enemy's camps, and etc., expecting them to attack New York, but that he was too unwell to go, not having recovered from a recent illness, that upon a second application he had consented to go, and said I must go as far with him as I could, with safety, and wait for his return. Accordingly, we left our camp on Harlem Heights, with the intention of crossing over the first opportunity, but none offered until we arrived at Norwalk, fifty miles from New York. In that harbor there was an armed sloop and one or two row galleys. Captain Hale had a general order to all* armed vessels, to take him to any place he should designate—he was set across the Sound, in the sloop, at Huntington (Long Island) by Captain Pond, who commanded the vessel. Captain Hale had changed his uniform for a plain suit of citizen's brown clothes, with a round broad-brimmed hat, assuming the character of a Dutch schoolmaster, leaving all his other clothes, commission, public and private papers, with me, and also his silver shoe buckles, saying they would not comport with his character of schoolmaster, and retaining nothing but his college diploma, as an introduction to his assumed calling. Thus equipped, we parted for the last time in life. He went on his mission, and I returned back again, to Norwalk, with orders to stop there until he should return, or hear from him, as he expected to return back again to cross the sound, if he succeeded in his object." So far as there is any other evidence, it tends to confirm this part of Sergeant Hempstead's report, and he is today considered one of the most valuable authorities on Hale's last intercourse with brother soldiers. Of the details of his captain's arrest and execution, which are told in the last part of the account, and of which Hempstead had no personal knowledge, he declares that he was "authentically informed" and did "most religiously believe" them. Some of the incidents he gives appear to have been proved since to have no basis in fact, others that vary from reports now accepted may yet, with more light gained, be found to be true. The second letter sent by Sergeant Hempstead to the *Republican* deals with his experience in the army in 1781, when he was one of the victims of the brutalities inflicted upon the hapless prisoners of war at Fort Griswold, Groton, Connecticut. The injuries he received there were, as he tells us, so severe that his own wife, having searched for his body in the fort among the dead, scanned carefully the face of every wounded soldier sheltered by pitying neighbors, passing him twice without recognizing him—he too ill to make any sign—and then resuming her search among the dead. Later she found him, and after a time he regained sufficient strength to be carried to his home. He was, however, incapacitated by his injuries for service in the field, and was thenceforth able to perform only duties calling for honest watchfulness rather than personal labor. After the removal to Missouri the whole family prospered greatly. He settled on a farm near the city of St. Louis, where he lived many years, respected by all who knew him. He died in 1831.

Asher Wright. Near the place where the Hale family lie buried is another grave covering the dust of Asher Wright, once Nathan Hale's attendant. He was so strongly attached to Hale that his [Nathan Hale] tragic death is thought to have unsettled his mind so that he never was quite himself again, and never able to earn his own living. For several years after Nathan Hale's death Wright was not heard of in his early home. Then he came back to Coventry, bringing with him some of Nathan Hale's effects that he had doubtless carried with him in his wandering, giving them, on his return, to Deacon Hale's family. Asher Wright died in his ninetieth year, having lived all his later days in his house not far from the Hale home. His pension was so supplemented by the Hale family, and by David Hale of New York, editor of the *Journal of Commerce*, that his last days were very comfortable. His grave is marked by a marble headstone giving his name, age, and former connection with Nathan Hale. His farm adjoined that of the Hale homestead and has now become a part of it.

Elisha Bostwick. One letter concerning Nathan Hale comes to us with a curious and interesting history. Not long ago, while in the city of Washington, a loyal friend and warm admirer of Nathan Hale, George Dudley Seymour, Esquire, of New Haven, had his attention called to a remarkable tribute to Hale. It proved to have been written by a fellow soldier in the Revolutionary War, Captain Elisha Bostwick. This remarkable document was found in the musty records of a very old pension list, and the portion relating to Nathan Hale is here given. It came to light a hundred and thirty-five years after Hale's execution. We give this valuable able record of Captain Bostwick's as it appeared in the *Hartford Courant* of December 15th, 1914, "*I will now make some observations upon the amiable and unfortunate Captain Nathan*

Hale whose fate is so well-known, for I was with him in the same regiment both at Boston and New York and until the day of his tragical death, and although of inferior grade in office was always in the habits of friendship and intimacy with him—and my remembrance of his person, manners and character is so perfect that I feel inclined to make some remarks upon them—for I can now in imagination see his person and hear his voice—his person I should say was a little above the common stature in height, his shoulders of a moderate breadth, his limbs straight and very plump—regular features—very fair skin—blue eyes—flaxen or very light hair which was always kept short—his eyebrows a shade darker than his hair and his voice rather sharp or piercing—his bodily agility was remarkable. I have seen him follow a football and kick it over the tops of the trees in the Bowery at New York (an exercise which he was fond of)—his mental powers seemed to be above the common sort—his mind of a sedate and sober cast, and he was undoubtedly pious—for it was remarked that when any of the soldiers of his company were sick he always visited them and usually prayed for and with them in their sickness.—A little anecdote I will relate, one day he accidentally came across some of his men in a bye place (out of the way place) playing cards—he spoke (asked)—what are you doing—this won't do—give me your cards, they did so, and he chopped them to pieces, and it was done in such a manner that the men were rather pleased than otherwise—his activity on all occasions was wonderful—he would make a pen the quickest and best of any man.—Innumerable instances of occurrences which took place in the army I could relate, but who would care for them. Perhaps it may be thought by some that I have already been at the expense of prolixity (speaking too much). Nobody in these days feels as I do, left here alone, and they cannot if they would, but to me it is a melancholy pleasure to go back to those scenes of fear and anguish and after the laps of 50 years (1826 was in my 78th year) to ruminate upon them which I think I can do with as bright a recollection as though they were present. One more reflection I will make—why is it that the delicious Captain Hale should be left and lost in an unknown grave and forgotten!—The foregoing statements were made from memory and recollection and from documents and memorandums which I kept."—Elisha Bostwick

Edward Everett Hale. Of the subsequent records of the Hale family no trace remains that is not honorable. Nathan's brother Enoch was settled at Westhampton, Massachusetts, in 1777, where he remained a useful and beloved pastor for sixty years. Enoch's eldest son, Nathan, graduated at Williams College in 1804. He was editor-in-chief of the *Boston Daily Advertiser* for more than forty years. Nathan's son, Nathan, a Harvard graduate, became associate editor of the *Boston Advertiser*. Lucretia Peabody Hale, a well-known writer in her day, whose delightful and amusing *Peterkin Papers* are still read and remembered, was a granddaughter of the Reverend Enoch Hale. Edward Everett Hale, a man beloved by everyone who knew him, was the son of "a great journalist," Nathan, grandson of Enoch, and therefore grandnephew of Captain Nathan Hale. He, too, had a son Nathan who died in his early manhood. Edward Everett Hale was one of the most commanding and admired of men, with rare endowments as clergyman, author, editor, and patriot.

Those interested in the study of his grand uncle, Nathan, owe to him the preservation of many records of the Hale family, and an arrangement of the genealogy of the Hale family, made while he was a Unitarian minister in Worcester, Massachusetts, and kindly lent to the Honorable [Isaac William] Stuart, one of Hale's early biographers. It will be long before some of Edward Everett Hale's vital words are forgotten, longer still before his marvelous story, *The Man without a Country* (first published in December 1863 in the *Atlantic Monthly*), shall cease to thrill its readers. The impassioned sentences in which he cites its unhappy hero as speaking to a boy—a midshipman—while under heavy stress, read, "For your country, boy, and for your flag, never dream a dream but of serving her as she bids you, though the service carry you through a thousand hells. No matter what happens to you, no matter who flatters you or who abuses you, never look at another flag, never let a night pass but you pray

God to bless that flag. Remember, boy, that behind all these men you have to do with, behind officers, and government, and people even, there is the Country herself, your Country, and that you belong to Her as you belong to your own mother." No one justly comprehending the bedrock of Edward Everett Hale's boundless patriotism can doubt that if the same call of duty had come to him that came in bygone days to his relative, Nathan Hale, he would have done exactly as Nathan Hale did. That call did not come, but to the end of his days Edward Everett Hale lived for his country as nobly as Nathan Hale died for it.

□□□□□□□□□□

Family Background of Nathan Hale

Robert Hale arrived in Massachusetts in 1632. He was one of those sent from the first church in Boston to form the first church in Charlestown in 1632, and was a deacon of this church. He was a blacksmith by trade. He also had a gift for practical mathematics, being regularly employed by the General Court of Massachusetts as a surveyor of new plantations. His son John, of whom mention has been made in connection with the witchcraft delusion was a graduate of Harvard in 1657. Samuel, the fourth son of John, was the father of Richard, father of Nathan Hale.

Elizabeth Strong, wife of Deacon Richard Hale and mother of Nathan, came from a family more notable than that of her husband. Her grandfather, Joseph Strong, represented Coventry in the General Assembly of Connecticut for sixty-five sessions and presided over town meetings in his ninetieth year. Mrs. Hale had four immediate relatives who were graduates of Yale College. Three of the sons of Deacon Richard Hale and Elizabeth Strong Hale graduated from Yale—Enoch, the fourth son, Nathan, the sixth child, and David, the eighth son. Three of the sons were officers in the Revolutionary army, and the husband of a daughter was a surgeon there. John was a major, Joseph, who died as the result of the privations endured there, was a lieutenant, and Nathan was a captain. Elizabeth, daughter of Joseph, married Reverend Abiel Abbot, for many years minister in Coventry.

Three of their sons were college graduates—two of Yale and one of Dartmouth. Rebekah, another daughter of Joseph, married Ezra Abbot of Wilton, New Hampshire. Three sons were graduates of Bowdoin. One son, the Reverend Abiel Abbot, was settled in East Wilton. Two daughters also married clergymen. Another daughter of Joseph, Mary, married the Revered Levi Nelson. For a man who died at the age of thirty-four, Lieutenant Joseph Hale appears to have been well-represented by his descendants. Surgeon Rose of the Revolutionary army, and Elizabeth Hale, daughter of Deacon Richard Hale, were the grandparents of the distinguished lawyer and statesman, Washington Hunt, and of Lieutenant Edward Hunt, United States Army, first husband of the celebrated author, Helen Hunt. Enoch Hale, Deacon Richard Hale's fourth son, graduated in the same class with his brother Nathan, became a minister, and spent a long life in his first and only pastorate. One of his sons, Enoch, was educated at Yale and Harvard and became a noted physician. A son, Nathan, was a graduate of Williams College and editor of the *Boston Advertiser* for more than forty years. His son Nathan, a Harvard man, became coeditor with him. One of Enoch's granddaughters married a minister named Montague. David, another son of Deacon Richard Hale, graduated at Yale, and was settled in the ministry at Lisbon, Connecticut. Joanna, the second daughter of Richard Hale married Dr. Nathan Howard. One of Enoch Hale's grandsons was president of the Continental Bank in New York City. The most noted of Enoch Hale's descendants was the Reverend Edward Everett Hale, clergyman, editor, and [noted] author, and a graduate of Harvard. The writer, Lucretia Peabody Hale, was one of Enoch Hale's grandchildren. David Hale, a grandson of Richard Hale, was long in control of the *Journal of Commerce* in New York City and noted for his charities. Alexander and Charles, grandsons of Enoch, were graduates of Harvard. As this list of college graduates and professional men is not extended beyond the year 1850, a little past the limit of a century after the marriage of Richard Hale and Elizabeth Strong, one is inclined to wonder whether any other farmer's family within that, or any other, period in American history, can show a more remarkable record. One is impressed, too, most profoundly, by the realization that, although Elizabeth Strong Hale died so early, as lives are now measured—she was only forty—to few women in any land who have reached the appointed limit of human life have been given the remarkable power of leaving to so many descendants such warmth of feeling and such nobility of nature as passed through that century of her descendants.

◻◻◻◻◻◻◻◻◻◻◻

For some time after the death of Nathan Hale a report was circulated, and apparently substantiated, that he had been betrayed into the hands of the British by a Tory cousin. Ultimately this report was printed in a Newburyport (Massachusetts) newspaper of the day, and read by Mr. Samuel Hale of Portsmouth, New Hampshire. This Mr. Hale was a prominent teacher and a strong friend of the American cause, and uncle, both to Nathan Hale and to Samuel Hale, the cousin who was said to have betrayed Nathan. Mr. Samuel Hale never for a moment believed the report, and set himself at once to disprove it. This appears to have been done in the most effectual way by the combined efforts of Mr. Samuel Hale and Deacon Hale, who furnished proof that the supposed betrayer of Nathan Hale had never visited in Deacon Hale's family, and, not being in his uncle's house when Nathan visited there, had never so much as seen Nathan Hale. There were, of course, at the time, strong animosities existing between those who supported the British cause among the Americans, and the Americans who were opposing England. As at all such times, some members of each party were not only unjust but cruel to the other party, and in some respects, this nephew of the teacher, Samuel Hale, and asserted betrayer of Nathan, paid very heavily for his loyalty to the English cause. We will let him tell his own story, only adding that when hostilities broke out he was a young and successful barrister practicing in Portsmouth, was married, and had one child. Unswerving in his loyalty to the English cause, he was soon obliged to leave New Hampshire, and eventually to go into English territory. He wrote to his uncle, Samuel, in whose family he had been reared, and later to his wife, neither letter is dated, but it is probable that when the latter was written he was in Nova Scotia. His letter to his uncle runs in part as follows, "My affections as well as my allegiance are due to another nation. I love the British government with filial fondness. I have never been actuated by any political rancor towards the Americans. My conduct has always been fair, explicit, and open, and I may add, some of your people have found it humane at a time when affairs on our side wore the most flattering appearances. My veneration is as high, my friendship as warm, and my attachment as great as ever it was for many characters among you, though I have differed much from them in politics. In the justness of the reasoning which led to the principles that have guided me through life, I can suppose myself mistaken. The same thing may have been the case with my opponents. Our powers are so limited—our means of information so inadequate to the end, that common decency requires we should forgive each other when we have every reason to think that each has acted honestly. Sure I am, this is the case with me and I hope it is the same with some of you. My conduct during this unhappy contest has been invariably uniform. I can in no sense be called a traitor to your state. I never owed it any allegiance, because I left it before it had assumed the form or even the name of an independent state, and when I neither saw nor felt any oppression. I must have been mad as well as wicked to have acted any other part than I did upon the principles I held. If I have been mistaken I am sorry for the error, and if it be error I still continue in it." This letter is certainly a good illustration of the truth that, in all great contests, perfectly honorable and consistent men are forced to take opposite sides, even at the cost of suffering heavy injustice. The letter to his wife is here given in full. [To Mrs. Hale] *MY DEAR GIRL, This you will get by Mr. Hart's flag of truce, who is coming to Boston for his family. I know the disposition of the leaders at Boston so well, that I doubt not of his success. I would have come for you and the boy, but*

I thought you would leave your father with reluctance—or am I sure that I could have obtained leave for you to come away, if you were disposed. I fear the resentment of the people against me may have injured you, but I hope not. I am sorry such a prejudice has arisen. Depend upon it—there never was the least truth in that infamous newspaper publication charging me with ingratitude, etc. I am happy that they have had [to have] recourse to falsehood to vilify my character. Attachment to the old Constitution of my country is my only crime with them—for which I have still the disposition of the primitive martyr. I hope and believe you want no pecuniary assistance. If you should, you may apply to some of my friends or your relations. You may then use my name with confidence that they shall be amply satisfied. I believe I shall have the power, I am sure I shall have the will, to recompense them again. I somewhat expect to see you in a few months—perhaps not before I have seen England. In the meanwhile, my dear girl, take care of your own and the boy's health. He may live to be serviceable to his country in some distant period. Respect, love, duty, etc., await all my inquiring and real friends. I am, etc., Samuel Hale. These letters sufficiently attest the character of the man, and we can hope that in later days he was enabled to return to his family, and to prove that political differences of opinion had not changed the integrity of his life. Knowing nothing of his later days, we may rejoice that the base assertion that this own cousin had betrayed Nathan Hale was wholly without foundation, and that in him, also, the Hale trait of loyalty to honest opinions enabled him to make sacrifices as great in their way as those made by many of his kindred.

☐☐☐☐☐☐☐☐☐☐

If Nathan Hale was in many respects the most notable American martyr, another man, in the English army, four years later met a doom that to the English appears to have exalted him to a rank corresponding to Nathan Hale's. For a long time there was glamour about Andre that lifted him above the place to which, in the minds of many, he rightfully belonged, and comparisons have often been made between him and Hale, as if in reality their services and their characters justified such comparison. It has been our aim to describe Hale as accurately as possible. He has been presented as an educated, high-minded patriot, wholly intent upon serving his country to the full extent of his ability, ready to run any risk in her service, and fully comprehending, in his last supreme effort to serve her, that he was risking his life and facing the possibility of a dishonorable death. He expected no reward if he succeeded, save the consciousness of having done his duty. But fail he did—and we have seen how simply and bravely he accepted his doom.

His grave is unknown to this day, and his country, as a country, has made no recognition whatever of his supreme sacrifice. In regard to Andre, we know that he was of foreign parentage, his father a Genevan Swiss, and his mother French. He had not inherited a drop of English blood. Born, however, after his parents removed to London, he was, in ordinary acceptance, English. His parents were able to educate him thoroughly, and to fit him for what they supposed would be a successful commercial career. A disappointment in love, however, led him to seek a change of scene, and he entered the English army. Personally he was most attractive, charming in his manners beyond the average man, a fine linguist, and a brave man. He soon attracted attention among the English officers engaged in the war against America, and was eventually made adjutant general of the English army. So far as can now be judged, his life as a soldier had been most agreeable, and he had made friends with all his associates. While [Benedict] Arnold was perfecting his designs to betray West Point into the hands of the English, and thus in effect terminate the war, Andre was appointed to act as the intermediary between Arnold and Sir Henry Clinton.

Andre may have looked upon himself as an envoy from his own commander to an American commander, and he well knew that, if successful, high honor and a desirable command in the British army would be awarded him by the English government. He does not appear to have considered the fact that he was risking his life in the service of the English. Indeed, none of the

English officers appear to have thought it possible that the Americans would dare to treat as a spy an English adjutant general who had been invited to his headquarters by General Arnold, and by him provided with safeguards for his return.

So sure were they of Andre's safety that it is said the British officers treated with derision the suggestion that he was in danger, even after his capture. Once captured, they should not have been so sure of his safety. But neither they nor he had any idea that he would be captured. Indeed, we can hardly see how he could have been captured had he followed the instructions of Sir Henry Clinton, who strictly enjoined him not to go within the American lines, not to assume any disguise, and not to carry a scrap of writing. At first Andre had supposed that Arnold would meet him on the HMS *Vulture*, and that all their negotiations would be completed there. But Arnold, too crafty to run any personal risk, or arouse any suspicion in his own officers, insisted upon Andre's landing and conferring with him at some little distance from his own headquarters. Disregarding, through Arnold's persuasions, Clinton's first order to remain upon the HMS *Vulture*, Andre's other failures in obedience appear to have been inevitable, and taking the risks as they came, he went forward to his doom, to his death, to Arnold's ruin as an American citizen, and to the preservation of the infant republic. For the third time, Providence appears to have thwarted the shrewdest plans of the enemies of America. First came the fog in New York Bay, enabling Washington to withdraw his troops from Brooklyn without the knowledge of the British, second, the knowledge of Hale's fate and the preservation of his last words by a humane English officer, despite the malice of Provost Marshal Cunningham, third, and apparently most important of all, the capture of Andre, involving the defeat of Arnold's traitorous plans to ruin his country's cause. From the moment Andre fell into the hands of the Americans, he was treated with the utmost courtesy. Every possible opportunity for him to prove his innocence was given him, and an offer to exchange him for Arnold, who had fled to the British camp, was made to the commanders of the English. This, however, could not be done honorably by Sir Henry Clinton, and Andre had to face a fate he had not for a moment thought possible. He bore himself bravely, and he certainly won the hearts of those who held him prisoner. When he came to die in Tappan—not, as he had hoped, as a soldier, shot to death, but hanged as a spy—he seemed for a moment greatly affected. Then recovering himself before the fatal drop he said, "Gentlemen, I beg you all to bear witness that I die as a brave man." Self-pity, the desire to be honored despite the manner of his death, marked Andre's exit from the world. Hale had gone hence without one personal expression of regret save that he could not add to his service for his country. Andre had died pitied and lamented even by loyal Americans. England, remembering what he had done to serve her, and that he had died in her service, rendered his memory the highest honor.

She conferred knighthood on his brother, and a pension of three hundred guineas a year on his mother and sisters, already well-provided for. Forty years later she sent one of her war vessels to America to bring his body back to England, and then the doors of stately Westminster Abbey, in which lie buried the dust of those she most delights to honor, were opened to receive his remains, there they will lie till the old Abbey crumbles. Thus England honors the men who try to serve her in any line of heroic service, proving that if she "expects every man to do his duty," she, in her turn, expects to honor those who serve her, be they her own sons or the sons of strangers born "within her gates." October 2, 1879, the ninety-ninth anniversary of the execution of Andre, a monument, prepared by order of Cyrus W. Field and placed over the spot of Andre's execution, was unveiled. There were present members of historical societies, of the United States Army, of the newspapers, and various other persons. At noon, the hour of Andre's execution, the memorial was unveiled.

There were no ceremonies on the occasion. The epitaph had been prepared by the Reverend Arthur Penrhyn Stanley, the beloved and honored Dean of Westminster, at whose suggestion Mr. Field had erected the memorial. It is inscribed as follows.

"Here died, October 2, 1780 Major John Andre of the British Army, who, entering the American lines on a secret mission to Benedict Arnold, for the surrender of West Point, was taken prisoner, tried and condemned as a spy. His death though according to the stern rule of war, moved even his enemies to pity, and both armies mourned the fate of one so young and so brave. In 1821 his remains were removed to Westminster Abbey. A hundred years after the execution this stone was placed above the spot where he lay, by a citizen of the United States against which he fought, not to perpetuate the record of strife, but in token of those friendly feelings which have since united two nations, one in race, in language, and in religion, with the hope that this friendly union will never be broken." With this tribute we close, believing that the tardy justice accorded to our martyr-hero is destined to become a nationwide loyalty, that the day will yet come when our nation, as a nation, will recognize the nobility of nature displayed, and will assign a high place to the brave lad who so sublimely relinquished all that life held, and all that coming years might bring, to die for his country—our country—the immortal patriot Nathan Hale.

Afterword

Following the death of Pocahontas on March 21, 1617, she was laid to rest in Gravesend, England, inside the Church of St. George. She was buried in the chancel which was usually reserved for clergy and notable parishioners. In 1727 the church burned down in a fire that destroyed most of the town. It was rebuilt in 1732. However, the exact location of where Pocahontas lies buried today remains a mystery due to the rebuilding of the church after the fire. Rumors have circulated over the decades that she was actually buried at Westminster Abbey under her Christian name, Rebecca Rolfe, in a vault meant for King James but no proof have ever been found to verify that statement.

John Rolfe returned to Virginia following the death of Pocahontas but left their son (Thomas Rolfe) behind in his brother's care. He never saw his son again. Rolfe died in March 1622, though it's unclear if he died of natural causes or was killed in a brutal massacre of Jamestown colonists orchestrated by the younger brother of Powhatan. Thomas Rolfe returned to Virginia as an adult and later married a colonist named Jane Poythress.

Through Thomas Rolfe and his wife many prominent Americans have descended, including former First Lady, Edith Bolling Wilson, soap opera actress Anna Stuart, novelist Susan

Randolph Donnell Griffiths (Lady Griffiths), actor Edward Norton and former First Lady Nancy Reagan to name a few.

Centuries after the death of Pocahontas, she remains a part of history on both sides of the Atlantic Ocean. At the church where she is buried in Gravesend, a replica of a bronze statue by renowned sculptor William Ordway Partridge is displayed on the grounds of St. George's Church. Ordway is also credited with creating a statue of another American hero, Nathan Hale. The original statue by Ordway of Pocahontas is located at the Jamestown Historical Site in Virginia. In 1907 Pocahontas became the first Native American to be honored on a US stamp.

Today, Pocahontas is revered by both Native Americans and persons of European descent. Despite the passage of time and misguided efforts of certain groups to discredit her place in American history, she remains more popular than ever. Labeled by many as the mother of the United States of America, no more fitting tribute is needed. For better or worse, it can be assumed if she and Captain John Smith had not crossed paths in 1607—the history of the United States would have been a lot different.

The tragic death of Nathan Hale at such a young age may have put an end to what could have been a remarkable life, but in death he achieved immortality. His story is told and retold in both junior high and high schools across the United States. Hale's enduring mystique grows with each passing generation as heroes become harder and harder to find. Though the exact location of where his remains lie buried is unclear—it has done little to dim the portrait of a young man who gave his life for a cause without having to think twice about it or compromise his morals.

Over a century later the diary of a British officer named Frederick Mackenzie, who witnessed the execution of Nathan Hale was discovered. It detailed Hale's last hours validating what had been stated previously about his honorable demeanor.

It can be assumed wherever Nathan Hale is presently he's probably amused at the respectful attention given to him and his noble gesture centuries after his death in September 1776.

Additional Notes

Many inaccurate stories have been associated with the life and times of Pocahontas. Some were simply careless biographers wanting to "juice up" the life and legacy of the famed heroine of the Jamestown colony in order to sell stories to local newspapers or in attempts to publish her "biography." But for many others it was done with the intention to change historical records. Blame for such behavior can't only be placed on British and American historians, but also on Native American "storytellers" who added to the false stories throughout the years as well. While many Native American historians might assume they're telling the truth when they repeat oral histories as fact, the disservice they do outweigh any attempt to truthfully add to the voices of Native Americans. Oral history is what it states, stories repeated over the years as a way to keep history alive. That said, oral history is nothing more than gossip, which more times than not has been embellished by those who repeat it. Does anyone actually believe stories that were supposedly told to village elders in the late sixteenth century have remained unchanged centuries later?

Human beings as a rule tend to add to statements made when repeated and throughout centuries what may have started out as fact has become nothing more than a tall tale. Native

Hawaiians for example, are notoriously overly dramatic with their so-called "stories" about how the Hawaiian Islands were formed. Listening to them tell detailed descriptions about how the islands were formed by gods and various deities becomes laughable after a while when you realize such events never occurred and are best left classified under fiction along with *Grimms Fairy Tales*. Yet even in the twenty-first century many Native Hawaiians will swear on a stack of Bibles that these tales are true and consider it an insult to be told they are wrong for believing such things.

Native Americans are no different in many of their beliefs than are Native Hawaiians. Native Americans cling to delusional fantasies created by revisionist historians that they were wonderfully sweet—and always victimized by Europeans. In order to believe some revisionists accounts of the colonial era you'd have to throw reality out the window and believe that Native American stood helplessly by and watched their world slip away from them without fighting back when provoked or not.

Knowing what I know presently, I will not dare defend the behavior of seventeenth century Europeans and what some of them did in the name of religion and exploration. With that said, it would be hypocritical not to state that not all Native Americans were sweet and angelic despite falsehoods saying otherwise.

Some were downright vicious in their treatment of their own people as well as other tribes they came in conflict with long before the arrival of Europeans. It is a known fact the father of Pocahontas wasn't a decent human being. In fact, it seems by most accounts he was a two-faced liar, skilled manipulator, and murderer, who turned European explorers against each other when given the opportunity. More likely than not he saw his daughter as someone to use when it served him and whether he loved her or not is questionable since he left no writings behind to say one way or the other. But actions speak louder than words and from historical accounts gathered from the Jamestown colony archives, Powhatan is portrayed as a cold, calculating, cruel, and diabolical individual. It can also be said despite being held captive at Jamestown against her will at first—it seems that

Pocahontas chose to remain with the English because she felt more at home with them than her own father. One just has to wonder how cruel he must have been to her and her siblings before Captain John Smith crossed path with Pocahontas and changed British and American histories forever. Though much of what is known about the life and times of Pocahontas is limited due to lack of written history of that era, her story can viewed in various ways concerning the events of 1607, especially if you listen to what revisionist historians have stated occurred, when in fact they can only guess or assume such events happened.

Many of the statements made in books about Pocahontas written by Native American scholars should be viewed with a grain of salt since they were no more privy to the background of Pocahontas than are non-Native Americans. Unless of course you believe in the oral histories given in some of these so-called biographies that purport to be true when it simply is wishful thinking by those wanting what they believe to be true. Tall tales are everywhere in "factual" histories from around the world. But believing everything is truthful that was handed down through generations of oral histories is questionable given the fact how much embellishment is included each time a story was repeated. Seriously, how many times do you think the stories in the Bible were accurately repeated and changed with each revision of the story throughout the centuries when recopied? How accurate do you think the Bible is in terms of being factual since the first revision? It depends on what you're willing to believe.

Throughout the biography of Pocahontas by Elizabeth Eggleston Seelye, she mentioned several incidents concerning the Roanoke Colony (and a few others) that need clarifying. The incidents as mentioned in her book are based on fact but in many cases have been distorted by inaccurate material on the Internet or in published books over the last few decades. Sloppily-made documentaries have also distorted factual events in order to make their stories seem more interesting by misleading viewers with outright lies and retelling of historical events concerning the fate of the Roanoke Colony. Below are a few details of the events mentioned previously concerning the story of Roanoke's "Lost Colony" and its connection to Powhatan as well as Jamestown.

The story of the Lost Colony of Roanoke has been an enduring mystery from Colonial America that has provided plenty of drama for history buffs, Internet sites, so-called "case closed" articles and countless books that end the same way, no closer to the truth than before the first chapter began. Elizabeth Eggleston Seelye mentioned the "Lost Colony" a few times but never tried to claim either way she had an answer. There was no answer in 1879 when the original edition was published and there is no answer today over one hundred and forty years later. What can be assumed seems the most likely. The surviving settlers, fearing an attack, probably from Powhatan, ventured south and sought refuge from the Croatoan Indians who lived nearby after Captain John White left his daughter, granddaughter (Virginia Dare) and a small group of English colonists when he returned to England.

When he returned in 1590 the only thing he found besides a deserted island were the words CROATOAN carved on part of an abandoned fort. It's not clear if White searched further for his daughter and the rest of the colonists or if he gave up, assuming they had been killed by hostile Indians in the area. Regardless, the story of the Lost Colony would remain in the minds of future explorers to the region for the next century. Captain John Smith was aware of the possible fate of the Lost Colony upon his arrival in Virginia and briefly looked for evidence of survivors still alive despite a passage of almost two decades. From what can be gathered on several occasions Powhatan told John Smith and other explorers that he had murdered the Roanoke colonists.

Notwithstanding Powhatan's history of lying, two things can be true at the same time. If he did kill the Roanoke colonists as he claimed, he was only telling half the truth. From records gathered over a century later, reports from witnesses stated that Native Americans with red hair and English features were seen among several tribes in the region, some of which apparently could read from books and write English. Such statements could lead many to assume these "Native Americans" were actually the descendants of the original Roanoke settlers. More or less it seems apparent the surviving colonists successfully integrated with the surrounding tribes and their bloodlines endured over a century later when "red-haired Indians were observed."

Of the story Powhatan told Smith and other members of the Jamestown colonists about wiping out all the English settlers from Roanoke? He either outright lied in order to keep Smith and his people from further searching for the missing colonists fearing they were team up against his tribe—or he assumed he had killed the Roanoke settlers in an attack (one or many) but actually a small number survived and made their way further south to what is present-day North Carolina and thrived. That would clearly explain the sightings of "white-appearing Indians" in the early part of the eighteenth century. Of course if this outcome happened, the stories about the Lost Colony being wiped out by Powhatan's tribesmen are false. As is the "stories" that their ship was lost in the Bermuda Triangle during their escape. A lot has also been said about Virginia Dare too, the first English child born in America. But her fate remains unknown—one can assume she probably lived to a ripe old age, enjoying her life as the wife of a brave warrior who fought against Powhatan's treachery.

Last, but not least, the story of the "Dare Stones." This tale is best left for the pages of the *National Enquirer* than real news. Supposedly in the late 1930s a bunch of rocks were found in and around areas of the Southeastern United States. Of course this ridiculous story has given serious ammunition to people who are avid readers of whacked-out stories about UFO abductions and tales of real-life werewolves running amok everywhere. Are we suppose to believe that the Roanoke colonists wandered through the uncharted wilderness in what is today North and South Carolina as well as Georgia just dropping rocks everywhere with writings on it, hoping to be found by John White upon his return from England? The answer is no. The rocks were taken seriously at first but soon exposed as fakes. From writings from the early eighteenth century of eyewitness accounts it seems clear the Roanoke Lost Colony assimilated into the nearby

Croatoan tribe following their departure from Roanoke Island. The bigger question should be—why didn't members of the Jamestown colony make a serious attempt in locating their lost brethren once they had established themselves successfully?

OTHER INCIDENTS

Of the mentioning of Jamestown colonist George Cassen on page 54, the details of his demise was probably much too graphic to published in the original 1879 edition of this book and was only described in the briefest of descriptions by Seelye.

Cassen was apparently captured in a sneak attack by the young brother of Powhatan, Opechancanough, and tied between two stakes, stripped and tortured to death. His skin was scraped off or ripped off using seashells, his skin burned before his eyes, followed by having his fingers cut off piece by piece. Still alive, his internal organs were cut from his body and finally he was burned to death. This type of behavior was known to Native Americans for centuries as a way to exact revenge on their enemies.

In 1782 this similar type of torture and execution tactic was exacted on William Crawford in the Ohio wilderness by Native Americans of that region during the American Revolution. An account of a witness to the gruesome Crawford incident was published in a 2021 special edition of the book *Self Portraits*. An account of Cassen's fate was first published in Captain John Smith's 1624 memoir. Smith wasn't present but was told what happened by other survivors who witnessed this horrific event. Smith almost suffered the same disastrous fate but managed to outsmart his captors. A reason for why Cassen was murdered so brutally by the brother of Powhatan was never explained.

On page 145 the mentioning of Thomas Rolfe and the present-day descendants through Pocahontas is as follows. Due to the fact Pocahontas has many notable descendants of which several are mentioned in the Afterword, only one will be focused upon below, former First Lady Edith Bolling Galt Wilson.

John Rolfe and Pocahontas had one son named Thomas Rolfe. He had one daughter, Jane Rolfe, from his marriage to Jane Poythress. Jane Rolfe married Robert Bolling and had a son, John Bolling. John Bolling married Mary Kennon and had a son, John Bolling Jr. He married Elizabeth Blair and had a son, John Bolling III. He married Mary Jefferson and had a son Archibald Bolling. (Mary Jefferson was the sister of Thomas Jefferson.) Archibald Bolling married Catherine Payne and had a son, Archibald Bolling Jr. (Catherine Payne was related to former First Lady Martha Washington and is possibly related as well to former First Lady Dolly Payne Todd Madison through her father.) Archibald Bolling Jr. married Anne Wigginton and had a son named William Bolling. William Bolling married Sallie Spiers White and they had a daughter named Edith Bolling. Edith Bolling Galt Wilson would go on to become First Lady during World War I. It has been stated that she took upon the duties of President while her husband was ill, which would make her the first official female US President without the credit of actually being elected President.

On page 146 there is a brief statement concerning several Native Americans being taken by force to Spain, of which they were to be sold as slaves. One of the Native Americans sold was Squanto, who would later play an important part in the early history of the United States. Though ignored by most historians, this story has much interest to the story of Captain John Smith and Pocahontas, although not directly. The incident was mentioned by Smith, but he obviously had no contact with Squanto during the incident it can be assumed. Of course for history buffs, Squanto heroically figures into the history of Massachusetts through his connection to the intrepid Pilgrims.

Apparently, he was captured by English explorer Thomas Hunt and sold into slavery in Spain along with several of his tribesmen. He escaped and eventually made his way back to North America in 1619 where he came in contact with English settlers after they landed in Cape Cod in November 1620.

About the Series Editor

Gary Brin was born in 1965 and has lived in the United States Virgin Islands, Hawaii and California. He has edited numerous original literary works over the years—both new and revised. In 2019 he established Standish Press to bring forth interesting fictional and historical material usually ignored by mainstream publishers because of specific views or content. In addition to publishing books, he also created the Nancy Hanks Lincoln Public Library (named after the mother of Abraham Lincoln) in 2014 to make available hard-to-find books to a worldwide audience.

Production Notes

Written by Elizabeth Eggleston Seelye and Jean Christie Root with assistance from Edward Eggleston
Manuscripts edited by Gary Brin
Front cover design and book layout by Gary Brin
Cover layout and additional design by Victoria Valentine
Additional help provided by Carlton J. Young
Series created by Gary Brin

For free public domain books please visit
www.nancyhankslincolnpubliclibrary.org

Marie Laplace
February 13, 1892
August 16, 1981

Robert J. Questel
June 22, 1911
August 4, 1990

Marie Anicia Berry Questel
January 13, 1912
April 9, 1997

Eugene Albery Brin
March 21, 1932
May 26, 1977

Lucille Questel Brin
February 21, 1940
December 10, 2000

They never got to have the dreams they wanted or expected but their lives were important nevertheless.

Pocahontas
and
Nathan Hale

Published by
Standish Press

www.ingramcontent.com/pod-product-compliance
Lightning Source LLC
Chambersburg PA
CBHW071959110526
44592CB00012B/1138